BLESSED BY LIGHT-FILLED LOVE

THE CELESTIAL TEACHINGS OF ASHENTO

By
Mariam Massaro

Copyright © 2021 Spirits of the Sun

All rights reserved. No part of this publication may be reproduced, distributed, or transmitted in any form or by any means, including photocopying, recording, or other electronic or mechanical methods, without the prior written permission of the publisher, except in the case of brief quotations embodied in critical reviews and certain other noncommercial uses permitted by copyright law. For permission requests, write to the publisher, addressed "Attention: Book Rights and Permission," at the address below.

Published in the United States of America

ISBN 978-1-955243-18-6 (SC)
ISBN 978-1-955243-19-3 (Ebook)

Spirits of the Sun
99 Harvey Road,
Worthington, Ma 01098
www.mariammassaro.com

Ordering Information and Rights Permission:

Quantity sales. Special discounts might be available on quantity purchases by corporations, associations, and others. For details, contact the publisher at the address above.

For Book Rights Adaptation and other Rights Permission. Call us at toll-free 1-888-945-8513 or send us an email at admin@stellarliterary.com.

CONTENTS

ACKNOWLEDGEMENTS vi
PREFACE 7
The Teachings of Ashento 40
ABOUT THE AUTHOR 300
ALSO, BY THE AUTHOR 301
PHOTO GALLERY 304

Peru Lovers at Machu Picchu, by Cusi of Cuzco, Peru

Ashento is a spiritual being dedicated to guiding humanity through the Great Shift that is occurring now, by offering his wisdom and inspiration through Mariam, who co-writes his teachings.

<u>Excerpts from Blessed By Light – Filled Love</u>

Be at peace, in love with all that you are and will be, for the future, past and present are one, and fully fixed within you now. Love for the sake of love, trust that it will change soon.

What one does daily, reflects the choices made prior to incarnation, when there was a review, a process to choose which aspect of learning, giving, and receiving, one was to encounter on Gaea Star, (Earth).

As life unfolds, these prearranged contracts are revealed, however, at times, the plan is forgotten due to the densities of material life, which causes one to miss the true pathway.

Every day honor your chosen path, by nurturing your soul's deepest longings.

Soul travelers, we await your return to these heavenly realms, with missions completed and renewed enthusiasm for your next assignment. There is no rush. The pace you set, is directed by your motivation to weather through life's challenges.

Be peaceful in all that you encounter, cherish every moment.

Mariam Massaro

99 Harvey Road
Worthington, MA 01098

mariam@wiseways.com
mariammassaro.com

Printed on Recycled
Paper

Mariam as Isis in the filming of The Gaea Star Crystal, Awakening the Tribes of Light

Mariam Massaro

ACKNOWLEDGEMENTS

This book is lovingly dedicated to my parents, Pat and Marion Massaro who were absolutely devoted and happily married for sixty-seven years. They inspired me to be strong, yet fair and to believe there is nothing to prevent anyone from manifesting their dreams. I believe they are enjoying celestial life together. All of my family, three sisters and five brothers, have prospered with healthy lives, thanks to growing up in our loving, authentic Irish Italian family.

Heartfelt gratitude to the wondrous Creator, the eternal source of Divine loving light and to beautiful Gaea Star, Earth, who provides humanity with everything we'll ever need.

I cherish her powerful natural elements that inspire, sustain and nurture me, as I sail through this enchanting life, where every day, I live in the fertile serenity of magical New England.

I thank the following teachers and friends, for their loving support, Ashento, Dameron Midgett, Corrine Sharkey, Nancy Crompton, Jesse Massaro, Rudi Weeks, Charlie Thom, Charlotte, Teka Luttrell, Ray Taylor, Gail Krutka, Grandmother Diane, Robert Fish, Freddy Arevalo, Jay Lynch, Kuauthli Vasquez, Diana Noble, Sierra Bender, Gabriel Howearth, Kathrin Bateman, Robert Sherwood, Robin Rooney, Amanda Potluck, Lynne Massaro Davis, Diane McCormick, Gordon Michael Scallion, Cynthia Scallion, Cie Simurro, Sondra Lewis, Eve Christoph, Jaia Wise, Pedro and Paris Fernandez, Martin Jones and Barbara Robinson.

PREFACE

Ashento is a loving spiritual master, who dwells in the Seventh Celestial realm and offers inspiring wisdom through my hearing or dreaming his gentle voice within.

The following is the story of meeting Ashento, while on my journey of becoming a ceremonial medicine healer and visionary Creatress of the arts and music.

I came from a large Irish Italian family that moved many times, due to my father's Army postings, one of which was southern Germany, near the Zugspitze mountains. As a young girl I happily explored the majestic beauty of the German forests and Alps, inspiring me to someday live on my own farm.

I left upstate New York, after high school, to travel the USA during the 1970's. Embracing the alternative back to the land movement, I became a vegetarian, home birth midwife, organic farmer and pursued the study of herbalism, focusing on women's health remedies.

Learning about the earth's medicinal plants became my passion, when personal herbal experiences demonstrated their healing abilities, in natural ways.

After living throughout the US and traveling to India and Nepal, I finally landed in Western Massachusetts. Fueled by my herbalism interests, I co-founded the Blazing Star Herbal School with Gail Ulrich in 1983 and an herbal product line, Isis Herbs. I chose her name as I felt a connection to Isis, the ancient Egyptian Goddess, with her loving emanation of the Divine mother, a midwife and revered teacher of esoteric healing arts.

Teaching herbal classes kept me busy, but it was still necessary to do other job like midwifery, after birth family care and waitressing. I set the goal of manifesting my right livelihood to support what I love doing, joyfully and abundantly, without having to do too many things.

Mariam Massaro

An astrological alignment, called the Harmonic Convergence occurred for two weeks in August 1987. This was a time heralded as a spiritual awakening for humanity, to live more creatively and harmoniously. On the last day, August 15, I went through the forest, to a panoramic hilltop close to my farm in Williamsburg, Mass, to meditate alone.

I had a vision then and knowing it was significant, I scratched it onto my sitting pad and ran back through the woods, to ask my artist housemate to make a rough sketch of it.

A month later at a holistic health fair, I was drawn to the booth of a spiritual psychic, Gordon Michael Scallion and his wife Cynthia, from New Hampshire. I talked with him about the necklace he was wearing, which was like my vision. He said, "Oh, that is the ancient symbol of the Egyptian Goddess, Isis."

Now it made sense, why I used Isis for the name of the business. She was and still is a powerful guiding inspiration for me.

Gordon offered to create a medallion, using my design with gems that he ascertained were specific, to awaken my inherent gifts. On December 12, he called, "The medallion was ready." I wore it home, thrilled with the smooth silver piece made with Shattukite, a rare form of Lapis and Moonstone.

That night, I dreamed of a mineral bath formula, which became known as, 'Detox Healing Bath Crystals," and a best seller for years, by releasing environmental and chemical toxicities, via the skin.

I designed a logo using this new vision, with a local graphic artist, Nancy Crompton who finalized the artwork.

Blessed By Light-filled Love

We bartered her services in exchange for being her homebirth midwife. Nancy suggested that since the logo represented Isis, the goddess of unseen mysteries, why not change the name of Isis Herbs to WiseWays Herbals. I loved that idea and took it as the new name for the company.

I gave up my rights to the Blazing Star Herbal School to Gail Ulrich, my co-founder, at the end of 1987, to launch a new herbal business using the new logo. I created thirteen medicinal and body care products, made right out of my home in Williamsburg.

In late January 1988, Gail and I spoke at a lecture in Northampton on, "What is the New Age." I displayed the herbal products made with purple and white labels, that Rudi Weeks, my husband at the time, designed from scratch, the cumbersome way, before the advent of computer design programs.

The partner of the buyer from Cornucopia, a local health food store, admired my display. She suggested the owner, Bud Stockwell, maybe interested. When I presented the line to him, he asked, "What makes these any different from what I already have in the store?"

I replied, "These are my ideas, from years of herbal experience and unique enough for your store." He agreed to try them. Another buyer, Patty Waters, from the local Greenfield Coop also placed a large order.

What a profound feeling, to first envision a right livelihood, then be inspired with a great logo and take the subsequent steps to create a viable business, with little experience. It entailed dedicated, hard work, research, and constant expansion, for creating new products.

In the fall, I presented the line to the buyer of Bread and Circus (now Whole Foods) in Hadley. She was a student from Blazing Star Herbal School and agreed to pick up the products, if I used All Natural, a distributor rather than deal direct. The owner, Paul Peckham, complied and is still a distributors, after 33 years, as of January 2021.

That was the break I needed to launch the company, that has now expanded to national and international distribution. For five years in a row, I moved to keep up with the demand for more workspace. I longed for the oily salve messes, to be in a separate kitchen, free of the stress of keeping my personal kitchen clean.

My last move, to Huntington, included a basement room, to separate the two, at last! Even so, I started saving a down payment to manifest my farm and a bigger workspace for WiseWays Herbals.

In January 1992, we were asked to move when our house went on the market. Brr, it was cold, looking at farms, in three states. I consulted a psychic, who said, "Stop looking, your farm is there. You'll hear on February 14th. Go back to making the Radiant Rays Chakra oils." I liked that, rather than searching with a child in the cold.

Indeed, a special moment happened on February 14, when a former midwife client, called asking if I wanted to buy their 1800's farm in the hills of Worthington, only fifteen minutes from my home. Wow, it was the exact day said by the psychic.

I knew this remote farm as a decade before, I helped to deliver two babies there. I loved its peaceful beauty, forests, pastures and gentle brook, below the old rambling house. What a powerful sign, it must be my new home! Rudi and I decided to separate. It was on me to make this sale happen, but I was being guided so no worries.

I convinced the family that I would purchase the home, within a year. So, with a down payment to show I was serious, we did a lease to own contract in June of 1992. What a joyous feeling, to move in with my son, Jesse, and adopt their sweet cat they left behind, and enjoy lots of organic food in the abundant gardens.

It was exactly a year of hard work manifesting the funds to buy the farm. Thanks to business contacts and friends, in August 1993, Singing Brook Farm became our permanent home.

Blessed By Light-filled Love

Settling into country living was easy. I loved every moment of the quiet beauty, reclaiming the old house from disrepair and planting more gardens with veggies, herbs, fragrant roses and delicious fruits, while managing WiseWays Herbals. Over the years, I added additions for the business growth and planted trees, shrubs and put in water gardens with Koi and Goldfish.

The serenity of this nurturing land always fills me with peaceful contentment. I'm often inspired to create songs and poetry, during powerful full moons, blustery blizzards, thunder and lightning storms or crystal icy freezes. My dreams continued to impart messages, visions, or healing remedies.

When I wrote or sang what I heard, I often felt a different energy other than mine. I never questioned that presence, even though my pen moved without guidance, with poetic, spiritual words that flowed as a gushing fountain of love.

I did not realize that I was channeling these words from a high spiritual being, an ascended master. I knew others did though, from all the New Age books that I read.

I kept this to myself, until I understood the special connection with this guiding spiritual companion that I met in a dream while on a vision quest in 2003. He said he was my twin flame and has been united with me for eons.

In November 1998, on a fall afternoon, I sat on a pile of slab wood with my cool tailless Manx cat, Fu Manchu. We watched the colorful sunset with clouds drifting by in unusual formations. I heard a voice, "Create a play, a lively expression of what you feel and see at this moment of earthly serenity."

As I admired the majesty, I said, "Fu, look at Mother Nature's magnificent sky. I'm going to write a play to honor this spectacular beauty, to inspire others to preserve the Earth and her precious resources for future generations. I'll start today."

I ran down the grassy path with Fu following, to tell my son. "Hey Jesse, I was just inspired to write a story to save the Earth, do you want to help?" He agreed, "Sure, let's do it."

We sat in the kitchen, concocting "The Rainbow Crystals of the Earth" into an adventurous play with spiritual seekers who search for crystals, buried for safe keeping, by elders when the Earth became out of balance. The faery, animal, forest and plant spirit realms, unite with the seekers to find the crystals, helping to restore peace and harmony throughout the world.

We envisioned performing outdoors, in celebration of the regal Earth. Throughout the long winter, the story grew to include over twenty characters with all sorts of earthy adventures.

As I pondered which animal to represent the west, I looked out the west window. I saw the answer; a large black bear was crossing the narrow part of the brook. Now I knew where to build a bridge to access the inviting forest. Four bridges have been built on that same spot since 1999, due to the mighty rainstorms washing them away.

The play evolved into a musical when new songs came to me. The first, "Calling in the Elements," was inspired while watching the evening sky at my stone fire circle. The wonderful aspect of music is that a new melody or lyrics, can always be added to the original and it stays, as part of the song.

Years later, I helped Sierra Bender, an empowerment, yoga, and fitness teacher, by leading Stone People lodges for her Boot Camps for Goddesses retreats in the USA and Australia. We sang the song in the lodges and on our powerful hiking journeys to the Peruvian Andes.

Blessed By Light-filled Love

Calling in the Elements

We call in the wind, the breath of our mother

Gaea, Gaea Star

We call in the fire, the spirit of our mother

Gaea, Gaea Star

We call in the water, the blood of our mother

Gaea, Gaea Star

We call in the Earth, the home of our mother

Gaea, Gaea Star

We call in creation, the home of our souls

Gaea, Gaea Star

"The Rainbow Crystals of the Earth'" was performed on Earth Day, April 24, 1999, on a sunny day with friends and others who came to build a sweat lodge for Charly Thom, a well-known elder from the Karuk tribe of Northern California, who was coming to lead lodges for the Memorial Day weekend.

When we finished the lodge, we staged the play, as a prayer for the Earth and her tribes. We made creative costumes to go with our chosen parts. I played an earth goddess, the parts not filled and sang the songs, while Jesse and friends, were the rambunctious crystal seekers.

Elliot Tarry was the impromptu storyteller:

"Eons ago, the enchanted Earth had magical creatures that still roamed freely, not yet hidden by the veils of unbelief. Faeries danced in magical moonbeams, green elves played in the forest and regal unicorns pranced in lush meadows.

Crystals were revered for their great healing powers. Peace reigned throughout the pure fertile lands.

When simple ways of living, were replaced by the advances of technology, we lost the inherent connection to living in harmony, in community, with a commitment to preserving the Earth for future generations. The purity of the Earth became dangerously out of balance, due to uncaring greedy people.

Concerned beings gather, hoping that somehow, there is a way to heal this critical dilemma of the aching Earth, before it is too late. As imbalance spreads, the healing crystals are buried for safe keeping, by the wise elders all over the world.

Hobiton, one of these crystal guardians, lives in a remote cabin, high in the mountains with his apprentice, Okemo who went to the nearby village to get supplies. A great blizzard lasts for days preventing his return. Finally, after the storm breaks, Okemo climbs the steep mountain pass, to hear angels singing,

> *Reborn, reborn, I am reborn,*
>
> *I am returning to my sacred star*
>
> *On wings of golden light*

He is surprised to see Hobiton, his beloved master, in spirit form, floating above him as he must have passed away in his absence. Hobiton asks, "Okemo, are you ready to restore the Earth's harmony?"

He responds, "Yes, of course."

Hobiton says, "Then seek the wisdom crystals, they are essential to unify humanity. I am onto the celestial realms. It is up to you now."

Okemo sets out with hope, meeting crystal seekers, spirit keepers, animal and elementals, who all agree to help humanity on this important mission to help save Gaea Star."

What a wonderful staging a beautiful Queen of the Faeries, fluttering around with huge golden gossamer wings, while her faerie helper, playfully sprinkled magic faery dust throughout the farm.

Blessed By Light-filled Love

The audience followed, as we tromped through the forest, to meet Grandfather Pine, elves, and slinky watery nymphs near the brook.

As we emerged from the forest, a medicine man, invited us to sit by his glowing fire, in front of his tipi, where he shared wise teachings and herbal tea. Rose Queens led us into their lovely flower garden, to explain what their fragrant essences were used for.

When all the crystals were reunited, a festive celebration ensued, with the crystal seekers, doing a flamboyant sword dance to honor the four directions and the tribes of the world. Hope and excitement for a new peace, dawned for the Earth.

Everyone agreed the best part of the play, was when a boy wearing a fox mask, read the Fox part with little emotion. Just then a female fox, trotting down the road, veered into the upper driveway, coming to where we were standing in the field. We stood still, mesmerized, including a large dog, Thunder, that belonged to the Lady of the Beasts, from the story.

She had artfully arranged a cute collection of stuffed animals, as her little beasts on the ground. The fox sniffed each one before looking up, as if to say, "I see they are fake." She promptly hopped over the stone wall near her den, to be with her four cute pups, that often played in the gardens, to our delight.

People wondered, "How did that happen?" The mystery of divine timing entered my life once again. Sometimes the line between what is real and what is make believe, just disappears. Nature joined in with us, just like in the story.

I'm sure it happens often, but is not understood or accepted, except by children who never forget, that we all enjoy the same vital essence of life, on this wonderful planet.

Weeks later, the story came to life, when Charly Thom, the elder, arrived with a handsome fire keeper, Bob Fish. Smiling, he offered to do what was needed to prepare for the large crowd coming for the weekend lodges, which could possibly be over hundred people.

He completed the list I gave him by the next day and asked for more things, with a wink, which made me look closer at this wild cowboy, a type I never dated.

By the end of the intense lodges with Charly, Bob persuaded me to be his new life partner, and to wait for his return, since he was going to participate in a Native Sundance ceremony in California after the weekend was over.

Shortly after he left, he called, asking me to come to California with Jesse, to support him in the Sundance ceremony. He had received two airline tickets, by giving up his seat twice. It was like a rocket blasted with full force into my peaceful life.

Always up for an adventure, Jesse and I went for the experience of a lifetime. We camped at the base of mighty Mt. Shasta, with a magnificent view of this incredible power center. It was an amazing time, praying for ourselves and the world, with so many diverse people, from different countries.

When Bob returned, he barely escaped serious injury, when his truck rolled while being driven by Charly Thom's daughter, on his way here. I had to send for his crunched belongings, that were strewn over the highway, including rocks from Mt. Shasta for the lodges. What a way to begin a new relationship.

Charly Thom continued to come east, to lead sweats for years. We happily shared in these healing ways, while enjoying this beautiful farm, raising horses, llamas, sheep and angora bunnies, along with gardening, sewing tipi's, spinning, weaving and knitting clothing and blankets with my animals' fiber.

"The Rainbow Crystals of the Earth" play was shelved, and I nearly threw it out, but heard a voice, "Wait, hold it, you may make a musical or movie out of the story someday." I put it back on for safekeeping.

We sponsored other elders from North and South America, who came to share the "Red Road and Green Way," plant teachings with our community.

I immersed myself in these plant medicine teachings, enjoying it as a spiritual path. It eventually led me to Colombia and Peru, to study with shamans from the jungles and the Andes.

Through these ceremonies, I discovered another passion; singing prayer songs, which evolved into musical collaborations with inspiring messages, honoring beautiful Gaea Star and our connection to our loving Divine spirit.

The Vision Quest

It was an especially cold spring in late May 2003, when a small group from our prayer circle, ventured deep into the forest for a Vision Quest with Freddy Arevalo, a shaman from Peru. The year before, I planned to participate as a quester, but just as it was starting, I decided to back out, as I was not ready to be in the cold forest alone.

I helped instead in the base camp, making food and bringing herbs into the nightly lodges, where we prayed in support of the questers. It was a perfect preparation to feel brave for the next year quest, as a prayer for my life. I felt more confident now that I was more prepared.

After we did a short sweat to bless our intense journey, we walked into the woods, where each quester was placed in their own spot with only necessary clothing, bedding, and a tarp, to stay four days and nights, praying and fasting.

Immediately, a powerful thunder rainstorm burst upon us as we put up my makeshift tarp. I was left with intense bolts of lightning crashing around.

Mariam Massaro

As I witnessed the wild storm, I was grateful, for my tarp, thinking, "Wow, what a way to begin, a good way to go, in the prayer, in the moment, in nature." I sang, rather than be afraid, and the first of thirteen songs, was received on this quest.

Thunder Beings

Aho, aho, aho, thunder beings, aho

Lightning in the sky, changing the night into day

Shaking me to my core, with your mighty roar.

Rain, rain, rain, rain.

Restoring life to the earth, to the beauty of the plants

Moisture is in the air, wet dripping everywhere

Aho, aho, aho, thunder beings, aho You

purify my life, you cleanse my fears You

purify my way, you teach me

Aho, aho, aho, thunder beings, aho

I sang softly to not disturb the other questers, although no one could hear me anyway in the storm. I wanted to remember the song, so I took out a recording device which promptly failed to work. I realized that I was not supposed to use it, but how was I to remember the melody? I invented a unique method by translating the melody into syllables that actually sounded like it.

For example, 'Aho, aho, aho, thunder beings, aho.' When I see these words, I sing them until the melody returns. The sounds of the letters carry enough of the vibrational essence of the tune, to jog my memory.

Blessed By Light-filled Love

I remembered all thirteen songs with this technique. It has helped me since then when I am inspired with a new song and have nothing to record with. After returning home, the recording device worked, which seemed to say, "See, you had to teach yourself."

It was an intensely empowering time, even with hordes of mosquitos, no tent, and only a dripping tarp to try to remain dry from the nearly continuous rain falling the whole time. I had never been alone at night in scary sounding woods, far from houses.

That night I heard a cougar scream, and someone calling me, but eventually I fell asleep and awoke grateful for being in the quiet of nature, undisturbed, to listen and observe the serenity everywhere.

Somehow in my sweet little sacred space, in the peaceful forest, I fell into a trance, spending time immersed in prayer, reviewing my life. Eventually I figured out how to adapt to thirst, hunger, cold and being wet, while lying on the uncomfortable ground, full of tree roots. Yes, it was very difficult, but I knew it was good to try to manage the challenge, as it was the hardest thing I would ever do on my own.

After days and nights of aloneness, I was not afraid, even at night. I discovered the wonder of the majestic forest that I never noticed. Faces peered from the trees, in the bark, in the leaves, and in the sky, inspiring a new song I named - Spirit of the Forest

Hoye, hoye, hoye, ho ho ho ho ho

Spirit of the forest, spirit of the plants

Everywhere, your faces are looking at me.

I am in the presence of holy creation.

I am in the presence of divine spirit

Hoye, hoye hoye, ho ho ho ho ho

I hear you in the wind, I taste you in the rain

Mariam Massaro

I lie upon your gentle earth and feel renewed again

I feel renewed again

I am alone, seeking a vision, in the wonders of nature

In the wonders of your beauty, in the wonders of serenity

Mother Nature, you heal my body,

Mother Gaea you make me whole

Pachamama, you heal my soul, Pachamama, Mother Gaea,

I am in the presence of holy creation

I am in the presence of divine spirit

I align with my true nature

I'm awakening my courage and all my strength

I hear the owls in the holy forest

As I lie upon your gentle earth, I feel renewed again

And I feel renewed over and over again

In the wonders of nature, in the wonders of beauty,

in the wonders as far as I can see

Hoye, hoye, hoye, ho ho ho

On the fourth morning, miserable from the constant dampness and dripping rain, I wrote, "I am cold and thirsty. I don't know if I can stay here another day, but I'll try."

That night I dreamed I was walking in a hallway alongside a tall handsome blue skinned man with long black hair and piercing dark eyes. We reached for the handle of a wooden door at the same time and together with his hand on mine, we turned it, then walked through the door, laughing.

Blessed By Light-filled Love

I had never seen anyone that looked like him. He had intricate tattoos on his chest and back that were multidimensional green and blue unfamiliar geometric patterns. There were beads, feathers and sparkling stars on the points of the design. The majestic ocean swirled with colorful fish and other sea creatures on his right arm. The beautiful golden sun, and the luminous white moon were shimmering and reflecting in flowing rivers on his left arm.

"Hello, my sweetness, it is good to see you again," he said, smiling.

I was speechless, as I did not remember meeting him. "Who could ever forget such an incredible looking being?" He came close to gaze intensely into my eyes, "My sweetness we have divine loving destiny."

I took a deep breath to ground myself as intense warm currents of his powerful energy, flowed through me. I was stunned at my feelings for him so quickly. It was true love at first sight, and not easy to ignore.

"Well, you are very attractive, with profound charismatic, energy but I already have a husband."

"Yes, I know. He is fortunate for you are a Goddess with great power. I will wait for you, as I am not of Earth and never will be."

"I will certainly remember you. What is your name?"

"Steward," he replied.

I asked, "What are those unique tattoos all over you?"

"It is a strong prayer," he replied.

"Yes, you are quite a vision of elemental beauty." I spoke.

We part with difficulty, almost hugging, but I just walked away. I told my husband about meeting Steward, as I did not want any feelings or desire for him to interfere with our relationship. Still in the dream, Steward called my husband, to encourage them to meet, as one strong warrior to another, wishing to diffuse any source of jealousy.

He said, "Since I am not embodied in this world, I invite you to accept my energetic presence, to embrace my grand love flowing, and to know this divine love."

Later in the day while I was awake, but resting, I heard Steward whisper, "Lie on your stomach, I'll rub your sore back with your fingers." When I did, it felt so good to feel his love. Joy flushed over me when he said, "I am your twin flame. I will always love you."

He sang a love song that I named "Let Me Love You." I cherish singing this romantic song. I have had the pleasure to sing it at three weddings, including one in Machu Picchu, Peru, while our wedding party was overlooking the panoramic cathedral like Andes mountains.

Let me love you, let me hold you.

Let me love you with my eyes.

Let me touch you, let me kiss you.

Let me love you with my heart.

I will always be there in the morning.

I will always be there in the night.

I will always be there when you need me.

I will always be by your side.

Let me walk with you, let me talk with you.

Let me love you with my mind.

Let me laugh with you, let me cry with you.

Let me wipe away your tears

Let me dance with you, let me sing for you.

Let me whisper in your ears

Let me lay near you, make love with you.

Let me love you with my touch.

Blessed By Light-filled Love

I am from your dreamtime,
Look within and it is me you shall always find.
Wherever you go, I'll follow
now that I've found you again.
You're the treasure within my heart, I'll love you forever.
I'll love you eternally. I love you.

On the last morning of the quest, Steward whispered, "Close your eyes for another vision as we walk." I enjoyed the pretty vistas of stately western mountains and regal splendor all along the pure flowing rivers. We rode horses past sacred temples and meandered through glorious gardens of exquisite flowers. Steward said, "These are the earth times where we lived joyously in love."

He returned to me later in the day, "Let us walk again." This time I saw ancient beings and golden and white animals, with unusual faces, dancing around a circle of females wearing ceremonial regalia.

One spoke; "We are grandmothers from the Star nations. You are a medicine healer from distant realms, Shoshoni Tolani, she who walks with the buffalo and owls. Use your voice, touch, eyes, heart and healing plants as you walk this sacred path."

A beautiful woman in a beaded white dress, carrying a drum, began singing a native style song. Those gathered, sang, and danced, as they circled around me.

Yani yatu heyo, yani yatu heyo, yani yatu hey hey,ho
Awu au heyya, awu au heyya, awu au hey, hey ya
Yahey, yahey, yahey, yahey, yahey, yahey, yahey, heyya
I am an ancient one, behold from the stars I come,
a golden maiden of peace.
So, take my hand to walk with

me upon this sacred ground in unity
Release your fears, release your
cares as you learn to share
This holy path of peace, upon this sacred ground,
From the East and South, from the West and North
The holy path of peace.
Celebrate mother earth, her healing plants,

Holy fire, pure water, pure air
Seek your strength praying in nature, for a holy vision
May you find your powers praising creation beneath
the moon and the sun
Love each other day or night
as you walk in truth and light
Yani yatu heyo, yani yatu heyo, yani yatu hey heyo,
Awu au heyya, awu au heyya, awu au hey, heya
Yahey, yahey, yahey, yahey, yahey, yahey, yahey, heyya

What an honoring experience to hear this healing power song and feel the support from these spiritual beings. I sang it and wrote it to remember it. I still sing this song in ceremonies and performed it in the Gaea Star Goddess show which evolved years later.

Steward returned that day as I lay in the pine forest. He whispered, "Watch yourself breathe."

I closed my eyes, taking slow deep breaths and saw tiny balls of golden light growing larger, then floating away. "Does that happen whenever I breathe, warm golden energies of light flow out?"

"Yes, the human body releases energy like this all the time.

Blessed By Light-filled Love

It is good to acknowledge this, to pay attention to your words, for what you say has powerful effects."

Lulled by the soft rain, the stillness of the forest, the women's ceremonial song, and Steward's healing words, I easily made it through the rest of the quest in a gentle trance. After leaving the woods, I was proud to have completed the challenging prayer. I felt changed forever by experiencing such an empowering vision quest.

Meeting Steward in that powerful manner touched me deeply. After resuming my busyness, I did not commune directly with him as during the quest, although I kept writing inspirational messages of wisdom in my journals. Thinking of Steward as a celestial twin flame from a distant star, always gave me an uplifting warm feeling, and even inspired several new spiritual love songs.

During the quest, I brought a photo of a beautiful waterfront farm that was possibly for sale, in upstate NY, "To the right person," according to the Florida owners. They said we were "first on the list when ready to sell." We wanted more land for our animals, and this was a perfect choice, since it was near my family who still lived in Watertown, only nine miles from there.

It was a lovely 1800's homestead with 185 acres and huge post and beam barns, at the mouth of the Black River Bay, where it flowed into Lake Ontario in Dexter, NY. I always longed for a waterfront farm in Maine, but when Singing Brook Farm turned up, I settled in Western Massachusetts and created a prosperous peaceful life there instead.

I placed the photo under my tarp to keep it dry. It was what I focused on, to manifest the ability to buy it. I prayed often, as there was nothing else to do except sit and pray, lay and pray, or sleep and dream.

Three days after the quest, the owner called asking us to come to New York to talk about the property.

We went immediately and to our joy, the lovely couple agreed to sell the farm for a "fair price" which was an incredibly affordable, "deal of the century."

I had my home reappraised, to see if there was enough equity accrued to not have to sell it right away. What a surprise when the appraisal was exactly what I needed to buy the farm without having to sell Singing Brook Farm, which had doubled in value in ten years.

On August 15th, 2003, the same closing day for my first farm in 1993, I bought the NY farm. We were thrilled to go to our new home that day. While looking out the window, I saw two eagles flying in a love ritual above several pine trees by the water. We ran out to watch as they magically mated, with enormous wings holding each other. They fell toward the earth until the last moment, where they split apart, flying up high into the sky to repeat the ritual over again.

'Eagle Bay Sanctuary' became the new name of the farm. Those eagles nested in the tall pine and oak trees for years, right in full view from the house where we watched them fishing the majestic Black River Bay. A few times there were two cute eaglets in their nest, a rare occurrence. They were unafraid to look at us, as we walked by on the way through the woods to the waterfront area.

My partner Bob, moved there, while I went between NY and Massachusetts. I was planning to relocate once a post and beam building was completed to move the herbal business too. My dream of waterfront living was becoming a reality, or I thought.

It was years before the building was finished, which strained our relationship from living apart for so long. Plans to relocate to Eagle Bay Sanctuary changed after we decided to separate in 2006. I still went for trips as I loved the inspiration from the waterfront. We held tipi ceremonies, sweat lodges and my fourth and final year of Vision Quest there. I loved my idyllic spot I chose along the peaceful waterfront to pray. It rained but not as much as during my first quest.

It was a busy time, with two farms, gardens, fiber animals, the herb business, and music making. I knew I needed to slow down, to make life simpler, with more downtime. However, I was just not ready to make big changes.

In January of 2007, I met Dameron Midgett at a contra dance. Feeling an attraction, we soon became dynamic musical, and spiritual life partners and enjoyed making a wonderful life together.

That fall, as I awakened, I heard, "Revise 'The Rainbow Crystals of the Earth' to give to the world. Now is the time." I took it from the bookshelf to figure out what to do with it.

A friend of Dameron's, Charlotte, offered to scan the play into her computer, since the original version no longer worked in my newer computers. She sent it back, excited. "What a great story! You should rewrite it into a screenplay. Can I send it to my friend, Teka? I'm sure he will like it too." "Yes, of course." He loved it and offered to be involved in the project as the art director.

On December 31 as I rested from a headache, I heard, "Get up. Pay attention. Look at the starry sky." I looked out the east window to see a glowing red star rising above the trees. It was Mars, closest to the Earth in years. A green comet was also visible. It was a while before I realized that my headaches indicated I needed to listen to Spirit. They stopped once I paid attention to the many messages coming my way.

I heard, "Change the name to the 'Gaea Star Crystal. Begin before the beginning, where the grand council, confers in heaven about Gaea Star, (Earth). Express the Angelic Ones are guiding humanity to awaken to their true missions upon Gaea Star."

I was excited to rewrite the story on with Dameron. We finished Act One at midnight. I rewrote it seven more times before completion. I titled "The Gaea Star Crystal," on the cover of a sparkly blue notebook, that I used to write ideas and songs in. My creative abilities awakened more than ever.

When I wrote the messages from Steward, I understood his teachings better. It was like holding a flying kite, and pulling down the string that was dangling, for the clues, to become tangible and easy to work with.

In January 2008, we celebrated our anniversary skiing at a cross country lodge in Vermont. After exploring the gorgeous woodland trails and feasting on delicious food, Dameron slept, so I wrote. I had an idea to introduce a love element into the story. It seemed like a good change to transform the original character, Okemo, into a star medicine woman, Ayalasha, who meets her twin flame, Steward as the eternal love of her life.

Yes, that was good but was his name Steward? It sounded serious and not celestial. When I told a friend about Steward, she had said, "He is a steward in heaven. I bet he has a different name."

Now was the perfect time to ask, so I wrote, "Steward, what is your name in heaven?" I heard, "Ashento." I liked it. What a perfect fit. We checked the internet for info on "Ashento," and to our surprise there were only two hits.

One was the Erasmus Foundation quoting Dutch philosopher,
Erasmus from his twelfth century <u>Book of Wisdom</u>:

"This time it is not to the great and glorious, nor they who ride hard above the height of others, that I look for my land to be reclaimed, not so. I have sent Apodura Ashentos over the tides; you have reviled them. I have sent messengers. You have destroyed them. Small people of the Earth, the task is yours." We wrote to this link but no response.

The other was the Glade Foundation in England, which offered spiritual courses that included an Ashento level. I wrote, asking what "Ashento" meant and explained how I received it.

Ray Taylor responded:

"The seventh plane of light is known as the Zenith or pre-Ashento plane. To reach this level, the requirement to take lives on Earth would have long passed. The 'ordeal' is personal to each spirit, but on completion that spirit may be called 'Ashento' 'Ancient' or

'Master.' They then have the gift of being free, roaming through all the dimensions of 'Home' and do not require permission. They have received wings.

"However, that is not the end of evolvement for that spirit, for when that spirit has attained perfection (which could take eons) then it might be permitted to approach the 'Crystala' one of the seven aspects of the Great Mind, which is a multifaceted pear-shaped crystal.

"The Crystala will open and that spirit will enter and then be one with the Great Mind. It will have to be of utter purity; otherwise, it will be destroyed by the power. It is, of course, free to leave when it wishes, but it will then be given the title by the Great Mind to be addressed as ('Lord' and its name) and given its own "Rill of Power."

"The irony or beauty is that when one no longer seeks power for its own end, it is given in the fullest measure. It is unlikely that you will find this information elsewhere. It is time for these teachings to be given and it seems that our foundation is to be one of the channels used. I am delighted but surprised that you found our website, for we are in the final stages of completing courses and then we were going to launch it with search engines.   Regards, Ray Taylor"

My response:

"I am inspired by the "Gaea Star Crystal" story. With permission, I want to use aspects of an "Ashento" to develop my "Ashento" character, to share a message of peace, compassion, and love, while expressing our soul's longing to restore needed balance to Guea Star."

His response:

I understand why you are so affected by your experiences. The following will help your endeavors; Religions on Earth have failed simply because they were based on the messenger instead of the teachings. It is clear, that was always going to be the case. Three thousand years ago (in our terms) several ancient highly evolved spirits were summoned to the Great Mind (God) and were told of lives that they would live on Gaea Star.

They would be known as Crystal children, becoming the next leaders, helping to transmute the intensities. This will happen on Gaea Star due to their great wisdom, love, strength, and humility. It is a paradox that only the young and the old are told to take certain lives.

When the time comes, all of these special crystal children, light beings, and their groups will combine powers for the new phase of humanity to evolve on its way. We are part of the Great Mind, created individually as eternal beings which is why we are in reality all one."

"However, we were not created at the same time. Consequently, we are at different ages and levels of spiritual evolvement, which explains human behavior.

Religions will pass and be replaced by methods in which each individual will identify more with their own spiritual self and develop the latent intuitive (I prefer this word to "psychic") abilities which we all possess. Because we are a part of the Great Mind, we can of course, talk direct to God and do not need intermediaries.

In the meantime, as the world descends into chaos, healing will be needed. We decided to set up a spiritual organization that offered free healing and trainings in listening and helping and advisory skills."

We were impressed by his words and thrilled to commune with Ashento - such a high being of light. I delved into esoteric books from all over the world to understand more the higher purpose of humanity.

In *the Flower of Life*, by Drunvalo Melchizedek, Clear Light Publishing, 1998, I discovered that Ashento's geometric tattoo represented an ancient symbol of the DNA blueprint, or Tetrahedron of the Earth's soul, known as the Tree of Life, the Merkabah or Metatron's cube. The design indeed reflected Ashento's remarkable strong prayer for his love for Gaea Star as an Earth steward.

I was on high alert, receiving, breathing, and creating this story in a totally unconventional, existential way. Books, music, and friends, came to me, with lots of information to work with. It was as if word was out in the higher realms and on the earth that I was seeking answers and ideas for the evolving story.

Crystals appeared in dreams; Satyaloka Quartz from the mountains of India, believed to enhance spiritual awakening and Morganite, the Pink Emerald, enables connection with the angels.

While in Maui in the remote area of Kipahulu, we were enjoying the panoramic beauty of a retreat center in the outdoor kitchen with a large tree growing through it. Just then a robust man, walked up a steep hill carrying drums over his head. We laughed as 'Bubba' was a perfect rendition of an exact character from the story.

The next day, a friend said to meet an artist who lived nearby, as he may be another character. Since I follow any leads, we went on an adventure to find John in an isolated area by the ocean. It took two tries before we found him. He was an older artist living in a rustic homemade cabin, surrounded by his carved statues and stunning expressive visionary paintings. Yes, he was a perfect emanation of Hobiton, the wise peaceful artistic elder from the original story.

John and Bubba agreed to be in the movie. I wish we had filmed them right then, because as years pass it's harder to return to that magical moment with the same people, as lives changed.

We also met characters in Western Mass. Some have become my friends.

Mariam Massaro

I believe that we star in one another's lives without realizing it. You know when you meet someone who is so familiar and easy to get along with and co-create and share life with. When the connection is so strong, it flows into friendships, or love for a long time.

How do we explain this? Was it another life, that we knew each other and agreed to meet again with a touchstone signal? Once we see each other, those far-off memories flood back to us. This time, there's no forgetting, since many believe, that before we came to earth, we chose our lives and now we have come to fulfill our spiritual contracts with these prearranged loved ones.

I finished the screenplay in July 2009, thanks to Ashento, Dameron and Teka Lutrell, who moved from California to assist in the screenplay project.

Our editor friend, Charlotte, gave us a fascinating book on Damanhur, a spiritual artists' community in Northern Italy, that built a series of astonishing underground temples, brimming with their incredible art. She suggested the celestial scenes could be filmed there.

After delays in connecting with her contacts, I wrote to Damanhur to ask permission to film there. To my surprise they agreed. Plans were completed to go in March of 2010 on a filming mission.

Three friends asked to join our trip. The visit turned out to be a powerful haven from the harsh realities of this world, where creativity was encouraged as a vital means of self-expression.

We had a creative artsy experience filming some of the scenes in their fascinating outdoor temples along with volunteers from the Damanhur community, where we dressed as celestial beings. What pure inspiration to connect to such a kindred musical, spiritual, artistically positive community!

The founder and teacher, Falco Tarassaco, (Oberto Airaudi) (1950-2013), inspired the Damanhurians through his weekly lectures, meditations, writings and unusual artistic creations. Their communities and supporting ones, now number over 25,000, in Italy and throughout the world. They believe that every day, one is to realize their true self in action by releasing their soul's artistic expression, or by serving their community.

I returned to America, inspired with a renewed awareness, to open more to my creative flow every day. I noticed a difference, as it became effortless to hear melodies and play instruments easily. It seemed as if the music was singing all along, showing that I was always tapped in, but I just had the volume turned down.

Ones that I never played, revealed how to bring out their sweet sounds, like the sitar, which I had not figured how to tune or play yet. I dreamed that an Egyptian priestess, Shahiraba, was sailing down the Nile, singing about healing blue lotus flowers. When we looked it up, we discovered blue lotus was an ancient temple flower used for centuries in Asia and Egypt for its sacred divinatory and healing properties. I picked up the sitar that morning, tuned and played the song, Shahiraba. It was as if I knew it from long ago in a different lifetime.

Dameron and I recorded and released our first CD, 'Gaea Star Crystal,' in January 2009. Several songs from the original 'Rainbows of the Earth' story, were included.

We realized it was easier to create a CD rather than a movie, which was a daunting idea. How do you get a screenplay into production? We decided to do it ourselves rather than waiting for "the one" to come along to manifest it into a movie.

Friends say I am a woman of action. Yes, that's true. I just do it. When we realized how expensive and complex it is to make a movie, we took on making the movie to maintain the control.

Mariam Massaro

In the summer of 2010, we bought a digital camera, and with a friend, Diana Noble, we gathered actors and friends to film locally. It was fun and exciting creating costumes and a magical happening just like in 1999 when we staged 'the Rainbow Crystals of the Earth.'

Again, we wandered through the farm, in fields, forests, and elsewhere, as faeries, wizards, spirits, villains and goddesses, with accompanying musicians. Even though we were novices at the technical things, we filmed like an improv theater, in our favorite setting, the glory of nature, while enjoying the magical Faery realms. It was challenging to stick to a script with children, so we set the intention for a scene and went with the flow.

There were remarkable mystical moments captured with flashing crystals, dancing orbs and people freely expressing themselves as their characters they chose.

That fall, we hiked in the Peruvian Andes. We made it nearly 16,000 feet, where I dressed in gold to be Shalaya, a priestess from the Gaea Star Crystal story, while Dameron filmed. I hiked high up the magnificent Ausengate, which is revered in Perus as a sacred mountain. It was powerful to take in the almighty, as a golden priestess in that astonishing splendor.

In 2010 I met Robert Sherwood when he came to work as a graphic designer for WiseWays Herbals. His vast musical resume especially interested me. Months later, I had a dream that I was learning piano from him. Since he is a master player, I asked for lessons. Something clicked between us, as I loved singing while he played. He is excellent at knowing exactly where I want to go musically without any effort, and thus began our long musical collaboration together. I never imagined it would lead to playing together in our Gaea Star Band, along with Dameron, Craig Harris, and others.

Blessed By Light-filled Love

Through these creative inspirations, our live musical, the Gaea Star Goddess Show, was performed at the Academy of Music Theater in Northampton, Ma. and elsewhere for the next four years. The flamboyant show, expressed the colorful Divine Feminine, honored in different cultures throughout the world; Pele, Inanna, Isis, Pacha Mama, and others. Each song was inspired from nature, dreams, and travels to India, North and South America, and Hawaii.

We have recorded seven CD's and over 455 "Gaea Star Crystal Radio Hour" podcasts through the Dreamvisions7 radio network as of August 2021. Thanks to Bob for his piano and excellent engineering skills to create such technically good music.

To celebrate the twenty-fifth anniversary of WiseWays Herbals in 2012, we compiled a movie trailer from our filming. The song, 'Sail to the Realms" from our first CD was the soundtrack. The faeries are singing, excited to sail to Gaea Star to assist with the lightworkers mission to help humanity rebalance life there.

I submitted the film trailer to the Hollywood and Vine Independent Film Festival in June 2012. To our surprise, it won for the best trailer and was showing in December. What? How could that be? I was booked on another hiking trip to Peru, so I canceled it to go to Hollywood with Dameron to receive the award.

It was exciting to glimpse the Hollywood scene. The trailer was shown in a small theater with other films. We were inspired by the unique films that won and made connections for the filming of our movie-to-be. Sad though, to see how filmmakers still used violence, revenge and suffering as the themes for their movies.

I really feel that honoring the peaceful goodness of life through love and compassion is the only truth that will set humanity free and lead to harmonious living. We have to reconsider making art to change this troubled world, as violence is never the solution.

We enjoyed staying in a funky hotel from old Hollywood days.

After returning, the momentum for the movie fizzled out, as things do when life gets busy. Although the film took a back seat, the feeling of the theme remained. It was the baby I always wanted, never forgotten, always hoping to be born to gift to the world. I feel imprinted with this message to share it through the creative process, to inspire beauty with costuming and passionate, uplifting music.

I wonder why we put down dreams, when they are halfway there, with positive results already. Then the day dawns when we say, "I am going to do this right now, to finish what I started, before I leave this planet." It took me a while to arrive at that point. Now I have managed to bring it through even with the many distractions a full life brings.

First, I made peace with saying goodbye to the spectacular Eagle Bay Sanctuary, in NY. I knew that Spirit was telling me to let it go after the beloved grandpa barns burned down in 2010, only a few days before we went to Damanhur, due to a misplaced heat lamp for baby animals. What a loss of the buildings and precious items.

After endless zoning issues over retaining a small parcel, the way was cleared to sell Eagle Bay, except for the cottage site. In 2013, the farm sold, ten years after buying it.

Yes, it was hard to let that waterfront living fantasy go. One never thinks that a dream we truly desire may not always bring us what is the best and highest for our soul's well-being, and peace of mind. Sometimes lessons in life are difficult but essential for our growth even if we do not know why at the time.

I always loved the idea of a store/cafe along a river, where I could express my artistic passions. So, with the upcoming sale, I found a place close to my home. It was a funky lodge in picturesque Cummington on a scenic river.

When the purchase was held up in Mass, I meditated to resolve it by invoking all the beings, elementals, stones, and rivers, to release me as the NY owner and accept me as the owner here on the river site.

The next day, my lawyer called, "Good news, I found a lawyer who's willing to assist with the sale, and he lives near you." He did clear the legal way for me to purchase it in March 2014.

There it was an old lodge, on the Westfield river, in an 1800's village, with an unusable rusty metal bridge in the backyard. At first, 'Rainbow Bridge' was to be the name, but after learning it was the term used to bury deceased pets online, I decided not to.

I like the word 'singing' as all rivers sing prettily as they flow on. I recalled that metal bridges hummed when you drove over them. I checked online and yes, there were photos of similar bridges as ours and so the Singing Bridge Lodge name was born.

I went to the town board to introduce myself and ask if they could restore the bridge. They were pleased with my plans to reopen the lodge and agreed to repair the walk bridge by the fall. They redid it with donations from the local lumberyard. The owner had fished off the bridge when just a young boy.

After renovations, the lodge/vegan cafe opened in spring of 2015 for Sunday feasts. We built indoor and outdoor stages and a stone dragon pizza oven. I was chef for our popular pizzas. After years of being super busy, I closed the cafe to have more personal time and converted the lodge into a popular Airbnb site. Our band, Gaea Star, continues performing most Sundays since we love playing along the river and in the cozy indoor music space.

This book was published in 2014. When editing it for an E-book in 2016, I discovered missing journal entries. As I typed the additions into the new version, I skimmed past an entry from 2012. I heard, "Go back. Reread the entry." I was surprised when I did that to see a dream I didn't remember, where I heard, "Stone Villa." I was running an artsy star nightclub, surrounded by stones inside and out, where people celebrated music in a creative atmosphere - a portal of love and healing for the earth.

I realized Singing Bridge Lodge was that villa, with its stone walls, fireplaces, and a sunroom with a stone floor. Yes, a refuge, with food, music, mermaids, children, and guests enjoying the peaceful place.

After the elections of 2016, I had the impetus to rewrite the Gaea Star Crystal screenplay into a novel, now that the new administration was destroying Earth's resources, exactly the stories' theme. I still desired to birth this relevant story, to let it drift like a pretty butterfly, into the blue sky. Delays set in.

In August 2018, I moved through the blockages with a strong drive to write in the morning before life distracts me. It was fascinating to see how my life has progressed since I first wrote the original story and continued to embark on a creative and spiritual path

Enjoy the moment right now with happiness - no looking to the past as if you can change it.

May all nations reclaim loving ways to celebrate life, free of strife, in blissful harmony for humanity. Let us merge into one loving family, for all of our hearts and minds to realign with peace.

Be blessed with seeds of loving light to plant in the fertile gardens of your heart. May we live in peace now that humanity moved into the age of Aquarius on December 21, 2020. Yes, dynamic changes are in store, especially after the planetary alignment of Jupiter and Saturn, that blazed as one star in the western sky. An event which has not happened in over eight hundred years.

What a beginning for 2021. Forces of light and dark at odds. Those who care are rising as powerfully as those who are desperately trying to hold onto misguided beliefs of inequality and oppression.

Blessed By Light-filled Love

Let's sail through this challenging time as we stand strong, breathing in the beauty and feeling love overcome all that binds us. Let's continue shining the light ever brightly. Loving warmth to all.

Mariam Massaro, September 7, 2021

The Teachings of Ashento

August 15, 1987 - Inspiration from within

Time is of the essence.

Many who understand the truth will listen now.

The world awaits the dynamic gifts of those who hear the message to express their divine missions and accepting this role as creators of inspiration.

Some will not succeed, as they must overcome their own illusions.

March 5, 1988

Many lifetimes ago in an age of flowers, majestic fountains and singing choirs of healing herbs, the Goddess of the Blue Lake, stepped from the peaceful waters to move toward the light.

As she/you reached the inner flame of knowingness, a memory was awakened that gave you a glimpse of healing practices, brought to Earth, from a distant planet.

The Guardians of the Ionosphere helped to open the channels of communication at that time. A blue ray destined for you, emerged covering your spirit within, in happiness and healing vibrations.

You received the name, Lucretia, healer of the magic waters, goddess of rainbow healing light. These rays activate and open the ones who make their way to you, to help them attune to their inner spirit. As a beacon of blue light, you will attract many souls for inspiring and reawakening their inner light and for giving gentle healing services.

We represent the inner realm. We have heard thy call, Lady of the Lake. It is a grand reason that you are here, to assist in opening the way for healing humanity and channeling loving messages.

Your destiny is changing shortly. It shall be revealed soon, until then, continue hearing, listening, helping and singing.

Blue Maiden, Goddess of the Lake, allow her to manifest, to arise to the world of light. We are within, we are one. Thank you.

Early 2007

Begin the Shaman's journey, by opening the way for your life force to flow and release its power.

Evaluate life's details, let go of excess accumulations, lighten responsibilities, prepare to change your life.

February 23

Welcome Home

Welcome home. We circle around,

we circle around, one by one.

Amor, amor, amor, love, love, love.

We circle around the world today with love, love, love

We dance with peace.

We dance with love, love, love

Welcome home, welcome home, welcome home.

Humaya, Humaya, Humaya, Peace to the Mother Earth,

Welcome her with light, peace and hope, and joy

We circle around this world today in light, in love

Welcome home, welcome home, welcome home.

March 5

In the brilliance of the Full Moonlight, I hear these words,

Wear white to radiate light. Create a moon temple to honor her silver beauty. Many will come to awaken to the source of light, to all that is as you share her lovely healing emanations of the Sun.

Connect to the Moon's monthly essence to honor her message.

For example, March Full Moon reflects Mars, active, fiery, creative.

Let Spirit help you release what no longer serves your higher purpose. As messengers, focus on your starry selves, to anchor in transitions, to surrender without fear, to seek wisdom within.

Now that energies are unifying, helpers are coming to assist. Let the divine flower of love blossom to help all weak parts to grow, prosper and be nurtured. Be peaceful.

You are the light. Distill the light. Discern the light. Inspire humanity to reconnect with Spirit to restore balance and peace.

June 13

During a healing ceremony, I see a book of my songs with gold letters on the cover with a radiant star and sparkling rays. I hear, "Star Being, Star woman, Blazing Star, Star water." I see starlight illuminating and hear beautiful singing of my songs that carry the wisdom of the stars and light.

July 4 - 26 -26 - 29

The essence of creation remains a mystery when two souls create a child out of passion and love. The history of their union is eons old, long before they began their new voyage into physical manifestation of light body creation.

Reclaim messages from the spiritual realm, as you restore and renew your wondrous connection to the energy of the light.

Creation flows through you in the morning, as surely as the sun rises with the healing force of love, light, beauty and warmth.

"When we worry about life, what have we to look forward to?"

How can this be? How can you worry? Why not live to enjoy a pure life of heaven on Earth, embracing each moment as it flows to you as a precious treasure to love, to appreciate and expand even closer to the source of your creation of pure love.

Say these words often, "I awake to the Divine presence within my everlasting soul. Oh, holy light you are the source of life, of breath, and our unlimited energy that flows through our veins."

The choice as an enlightened seeker of knowledge, is to stay connected to Source through prayer and attunement.

The love that flows from your heart, meets mine in the realm of holy divine light. Open wide to all that you are, to the holding, healing light of the prince of love. Surrender your physical, mental, emotional and spiritual selves, to liberate the light within your souls.

In every moment of Earth life, you're slowly evolving into who you came to be, to manifest your sacred contract with self-realization, of your Atman, or Divine soul.

ssYes, ask Archangel Michael for guidance when you reach a portal

that is unclear or difficult as you stand, searching and confused.

The voice says, "Oh, what shall I do?" It's only fears of the unknown that prevents one from stepping through the veils of illusion. Despite the appearance and the dramas that you allow yourselves to be caught in, believe that all is not as it seems.

The illusion is like a sheet of water, a barrier before us. It's not even there when you wave your hand, or step through.

We're so full of ourselves that we don't think we can change.

We say, "Help, I don't know which way to go, or what to do," when all we must do is step through, and there we are in the light, free and clear.

The reason why we don't realize we have a choice is because there's nothing there, no picture in the etheric realm, only pure light. Many believe that life is far more important than the spiritual.

Look at the rocking chair that is awaiting someone to sit in it. Even though no one is, isn't it still a rocking chair? It's that simple, to be comfortable with light as the vehicle of transformation.

August

Why persist in situations that do not serve you? You are called to create beauty, to release material density and to flow into the next chapter of your radiant life to help people.

Pursue a ministry, as a singer, with no strings to the interests of the past years. Surrender to what is next in your destiny.

Remember you're the one who can love you the way you want to be loved. Set your life free, to walk the path of your destiny. Simplify, give away what is no longer needed. Be happy that your life will unfold for you, sister of the light.

Clear clutter, chaos and disruptive patterns, by solving sticky situations when they arise, do not allow them to linger. Stay focused on the journey, right in front of you.

September 4

A dream - I helped build a temple to the Divine Mother, in Kipahulu, Maui with beautiful flowers growing everywhere.

The Divine Mother awaits communing with her as an expression of your work. Draw a design and place the statue that stands alone. Spirit emanates through the Divine Feminine even in your home, so create altars as a place of refuge, a portal for her other beautiful incarnations to flow through; Mary, Kuan Yin, Tonansti and others.

September 24

Dominion over Earth life begins at home.

Acceptance of one's reality is truly perfection as you learn how to cope with the challenges of human life.

Adornment of one's immediate environment brings satisfaction, contentment, and calls in the forces of spirit.

Life energy flows through your surroundings.

The path to one's home is the path to one's goals.

Clear it to be unobstructed, vital and open for harmony to flow.

Release chaotic energy, replace stagnation with beauty.

All rooms need the same attention to detail and care.

Remove obstacles to open each space.

Release dense materials from the past.

If there is no room or no time to realign them, then there is no reason to keep them.

What hinders anyone in the journey along a spiritual path, are their attachments.

They act as log jams in the river of life.

The more useless the objects, the more they collect along the way, creating barriers to open to receive the beauty of life.

September 30

I am the source and the power. I reflect the loving light of the divinity of Sol, of the radiant rays of Master Kuthumi.

Remember ask the higher realms for loving guidance and to access wisdom. They are available to everyone.

When the moon is radiantly full, it is a powerful time, to bask in her beauty and to seek her guiding inspiration.

I talked with a friend who was upset over the unnecessary war in. Iraq. I received this message.

To embrace peace is to walk in the grace of God, the source of light, the source of creation.

Is destruction not part of creation? Is natural the only form? Is not all life, in all forms, life? Whatever it takes? Pele's volcanoes, tornados, men warring, is it not the same?

What are the true issues here, compassion and righteousness, not being good to humankind?

Does your friend not trust in creation, in life's true purpose? In leading a spiritual life despite mundane, circumstances?

March to the beat of the truth within, for all life matters, no one is above, even the animals that humans eat every day.

Isn't that warring on innocent creatures, eating less life forms?

Peace is within, and everywhere, in the crickets, in the quiet, in the rivers, in the sighs of love, in the beauty of the new day.

Blessed By Light-filled Love

There is nothing, absolutely nothing to despair, only to pray, attune and join in happiness to pray for humanity, to reaffirm that life is wonderful, on your sacred journey home. Om.

October 11 - 17   *Eagle Bay Sanctuary, New York*

Just Breathe

We're on our way, every day, to the source of light.

We're on our way, every day, to the home of our soul.

Every day when we wake, all we do is breathe, breathe, breathe

So just keep on flowing like the river into the sea

We're on our way, every day, to the source of love,

We're on our way, every day, to the home of our soul.

Every moment is a precious gift of life

Every moment is a treasure of pleasure.

We're on our way, on our way, on our way back home

Each of us, returning to the source of love.

So just breathe, breathe, breathe.

On our way back home, om, om, om

Is there a purpose connecting to God, the Source of Life?

The transformation of one's life, happens in different ways.

The first step is to realize that forming creative thought into manifestation requires ultimate concentration.

Open to the will of heaven, to commune with Spirit.

Divine Force is present only when the mind accepts silence as the final word. Where to go when human life is confusing, calling in so many different ways? Simply stop struggling. Simply be.

Embrace the day, the moment, with complete awareness.

You are who creates your life by turning thought into action.

The human body is a tool for the manifestation of Life. This is what the mind does.

Disregard those who are bent on hurting humanity; all will right, itself in the end.

Shadow – Light, left – right, Yin – Yang, all is in balance.

The Earth is living, she was not created to live forever.

November 15 - 16

Each rebirth on Earth takes many forms. The essential lesson is to accept everything that comes along, to assimilate all the very deep, healing and beautiful aspects of the journey.

Many people funnel all they do into a narrow existence of daily duties with a total lack of love or connection to the Divine. It is vital to transform into aware, compassionate, loving beings.

When you step aside, allowing the radiance of the golden peaceful light to flow through, you open to great possibilities within.

You bless yourself as the veils of illusion fall away, revealing the sweet morsel of life's mysteries growing within all along.

The great awakening is happening right now. If you slow down even for a moment, you'll hear the wind whisper that all is flowing, returning, transcending and healing into oneness, for it is so.

The music of Mother Nature sings through her natural elements, opening the floodgates of heavenly bliss.

As winter ice appears, life draws inward. Living a spiritual life is within everyone's grasp.

Feel the call to stand strong as you pray for healing yourselves.

Help e a c h other to overcome the illusions of darkness right now as the veils are thin. T
The light is showing, illuminating all things.

December 6

Mother Earth is alive with healing energy that invigorates and bathes the body and mind with elemental vitality and wisdom.

As a carrier of knowledge, it is necessary to purify, to recharge.

All life begins with love, with a reason for being.

It is essential to the form, to the fabric and the essence.

Divine Source is formlessness, yet loving healing light.

One is under the dense material condition of life. The path may be difficult at times however, the reward to be free is beautiful.

When you tap into the spiritual essence that dwells within, you will receive love through all the senses.

As you discover the light of your spiritual self, you will achieve mastery over the imbalance of human conditions that cloud and confuse your true purpose of being on Mother Gaea.

Say often, 'I bring light through actions. I need so little as life renews me constantly through blessings of love, spirit and communion with the source of my existence. I strip away conditioning that prevents my awareness into oneness.'

January 16,   *Song - We are the Light*

We're the darkness and the light.

We're early in the morning or late at night

We're the sky on a cloudy day

We're the earth after fire burns it all away

We're the ground after the lightning touched down
The Earth beneath the apples that fell to the ground
We're the water at the oasis, the light at the end of the tunnel.
We are everywhere, we are the light

Life is manifesting will into action. It is important for Light Beings to bring union, healing and non-separation to humanity.

To receive knowledge, is to assimilate and surrender to the will of heaven, to the beauty of the celestial realm, where yes, there are flowers, love, healing, light and music.

We enjoy all the same aspects of being alive in the spirit, free from the encumbrances of the form in which you reside.

First release, then let go of the controls. Let us help you sail. You can ponder questions. We will attempt to respond naturally.

May we unite to work with you and the angelic realms?

We are pledged to work with you whenever you want to.

We are your guiding angels. You are a silver carrier of the wings of harmony through the beauty of your musical expression.

Writing taps into the wellspring of knowledge that existed before arriving, before you were selected, created and raised in a family on Earth.

When you write be at peace, light a candle and invoke our guidance. All questions will be answered.

"Why does Lucifer want to erase the memories of the

Light Workers who go to Gaea Star?"

Lucifer is a willing helper. He believes the human mind chooses to remain separate, as if that is the only truth. There is no duality here. Every soul is unique but remains as one, connected to the Divine Source.

He does not want the memories that souls have experienced on Earth to influence the outcome of their present life.

The challenges of life are to develop the spirit, to move into the higher realms of spirituality.

The ego grasps for power by feeling important and superior.

The more the past life memories are retained in the conscious awareness of each individual, the more likely their ego will feel they are better, stronger or more intelligent than others.

The egoic mind becomes deluded, refusing to unhook from the grip of life's illusions. To awaken naturally is to release the ego and express the beauty of the spirit's new lesson, becoming clear.

One of your gifts is imparting songs with inspiring, spiritual messages for humanity.

Each moment that you open to your purpose expresses your true Divine self. We will help open the way.

Everyone progresses by opening their hearts to love and believing they are spiritual beings in human form.

Remove obstacles to make a sacred space to work. Writing and singing daily helps inspire you even more.

The characters in your story are already aware, alive and responding. Just breathe in and open to their help. They will appear when needed. Call the Light Workers to begin their awakening.

Late January

As twin flames, our souls are united as we journey to the higher realms, into the inner sanctum of the seven celestial levels.

Wherever I go you can as well. To become aware, to cultivate this attunement, eat live food and less dense-vibration foods.

You are doing well, just keep releasing addictions to sweetness. Each level that is released, enables you to go lighter and higher in your spiritual pursuits.

The veils disappeared a long time ago for me. I see, feel and always know your presence. Please write in your journal daily. To develop your receptivity and voice. The message is important and is easier to reach you then.

In due time you must let go of all that distracts you from the goals you have set to achieve in this lifetime.

Release the dramas, to step fully into the expression as a great messenger, for you are in alliance with the star realms.

It is necessary to connect with the ones willing to assist in bringing important messages to help and to heal those who are stuck in the shadows of their minds.

Become aware, feel the role as a spiritual warrior of light.

Resume your heavenly role on Earth to rebalance and connect with all that arises from within.

Master your inner realms through prayer, yoga, and alone time. Commune with the angelic ones, to help remember your origins and why you are ultimately here in this life. Remain unattached.

Become your leading character. Do not wait for anyone. Let me hold you with these words as you sail into the light.

Every day, take yourself and others on a spiritual journey by singing, by awakening your souls through communing with the Creator, the Divine source of life.

I and the other Ashentos, await your return. Encompass my love in your heart, as you arouse the passion to inspire humanity and light the spark of desire to heal and release all that does not serve you.

Create rituals, prayers, and offerings. Progress is coming.

Create a Foundation of Light to connect the Light Workers.

Release, let go, attune, pay attention.

Hold me close in your heart to guide you, my sweetness,

love to you, I am on to another star.

February 8 - 11

Ashento of the golden sun, I commune with you. Dwelling in Spirit's radiance must be incredibly flowing. We are twin flames united. I realize now all the time you were guiding me, sending stars of light to everyone. Thank you, for sharing your healing wisdom.

Dare to shine like a brilliant radiant, royal star.

We are overjoyed to share knowledge as a bridge between heaven/earth, spirit/physical. Release your beautiful songs.

Inspire respect and awareness for all the elements of Gaea Star, to awaken not only the other Light Workers, but also the masses.

Many seek through books however movies reach more people.

Is there anything else to write for Act One?

Yes, in the realms of Sirius, there are other masters and dynamic leaders that are sending messages, not just the council, as part of the effort to awaken the Light Workers.

Reflect your knowledge of crystals, medicinal plants, music and

sound healing, by writing in many esoteric points of knowledge.

Thank you for weaving my essence into the story.

Now is the time of the great awakening, so be brilliant, courageous and hopeful for the new emerging dimension of life.

There is nothing to fear, all is unfolding along the divine plan, all governments come and go.

*The stars are twinkling through the windows, calling. I hear,
"Come my daughter, to the starry realms, to go beyond your limited view, release, dare to fly as spirit."*

Fleeting images race, with glimpses of future moments, ancient memories, recalling my promises of awakening. I ponder the Gaea Star Crystal story. When does it begin? Who called the council? Where did they all come from? When was the moment that humanity faltered for the first time? Have we been here before, repeating past mistakes?

Yes, the story begins at the moment of Divine Essence, proclaiming oneness, presence and multiple realities all at once.

Everything is as it should be.

Begin with the cold, fierce wind. What is the source behind her driving powerful force, as she spirals, swirling into vortexes of light rays, attracting more? All the while illuminating the darkness, with a humming softness and building intensity.

Sound ripples of waves upon waves, in blissful union with itself. Musical creation is an expression of its' Divine harmony, with frequencies of vibrational healing, each moment tuned to the next.

To begin beyond the beginning is to step through the portal into the dimension of timelessness. You are resuming the true journey.

Just look at the stars, to be reminded of your celestial origins.

Present Gaea Star as a gem of a planet, a diamond shining bright, a beautiful, alive, aware Goddess, a radiant aspect of the

Divine Mother, expressing her great power of all there is.

Depict humanity forgetting all things sacred, entangled in turmoil. Summon beings to Star Sirius for a council on the situation.

Trust every day to nurture and bless you. Awaken to each moment, as it will lead you home.

Follow your instincts to embody greatness, for a star shines brilliantly, even as it fades.

Send white light to heal yourself and inspire creativity daily. Writing is one of your paths of self-expression.

Humanity has to awaken so everyone can ascend together. Letting go is a part of it. Be content to create your unique vision.

Imagine blue ray or white light, soothing cleansing and purifying your throat. Breathe in the golden healing energy.

Believe I am radiant light, always loved and never alone. Think big, be big. Call in what you need to manifest dreams.

February 12 - 16

Twin Stars, Castor and Pollux, shine in the night. I remember a dream where I heard, 'Reverse the order, travel beneath the Earth through a long passage-way, to the crystal realms. It is a metaphor of seeking wisdom within where light exists with the shadows. The crystal seeker meets Grandmother Crystala spirit, in a cave, where she finds a small crystal, like a seed which is the essence of the whole, just as we are all part of the grand one, the great essence.

Consciousness becomes brighter, the closer one gets to the crystals, to the radiant, master generator of light.

All life is a journey home to the light, to the source of mystery.

Its' a predawn dream, when two stars dance together in the sky.

The seeker understands why her grandfather says to go within, as she realizes the jewel, is the treasure, within her mind.

She senses the spirit of the crystal, represents all that we are.

She is healed by the Crystala's rainbow light, master essence.

We carry the precious jewel of spirit within and have all along.

I hear a Star Trek name, Starship Regulus.

Movement through the universe requires spaceships, since each star system is a different composition. They make travel safe.

It is like a ship captain that uses navigation to know the

obstructions. All flows properly when star ships are the transport.

Opening to esoteric wisdom is difficult, for the mind searches

for a more tangible reality.

The mystery of the unseen is daunting to understand, unless you believe that all is not as it seems. Realize there are many illusions.

Let go of misperceptions even if eons old and entrenched within societies norms.

I wonder about Hilary Clinton running for the presidency.

No, she will not step through the portal of power at this time.

Female leadership of this country shall be in a different form.

They are beginning to rise in power in all walks of life.

The new leader will help unify and heal the wounds of slavery.

Write consistently in the morning when you are receptive.

The stars are familiar to your energetic vibration.

Release attachments to dairy and dense foods, as they do not carry nurturing healing vibrations, for your body.

Set up a crystal grid to anchor in your star ship portal.

The cold, fierce weather is fully engaging your attention,

demanding intense participation to all that needs to be done.

I must stop resisting and forgive humanity, by listening to the wisdom of the higher realms. I am surrounded by calmness, while creating this story, acknowledging my ability to write a successful screenplay. It takes composure, inspiration and release of the ego.

To help me flow, I set the tone with gentle music and open the windows to feel the breeze and hear the peaceful brook flowing.

Blessed By Light-filled Love

Come to me, Ashento, in the morning. I love to hear you speak softly.

Silence heals distractions, furthers mental stability, making it much easier to hear the sweet music of your soul.

Remove the veils of distractions to open to creativity.

Release reluctance to lose sleep, to write unencumbered. Throw off the armor of resistance to melt into the fire of truth. It's easier to work with imagery that you see from within.

Be not afraid to stand as a divine leader. Be simply smashing. Mountains of support flow to you, drawn by your inspiration. Follow instincts to gather momentum. Ask assistants to help.

Each creative act opens a portal, into a deeper connection which helps to share wisdom with you, and always carries my peaceful love.

We are pleased with your presence of mind, discipline and commitment. Even visions and dreams, are important, as they are the patterns of life.

Let words unfold, as we work to help you release the density of life, to open the way for inspiration and renewed zest for ideas.

Doors are slowly opening, even though some are creaky, heavy, and ancient. These are all the veils of misperception.

The portal of awakening the others, is coming soon.

My sweetness, look at all that you have. Say goodbye to your beloved sheep, for it is one less distraction in such a busy life.

Let it all go, becoming free as the silky wind on a summer day.

Your soul and spirit know no boundaries, just as the fire knows no boundaries. It comes to purge, to renew. Resist not the call.

Fatal illnesses occur to usher souls through the final stage of incarnation, back to their celestial home for rest and renewal.

The cries of humanity are heard everywhere, for we are all composed of the same essence, light and love.

You carry the seeds within to love, honor, restore dignity, respect all life, and improve communication with each other.

Stay focused on the Divine, for every moment, one is creatively engaged, fosters love, devotion and spiritual growth.

Feel the holy presence when you breathe, or walk, wherever you are. Yes, be happy, you are alive, for one more day.

Shine like a lighthouse, as a protector of those lost and fumbling in the darkness of their own shadows.

You're the Light

Hey hey ahey, hey hey 2x

Oh, hey hey oh, Oh, wey hey oh 2x

Open to wisdom within your heart

Open to spirit deep within

Create the light that you truly are.

Awaken, awaken, awaken to the light within

Shining, shining, oh peel away, peel away

Lift up the veils, lift up the veils

Be brilliant, radiant, oh so brilliant, radiant

You're the light, 2x, shining, shining bright

February 18

Full moon, icy snow. I change the character, Okemo to Shalaya, a crystal seeker who sets out to find the others. I see the Goddess Abuntia, showering us with abundance and tall turquoise crystals rising out of the Earth.

Blessed By Light-filled Love

In the silence of the night, one hears the mystery of life as they breathe in and out, one minute, gone the next.

The messages are within the songs that come to you.

The middle of the Earth is the same as your heart within, as the

Earth is a living planet of love.

Speak your truth every day, to all who care to listen.

February 21 - 25 - 26

I see circles of humanity, dancing in the moonlight, releasing love. Triangles of color are emerging like butterflies from the chrysalis of antiquity. Darkness is erased from the awakening ones as they circle around pulsating crystals, flashing brightly.

Oh, Holy Ones of Light

Oh, holy ones of light, you are the holy ones of light

Surround your love, surround your light

Oh, holy ones of loving light

Ahey yahey, ahey yahey, ahey yahey

You are the ones to shine the way, to show the others,

The long forgotten ancient ways

Release your minds, release your fears,

Open wide your hearts

Awaken to the mysteries,

Ahey yahey, 3x

Flying to Peru tomorrow. Any message for me, Ashento?

Yes, we are happy for your journey to the land of the condor. Renew, refresh and receive the inspiration of the sacred Andes.

Ashento wants to co-write a book on his teachings.

You are the pioneers and leaders for birthing humanities new cycle. We are here to guide you.

Opening to the light within your heart and soul, is the most direct way to understand life's great lessons. The portal is unfolding.

Release all that prevents you from hearing from the council, the words of wisdom that echo from here to there.

We are not so far apart, as whatever I experience, you do too.

Thank you for coming to Earth, for being devoted to creation and for loving humanity your entire life.

Go into the void, to the spiraling energy within. Merge with the light of creation. Be with the stars, as we radiantly shine.

As a star being, spread the light, as a reflection of love.

Do not succumb to the density. Enjoy nature and the moon on the snow, for it reflects the power and beauty of the celestial realm.

March 12

Are the rainbow auras I see around a woman always there?

Yes, you are already the sum total of all that you will ever be.

You are glowing radiant beings of light.

Each of you is a reflection of the other, what one person lacks is the other's gifts.

There is nothing ever missing. You are completely whole.

For what clouds the aura or rainbow light, are the shadows of the density of material life, lack of love and compassion, forgetfulness, or feeling depressed or abandoned.

Blessed By Light-filled Love

The light of spirit is in your heart and mind, in the eyes of each other, with nothing to fear or be sad about. Love is everywhere.

Life is love. Gaea Star is love. Lay upon her whenever you feel lost or confused. She will relieve your suffering.

Breathe in the beauty of fresh ocean air, revel in the sunshine and the stillness of the quiet forest to feel renewed.

In order to find one's way, accept what happens, as all a part of life, like a way station, you're here for a short time, even though it may seem lengthy before returning home.

I hike the Inca trail with seventeen women on Sierra Bender's Amazon Goddess trip. I see visions of ancestors, holy shamans of ceremonial ways, with colorful head dresses in sacred sites on the mystical trail. I return refreshed and inspired from the powerful Andes. I received the song, Pacha Mama, as I passed through a beautiful cave, carved out of the mountain that dripped with exquisite green moss.

Pacha Mama

Pacha Mama, I hear you calling, Pacha Mama I hear your song

Pacha Mama, I feel your power,

Pacha Mama, you're all around

Ahey yahey yahay yahay 3x

Pacha Mama, I see your beauty,

Pacha Mama, you're healing me

Pacha Mama, I taste your sweetness,

Pacha mama you are in me

Chocoquiero, Ukupacha, Salkantay, Machu Picchu, Ausengate

PachaMama, I'm in the Andes,

Pacha Mama, I'm in your cave.

Pacha Mama, I smell your deep earth,

Pacha Mama, I love Peru.

Pacha Mama, you're all around me,

Pacha Mama, you're deep within

Pacha Mama, Mother Earth, Pacha Mama, Pacha Mama

Released - Gaea Star Goddess CD, Spirits of the Sun Music, 2011

March 31.   Simply Be

Resume the journey from so long ago
Carry the message to the North, the South, the East and West
Fly with spirit, as you remember all that you know
Portals are opening, the light is bursting, brightly shining.
The veils are lifting, the holiness of self is becoming
The fires of awakening, illuminate the way
Shining, shining, to help you know the way
Arise, to unravel the mystery of life
Simply be. Be simple. Just be.

Those who direct their work to help heal humanity, are on a very tangible mission, some more intently than others.

Go within, to realize your role in this finale to the Earth's effort to right herself from such imbalance.

Self-realization is the ultimate expression of mortality. Resist not the calling of your inner souls.

Through sacrifice, you gain access to the spiritual principles.

Communion with creation, is to love the light.

Simply maintaining a peaceful manner, is all that is required.

Waste no time in useless endeavors. Every moment is special.

Seek to release control. When you develop the spiritual consciousness of your pure etheric soul, your Divine matrix appears thru the density and the body becomes less important.

April 11 - In Maui, Hawaii

Dream: We dance in a circle with star headdresses on, in a brilliant portal, holding star mirrors in alignment with Hawaii.

We created a Merkabah, an energetic field with others, from all over the world. The land was being revitalized to grow organic vegetables and healing herbal medicines.

The portal opened like an eye, as we used star mirrors. We received knowledge from Pleiadean energy fields to unify.

As I stepped through the portal, I saw realms that exist beneath the surface. Ancient Hawaiians stood in balance, between worlds. It was profound to look around as I awakened.

We stayed in delightful tropical splendor on the coast of Kipahulu. We hiked on a gorgeous day up a dry riverbed in a rugged canyon to a delightful deep pool with a gushing waterfall. Wow, we prayed to the wonder of that sweet, serene place.

Dameron jumped in and I gave my pearl necklace as an offering to Oshun, the goddess of the river and waterfalls. In a few moments, a trickle of water began to flow from the pool and into the dry riverbed. It was the Kokuai river flowing from further up the mountain now that the gates were opened there.

We walked with the river following us gently like a little puppy at our feet. It filled in the dry riverbed all the way behind us to the ocean. I sang, "Lead Me Down," as we climbed over worn boulders until the river met the sea. We swam in her waters in an incredible cave formed by the now gushing river flowing into the big waves.

Mariam Massaro

Lead Me Down

Lead me down the river of life, lead me down to the sea

Walking on a beautiful day, along the coast of Kipahulu Bay

Up the riverbed so dry, to a waterfall 70 feet high

Amrita flows from Mother Gaea,

Oshun, Goddess of the waterfall

Down she flows into the deep pool.

Wonder where the water goes?

Thank you for your beauty, for your flowing grace,

for you renew our lives.

Suddenly a trickle starts to flow, down the riverbed to the sea

When your life runs dry, did you forget to let your water flow?

Let your life flow with love, let your life flow with peace,

Let your life flow with joy

Why move the mountains, just flow around? Smooth

out the roughness as you wear your path down

Ohey yahey, Ohey yahey, Ohey ya hey, Maui

Lead me down the river of life, lead me down to the sea

April 15

In a ceremony with Kuauthli Vasquez, a medicine leader guiding me as a ceremonial leader, I received this powerful song.

Blessed By Light-filled Love

Oh, Heavenly Mother Earth, Gaea Star

Oh, heavenly Mother Earth, Gaea Star

I lay my life down upon your sacred soil

to walk the path of medicine healer.

I carry the flame of compassion, healing, and truth

To walk the path of star priestess

with my crown of fire and light

I carry your vision of peace, hope and love

Oh, heavenly Mother Earth, Gaea Star

You are shining your crystal of love tonight

You are the one who leads the way

I am your daughter of the sun and the moon

You shine through my heart, you shine through my soul

I lay my life down to walk the path of priestess,

to unify your people

from the sacred waters, from the river of life,

Oh, healing medicines

Oh, heavenly Mother Earth, Gaea Star

I lay my life down, etched forever into

the soil of your sacred fire

I give my heart into the spirit of the father,

of the mother, the creator of all life.

I return home to you.

May 8

I wonder about my recurring headaches.

Everything in the universe is composed of points of light. All that is within, is light. The cave is like a cabala of sacred geometry.

Surrender to the purity of the breath of life.

There are two receptacles and nostrils that receive and help you to breathe. When the breath enters it is transformed into regenerative healing effects on the body.

At times, the information that flows to you may be of great magnitude. Your body is restructuring to become a vehicle of light, from the stars, equipped to sail easily throughout the universe. Organize your mind. Resistance causes the suffering.

I see a star, with its' silver rays casting a brilliant essence on the center of my forehead. "Be that star, Sakweeanna, Star of love".

Time is of the essence for your divine manifestation.

The doorway is opened to activate your land, to anchor in cosmic flow. Direct your attention. Avoid unnecessary intervention.

May 11

Wings of Deep Blue

I awaken to the essence of my inner fire, warmth rising,

I feel the beauty of my soul flowing up the channels of light,

transformed into circles of radiant blue with gossamer wings.

Oh, cool me down, as I rise with my fire in the beauty of the night.

Up from the roots of my body, rising up the channels of light.

I awaken to my starry self, Satyaloka,

healer of the mountains high.

I feel the wind's beauty, blowing embers on my heavenly soul.

On wings of deep blue gossamer, I sail into the spirit of light.

I found Satyaloka in <u>The Book of Stones</u> by Robert Simmons and Naisha Ahsian, Heaven and Earth Publishing, 2005. It is a powerful quartz to open to our higher selves, from the mountains of India where monks from the Satyaloka monastery gathered it, to give to the world to encourage awakening and attunement to white healing light.

May 16 – *Dream*

Krishna and Radha, the Hindu god/goddess couple are surrounded by worshippers and pink light shining in a beautiful temple. Blue Krishna is beaming rays of love, as blue stars float by.

To see beyond is to go into the void of timelessness, where all is well in the inner planes.

Once you or any other soul, has committed themselves to sharing in the light of love, their lives unfold, unwinding from the chaos of self-imposed duties or responsibilities, becoming free.

When you open to inner light, the radiance illuminates your way. Belief in your true essential power, brings manifestation, with nothing to fear. Relax as you create warm, loving examples of love.

Remain at peace, drop the veils to become a radiant vortex of light, happily expressing your higher selves more fully.

As you or anyone else stand within their center, rays of light

flow from the core essence of your beautiful healing souls.

I am a Radiant Soul of Light

I serve as a soul of loving light

I hold the fire within to shine the way

I keep moving along the path of love

I am a radiant soul of love,

I am a radiant source of light

Alive, awake, aware I am

I ignite the fire of my way, I ignite the fire of my light

Ohey, yahey, yahey, yahey

May I walk through the portals of desire

as I step through the portals of fire

Returning to the way of love,

Returning to the eternal light

I am grateful for Teka's guidance in translating the messages. Planting seeds during the rains. All is well, as I express life into fullness and all that there is with dreams, songs and inspiration.

May 21 - 24 - 27

Dream - Chakra colors emanate in a circle of light, one by one. Colorful rays bathe the seekers as they pass by the glowing lights on the path on their way to the sacred temple.

May the clouds of illusion disappear more each day. The luminous moonlight wakes me at 3:30 am.

Listen to spirit for your spiritual growth. It flows even greater within, when you pay attention to the messages rather than forget or not act upon.

Dream - I see a large, five-foot crystal rolling towards a building, stopping nearby. I ran to see, meeting other crystal seekers. I ask to not do anything to it. We admire the sparkling powerful quartz crystal. I want to use that impressive crystal in the story. What fun it is to dream, then weave aspects of it into the work.

June 1 – 2

I see two rainbows shimmering, floating, turning into beautiful angelic women playing harps, wearing crowns and emanating golden auras. Angels sing and play peaceful music nearby.

Do you remember the way, you came from the stars, years ago, from galaxies beyond, deep inside the universe?

You were to be roused by fire, healed by the earth, soothed by the waters, breathing in deeply, the breath of life.

May your memories awaken within your soul, the reasons you came from a distant star.

Open the portal, to return to the light, to shine the way.

As I wrote, a chickadee perched on the railing, cocking his head, fanning his wings as if he heard me talking. So I wrote in a part where small birds warn the crystal seekers of an earthquake, causing a landslide, right where they were just walking.

I don't know if this will become a movie, but I love it when I create characters. Then they appear, as if we planned this story/ movie.

June 3 - 5 - 9

I am in the airport delayed on a trip to Texas, to assist Sierra Bender at her Bootcamp for Goddess retreat. I ask why the delay?

My sweetness, you are freeing yourself from this type of journey as it distracts from your purpose.

The path of illumination requires clear focused intention.

All cycles come to an end, as new one begins.

Walking through the halls of wisdom is so vastly different.

I feel your longing to find your way back home once again.

Fostering dreams into reality is the true work.

Write your ideas, visions and dreams down. They are powerful expressions of your artistic abilities.

Create artful collages with temples, dancers and crystals.

Walk in the blessings of creation to inherit all that you sow.

Everyone carries the key to open their portals of happiness.

Love who you are right now, as you are perfection.

May you always walk peacefully.

I love Teka's visionary art for the movie to be. Gaea Star, (Earth), is sailing through the galaxy with twin stars, streaking toward her. They are the radiant light comets that Ashento and Ayalasha are traveling in. I wonder about the ones, he calls "The Shining Ones."

Teka is the link to foster global intergalactic communication, with those serving humanity through the world wide web of light. Yes, it is the same channel that linked us, the vast web of light.

The Gaea Star Crystal is a powerful story to illustrate the spiritual aspects that humanity is striving to assimilate.

As the doors of wisdom open, the gifts of the teachings, from the beings of the Light, the Shining Ones, are revealed.

It is mastery over the body temple, unified with spirituality, that brings one to these celestial higher realms.

The presence of all of the elements Earth, Water, Fire, Air and Metal is conducive for creative writing.

I recharge within the grid of these deep energetic vibrations here.

As you open to your Divine expression, beauty surrounds you.

Your research and creation surpass our aspirations.

The weaving of such a complex message is joyful to witness.

The building at Eagle Bay Sanctuary, is acting as a beacon of light, for opening for communication of the high order.

You can release anything you desire, by saying:

"I release all that no longer serves my highest good as a daughter, or son of the Light. I release all that binds me to the density of human existence, in order to progress spiritually."

Sort through rooms to lessen congestion. Fill it with wonderful space instead. Pack boxes, as if moving into the higher planes. Review everything, to surround yourself with the highest vibration possible.

Continue to serve, to receive our support, to return to serenity.

Refresh, renew, and regenerate, to align to your original essence, to understand the important aspects of your soul's mission.

As you see, one can reach through all dimensions, to touch the essence of several realms at once, music, visuals and the teachings.

When you learn to understand the complexity of existence, you open to the multi-dimensional shifts that are occurring.

As a messenger, convey the knowledge that we are all light, composed of atomic energetic resonance.

The stories are written in the Akashic Hall of Records by the Ascended Ones, to be revealed in due time. We are here to serve.

June 11 - 14

You are one of the original ones that has always known you were encoded in your primary DNA to blossom and awaken at the proper moment of humanity. When all that was lost is recovered.

The longing to rediscover the higher planes of existence are strong for you and the other original pioneers, questers, healers, visionaries, wisdom seekers and truth bearers.

Whatever you do now in your awakened form, is attractive to those who come after you.

Many do not even know the way, as the veils are too heavy.

Even animals and plants species have become denser in waiting, but most are still united and parallel in being.

Shine like a beacon, as a radiant one of loving light. Remember all is well, even if it appears different.

Happiness and inner peace stems from trusting and letting the world evolve, as it orbits the universe.

Let go of what you think we are, or who you are.

Does what you do for money satisfy your soul's longing? If not, why not?

During yoga, I had an intense vision that I was dressed in ceremonial clothing as a movie character.

When Teka mentioned Ashento to a friend, she saw a vibrant blue ray - the room smelled of orchids. She heard, "He is going to write a large book."

Yes, I feel, we are twin flames and seek to enhance connecting. If we are meant to do great work, then I open to his teachings, to merge powerfully into oneness.

Thank-you, Ashento, for waiting for me to wake up. May I listen. I am touched by your spiritual presence. It is a journey, to rise above, to bless the world with our love. I surrender to you.

My sweetness, it is the stillness in the night, that fosters easier communing, away from your busy life. We can connect anytime, if you but listen or talk to me, for we are always flowing in oneness.

To awaken to heavens will, is to open to the will of your spirit. Oneness, compassion, love and forgiveness, emanate from the central source, the heart within, which is Divine Spirit.

Love is truth. It is all that needs to be expressed.

As the portal of realization opens, rays of pure intention, shower you with gifts of understanding and awareness.

To live simply, is to accept completely, that everything one encounters in life, underneath it all, contains the essence of love.

There is nothing to change, all is as it should be.

Difficulties are released, as one expresses their special gifts. It is what brings happiness and the fulfillment of your deepest longings.

June 16

Everyone loves Teka's art for the Gaea Star Crystal story - the movie to be. "Awakening the Tribes of Light" is added to the title.

Dream - Lakshmi, The Hindu Goddess, appears, "I bless you with abundance, for your service to humanity."

Lakshmi

Lakshmi, Lakshmi, Gayatri, Gayatri,

Goddess of Abundance, Queen of Vitality

Lakshmi, Lakshmi, sailing from the depths of the sea

You are the one who brings love,

You grace us with everything that we need.

Lakshmi, Lakshmi, Queen of Abundance,

Beautiful Queen of Abundance, you carry the grace of love

Lakshmi, Lakshmi

Yes, she loves wonderful avenues of creative expression.

June 19 - Full Moon

The screenplay is finished. I sent out copies, with Teka's colorful cover. Now I'll go watch the river flowing and check in with Ashento.

It is positive to present our love story as reuniting as twin flames, flowing throughout the eons, where the flames of our undying passion, are never to be extinguished, no matter who or what flows between us. We have reached a new level. The realms of this celestial haven await your visit. Thank you for returning to your higher self.

The ascended ones and the masters are pleased for the completion. Communication is necessary to produce a finely crafted, far reaching dynamic expression.

All is already set in the realms of creation. Return to your voice, to release the energy for singing, to let abundance flow freely.

Be the source of your own power. Writing daily releases feelings.

I am the Source of love

Attuning, attuning to the higher realms.

Resounding, resounding, hear the call of your soul

Echoing in the universe, throughout the realms of heaven

Waves upon waves, light rays, from the great source of love

Enter, enter, the portal is opening

, ready to receive, all that you are,

to help remember why you came from a star.

Leave the density of life, release the Earth you know.

Sail gracefully to your destiny, where only you can flow

Your spirit sails within, toward the source of love,

to release, to heal, to enliven life, with grace from above

I am the source of love, the source of light

I send myself to the realm of light,

on a radiant beam of love

I receive the love of Source deep within.

Blessed By Light-filled Love

My soul on wings of love, on wings of light,

softly illuminates my way

I'm never alone or left behind in the veils of darkness

I open my eyes, my mind, my heart, to the brightness

I am the birds, I am the trees,

I am the mystery, I am free

(Oh, hey ahey hiya, yahey, yahey, alleluia) 2x

I am the radiant one. I restore the way of light

I am I am I am, I am the light

June 22

Dream - A beautiful radiant Goddess with long light hair, wearing an emerald green sparkling long dress, sings this song,

Queen of the Stars

I am Queen Inanna, Queen of Heaven

Dream with me, dance along your journey, home to the stars

It's all the same, paradise from here to Gaea Star.

Breathe in light, love, and peace,

within your heart, within your soul

As you weave your web of life, in paradise, in the universe

Surrender to the beauty within, surrender to the beauty above.

To the beauty of the fertile ground, look around, look around

Nature's elements, wind, fire, water, earth

I am Queen Inanna, Queen of the heavens

It's all paradise from heaven to Gaea Star

You are alive, you are alive, in the wonders of paradise

As you weave your web of life, in paradise, in the universe

Inanna, Queen of Heaven, Gaea Star, Goddess CD

Spirit of the Sun Music - 2011

June 24

Dream, I see lights in heaven, like a movie going on. We are on the next phase, filming it. Is there anything from the higher realms?

Yes, we are pleased to see the gathering of the tribes of light, as you are manifesting your soul's expression.

The deeper you travel into the realms of celestial wonder, the further you merge into the light.

By breathing in deeply to flow out of drama into peacefulness,

challenges are released. You'll feel blissfully aware.

To move beyond thunder is to accept the sounds of love and life, for yes, it is all the same paradise, from here to Mother Gaea.

You can travel to any realm beyond the veils of illusion, when you sit in quiet contemplation, following your breath.

As you go deeper, each level is lifted, reducing the space a little more, until there is total immersion in the next higher realm.

When a twin flame does not dwell on the physical realm with the other, it may feel as if one is incomplete. The longing, the feeling that there is someone else really suited for you, never goes away.

Uniting with your twin flame, feels like total completion, resulting in great creative power, as you work together manifesting powerful visible art and wisdom for all to benefit from.

To be fully creating with your beloved twin flame, is an intense feeling of swirling colorful love and resonating sound frequencies.

Release the shackles of dense perceptions of life. Realities come and go.

Believe that the lighter you sail, you float ever higher.

Walk with me, as a luminous being, blessed by light filled

spiritual love.

June 27

Oh, radiant ones, look within to heal your souls.

Humans believe that their dramas are real, using terms like battle, fighting, can't. Without their stories where are they? What happens to their inner life?

The spiritual reason of existence is overshadowed, as if it does not matter. Treasure every aspect of earth life.

It is not until you become older and wiser, that one realizes the importance of fostering the spirit within.

To change one's life is to trust, that all is returning to normal. Open your inner eyes to see beyond the illusion of life.

Returning to the light helps you to remember the way from the stars.

As you walk the path of love, realize it is all only love that transcends all boundaries.

Take time to be alone, to rest, to walk in the deep forest and

seek the flowing waters, for nature leads you onward to bliss.

Responding differently to all that summons is a promising challenge.

Your soul seeks to reunite with your higher self, with the bright spark that continues to burn brightly here, awaiting your return.

There is a vast storehouse of esoteric wisdom, designed to impregnate the worlds of time with beauty, wonder and dreamscapes, from distant galaxies of celestial realms.

Revert to vastness. Release all restrictions that confine radiant, wondrous expressions. Dream on, Goddess of the Stars, once you awaken to your Divinity, why go on with what does not resonate in the highest level? Come home, my gentle one, flow upward, lightly like the ever-returning hummingbirds.

Do you not feel the pull, the longing for a deep spiritual existence, for time to enjoy joyful prayers, communing with nature, her wondrous waterfalls, magnificent beauty, celestial music and birds singing their morning concerts?

You are me. I am you. Together we are unified forever, in love as a balanced and strong team.

We have completed many spiritual deeds, in the realms far beyond Earth, my Untelia.

Past, present, future, all are the same. There is no difference, for each moment comes but once, with no repeats.

To remain stuck in one's life, is to walk in fear, tightness and uncertainty, from here to there.

Open to the light dawning. Trust that you're always fine, that all bills are paid on time.

Claim abundance, saying, "I am always abundant."

The learning is profound and immensely rewarding, on your holy journey back home.

To restore balance, is to accept attaining mastery over yourself.

Keep releasing, to step through the portal, even amidst busyness, to settle into the path of spiritual creative teacher.

May I retain and understand my dreams, as I slip back to Earth.

July 3 - 4

Rain falls, singing gentle roof rhythms, echoing patterns of resonation, in the dark night, soaking the Earth again. Thank you, Ashento for helping the story to unfold. It is being read in Korea, Switzerland, Hawaii and elsewhere.

Congratulations on a job well done, for assimilating your insights from nature, dreams and the high spiritual teachings.

We sense the veils have lifted for many of you.

The new energies of your awakenings, are sending out vast sparkling light waves, illuminating Gaea Star. It is happening, even if not easy to notice.

Meditate at least 30 minutes daily, to maintain one's spiritual focus after a busy day, to settle chaos, to access your true missions.

Rainbows are radiant rays of light and love. Each ray reflects love; powerful red, passionate orange, healing yellow, soothing green, calming blue, royal purple and white, for spirit flowing higher.

Radiant ones, you are reflections of love and peace, in beautiful rays of colors like never seen before.

Listen to nature as her waves flow to the shore, kissing the earth. Enjoy the river flowing in the dark, alive, aware, endlessly sailing to the sea, always part of the mystery.

The portals are opening, the layers are dissolving.

You're holding my heart in the depths of your soul, just like you have, since the dawning of our sacred birth.

I hear the chickadees sweetly singing in your farm.

Come, vision of splendor, of light. Shine the way for those dwelling in darkness, so they fly, from the familiar place they call home, leaping into formlessness, to begin the next part of their timeless journey, beyond boundaries of familiar faces, past the ropes of the deep end, to flow onward to that love in their hearts.

Why fill in the emptiness within? Listen to the quiet space once in a while, to hear the Universe sighing at its' own existence.

Shine like a radiant portal of light, a beacon within your soul. To believe in oneself, accept all that you are.

There is only one creation, one essence of all life, here and there.

July 9 - 10

I heard in my dream, Cohan.

Cohan is the name of an ascended being of the highest order. It is also the level you traveled this past dream time with me. Continue to seek knowledge beyond the physical realm.

This is the moment to open to all that lies before you. Take control as an angel of light, angel of love.

You are a master of the light. You can change it all.

As radiant ones prepare for the great changes coming.

It is easy to find one another by sending out a light signal from within the center of your heart space where the soul finds refuge.

It is not only I calling to rise above, to be the light. The Shining

Ones are summoning their sons and daughters, to heed the call.

Your powerful energy gathers in your circle, with teachings and communion with the elemental energies of fire, water, air and earth.

Release focus on the physical. Cast away what no longer serves. Organize resources to enlarge spiritual space as you soar to the heavens, on your favorite star with dreams of joyful freedom.

Be like the rushing river, complete, not needing a thing, for it only flows toward the sea, gathering momentum, yes.

Each soul rises from within, knowing it is not perfect, content it is only temporary, like the candle burning in, even as a small flame, until the wick is out, just as the soul leaves only when it is time to go.

I'm Rising

I'm gonna rise every morning, when the sun does shine.

I'm gonna rise every morning, when the birds start to sing.

I'm gonna rise to greet the new day, hey, hey, hey, ho

With the brilliant light shining, no matter where I go

Oh, what a day to be alive, what a day to just breathe,

to walk on the mother earth, to sip her sweet water,

to watch her fire all night long, hey hey hey hey ho

July 11 - 14 - 15 - 17

You are in the garden of loving manifestations, with devas, angels, and other Divine spirits, all sharing beautiful love.

All is well when you listen to insights, remembering predestined roles. The key is to write with colorful imagery, characters and action.

Carry our voices to the heavenly castle of our dreams, so, we may open to the wisdom within, to know the way home.

Open to heavens' will to maintain the starry connection.

Delve into the inner realms, seeking the mysteries of spiritual life. Establish an esoteric school to minister to the world, in need.

I'm rewriting the screenplay with new imagery.

Teach others to express their light by finding the way home, to their inner self, with love, willpower, devotion, awakening within.

I am, I am

I am the incarnation of love. I am, I am.

I am the incarnation of light, I am, I am.

I am the holy one of love, the shining one of light,

who came from heaven, from the great central sun,

to restore the light, to restore the love,

to restore humanity to their dignity.

I remember now, the holy council of love, sailing

in from everywhere, endless life streams, on

bodies of light, glowing like the moon,

to set humanity free, to free their chains,

to free their minds, caught in the webs.

I remember who we were, Guardians of the New Way,

Way showers, Shepherds, Bringers of the Dawn, Masters

, to teach the way, to find the keys to awaken, to gather,

to illuminate the radiant way home.

July 20

Sweep away darkness, the awakening of golden light is coming.

Resume the journey to the treasure of love, that is deep within.

It is the portal of new beginnings. Yes, the light glows brighter.

The veils are thinning, lifting higher. Love transcends all.

Friendships have no boundaries from far away.

Humans can save their world through radiant love, shining from Gaea Star towards the heavenly realms.

Awaken, arouse, anoint with intentions of greatness, brilliance and intelligence.

Release and cultivate higher feelings of love for each other. Recharge with water, the pure emissary of love, the embodiment of sweetness and vital energy.

May the river sweep your fears along the ever-singing waters of life, dissipating in the seas of love.

Rainbow ray of light, colors of creation, inspirations of love, eternally flowing.

Let the songs flow, arousing wisdom, sprouting like a tiny seed that is ready to burst forth with knowledge within, to be fully alive.

Aware. Awake. I am becoming whole, restored, in love with the part of my higher self, that remained in the heavens. I explore my true nature as a holy bright light, shining in the darkness, like a flashlight. I restore my batteries with eternal loving light.

There comes a time in every one's life, when they look within, to ask their soul, "Do I want to continue this. Is this why I came here?"

That thought is underneath the pondering, for the soul begins to remember, slowly at first, that there is something more to life.

The light turns on, to illuminate clearly, with renewed purpose. The spirit sings, "Yes, I hear you calling me. I sense I am rising from my long slumber, to open my life, to bring understandings, at last, aha moments, for me to truly see."

July 22 My Mom's Birthday

Atutenia is your ancient name from the highest order. It means one who pours forth.

Consider changing from business owner, farmer, and animal tender, to devoting more attention to what joyfully enlivens your soul, such as singing, writing, recording and playing sacred music, especially with the ukuleles, harp and flutes.

Dream - About Arcturus, a large blue planet, as if I came from there. I found books about the Arcturians, by Patricia Pereira. These teachings are intense. I feel the powerful depth of you, Ashento wash over me. I long for you in the physical, to happily walk Earth together.

I spread knowledge wherever I am called.

Life on Gaea Star requires great interactions with many souls. We encourage you but do not intervene, although it may seem

as if spirit does. We only point the way, to access the keys, to give the threads, to weave a positive reality for all who ask for assistance.

Restoring Earth to her true splendor is quite an undertaking by the higher levels. We focus our guidance to all leaders who came to anchor in this reality, to change the world, step by step, with songs, prayers, love, and lightness of being, for all to benefit from.

Continue imparting knowledge to those who listen and feel a spark of inspiration. Redirecting life is just the beginning.

The profound changes coming are a new way of connecting, where spirit is accessed through prayers and only telepathy.

Awakening to your divine holy selves, is really the first phase.

As you do this, the rest of your tribe will happily follow.

I love to connect with my family of light. May we link to sing in gatherings to honor Gaea Star, as music is the essence of life.

July 27

Dream: a lovely beautiful, Goddess appears, wearing a brilliant sparkling golden crown of stars, flanked by magnificent horses.

August 2 - 19

I see a movie scene, a large celebration with a crowd. A huge peacock struts around with crystals and stars decorating her wings, surrounded by colorful feather beings.

"All life matters" is a relevant important message to present. It's not what you do, it's who you love and how you open your heart.

I make Shalaya a character with the celestial name of Ayalasha, before she goes to Gaea Star. She remembers her past as a star priestess from the purple realm, with abiding love for Gaea Star. She plays beautiful music with Ashento, as they reawaken their celestial connection, rekindling memories of ancient times. Angels transform into trumpet flowers, lilies, and roses.

I sense Ashento when I meditated, watching my breath, seeing the golden orbs like on my first Vision Quest. Peaceful loving energy and magnificent healing light is floating all around.

September 7

Illusions

Illusions, illusions

When are you going to live beyond?

When are you going to look beyond the realms of time,

beyond dimensions of reality, beyond?
Holding visions of crystalline beauty, of radiant lives,
opening the portals of awakening,
within your hearts, within your mind.
Honor the will of heaven, to live within your true souls,
to love each other as never before, for there is so much more.
Step through the veils of illusions to walk the path of the priestess.
Turn away from all that no longer serves
Beyond, beyond, beyond,
Turn away, turn away, from all illusions, illusions

September 12

Dream: Ayalasha was in an exquisite temple, in realms of crystalline beauty, where peace, love and light emanated. Beautiful Goddesses were massaging souls upon their return to heaven after passing from earth, while singing and talking softly, "Release, relax, let go, your body is no longer with you. Open to your soul's essence."

October 2

Thanks, Ashento for the beautiful love song that came last night.

Sail into the Universe

Let's sail into the universe, together on our stars, united as one,
far from the folds of humanity, into the bliss of union,
Expanding our love, free of the veils of illusion.
Oh, my love, I long for you,
Oh, my sweetness, we'll never be through.
Carry our love on the wings of light wherever we sail.

Blessed By Light-filled Love

Bountiful wings of love, bountiful wings, free of the veils.

I have waited eons to hold you close to me,

with waterfalls cascading, dancing before us in beauty

Wiping away all those years of separation

Oh, my love, I long for you,

Oh, my sweetness, we'll never be through.

Carry our love on the wings of light wherever we sail

Bountiful wings of love, bountiful wings, free of the veils

Sail into the universe, together on our stars united as one

Oh, my sweetness, the bliss of celestial, celestial union, union.

Smooth Sailing Love Songs, CD, Spirits of the Sun, 2013

October 6 - 9 - 16 - 20

A dream - Filming in nature, with stars brilliantly shining. I placed a vase of roses on the soft Earth. We're having artistic fun with dashing and vibrant colorful costumes.

My sweetness, you are emerging with inspiring creative ideas. As you connect to the realms of heaven, you accept the role as high priestess of the stars, immersed in the magnificence of life.

Rise up star woman, send out powerful energy everywhere.

It's flowing faster now that the awakening is accelerating into multiple realities. All is not as it seems. The ascension is beginning.

Every moment defines all that we see or need to help humanity.

Bless all chaotic lives with pure love, light and sweetness.

Let's communicate daily through writing, as it is excellent for focusing, to create a light channel, a vortex of message filled auric fields. Thank you for opening to healing in the moonlight.

Life is complex and challenging. Humans develop their spirit, according to their free will and their subsequent decisions.

I ask why is it so difficult to remain connected to our higher self?

At times, the veils of materiality completely obscure a deep spiritual connection, causing the separation to widen from the higher self, which remained in the realms of celestial splendor.

As guides, we are always ready and willing to be in direct communication to assist humanity.

Release distractions through prayer, exercise and loving service.

Dream - Gaea Star has a swirling, toroidal field of magnetic energy. She is alive, pulsating and revolving as our lives changed.

I love wearing sparkling tiaras to celebrate Star Queen splendor. It is such an uplifting, regal feeling of magical delight. On and on we flow, filled with power and light. If only we knew the way home, there would be less suffering on Earth. How can we transform this mental anguish that is self-created?

Let the shining light be ever present in your warm hearts.

Cultivate the divine essence of love, joy, healing and nurturing union, with positive vibrations, that is the will of heaven.

Keep simplifying until what you have is easy to maintain.

Treat all life as a spiritual practice, a union with the light.

October 23 - 26

A prayer to humanity - Awake to the golden sunshine, in the morning.
Walk deep into the forest, to breathe in the beauty of nature.
Swim in cool waters. Play in green gardens. Smell sweet roses.
Eat peaches, strawberries, and blueberries where they grow.
Lay upon the soft ground with teeming life all around.

Blessed By Light-filled Love

Be under the stars as they glow in the silent night.

The most important relations are the connections of souls. What each person brings to the quest of life is the true reality.

For example, when Ghandi met the English government, they were adamant he did not have power to do anything. Look what happened. He united his country through his non-violent beliefs, forming a remarkable peace movement that overthrew the British rule.

You can do the same by inviting leaders, film makers and other talented people, to present the message of awakening.

What is there left to do, except acknowledge that the great change is necessary in this ripe and fertile time?

Creative harmony melds everything and everyone, which is the theme of the story, the council, elders, characters, the songs, all because of deep abiding love for Gaea Star and her living beings.

Separation, the absence of love is healed by compassion and nurturing without resistance, while undoing knots of ignorance.

Unification occurs by believing there is only one ultimate expression in all things, the power of love, as it flows from deep within the body's most powerful organ, the heart.

Let the creativity flow. Filming the story. Encourage participants to play aspects of previous lives, by pretending they are in a new time and place, and expressing that love and harmony is the only answer.

I enjoy opening as I write, making it rich with reality and tension.

As one uplifts themselves, life constantly changes.

To act as a graceful loving being, is to fly with the wings of heaven, the ultimate fulfillment.

Nov 4

Finishing recording the 'The Gaea Star Crystal, Awakening the Tribes of Light,' CD with Brian Johnson in Northampton, Ma. It was fun to use our own songs for the possible soundtrack, rather than trying to film the story. After the year-long project, the engineer asked for another song. Days later, after Obama won the presidential election, I dreamt this song about faeries going to Gaea Star to help humanity learn how to live in harmony.

Let's Sail to the Realms

Let's sail to the realms of Mother Gaea, on the path of the stars

Let's sail to the realms of Mother Gaea, on our divine mission,

to awaken humanity to live with truth and love,

To awaken the tribes of light to remember who they are

Awaken, awaken, awaken tribes of light

Awaken, awaken, tribes of love,

Oh heya, heya, heya, hey ya

We'll live in faerie realms of nature, her fire, water, air, earth

We'll live in the forest, in the trees, in the flowers, in the breeze

We'll live with the birds and the rivers and golden leaves

Growing gardens on Gaea with joy and inspiration

On to Mother Gaea, helping humanity,

remember their way home,

through love, light, love, only love

On to Gaea Star, awaken, awaken, tribes of love, of peace

Gaea Star Crystal, CD, 2009

November 9 - 18

Dream - A magnificent vision of Isis, the Egyptian Goddess, with her queenly presence, expansive rainbow wings and golden crown, reflecting the red disc of the brilliant sun. She teaches the mysteries of the esoteric realms while inspiring dynamic, creativity for Gaea Star.

Isis

Isis, goddess of the universe, goddess of the starry night

Isis, your golden wings, kiss the sun with radiant light

In your celestial palace you shine,

blue, purple, golden crystalline

Isis, queen of the universe, please guide us

Isis, teacher of the mysteries, of the healing arts,

Isis, Isis

Yes, there's always more to create but with your excellent

motivation, keep working on finishing what you started a year ago.

Honor the Lightworkers' profound awakening with the archangels.

December 15

Use imagery of a wood cabin, through the evolution of the wood, how it evolved from the tree, sprouting from seed below the Earth, from the rain and sun, back to the source of light and love, to oneness in the celestial realm above.

Journey with me. Feel free as you release all that binds.

Life flashes memories of warm creation, dancing in heaven, surrounded by golden, yellow, silver, turquoise and blue ribbons.

January 21, 2009

We have an anniversary party for WiseWays herbals and release the 'Gaea Star Crystal', CD, which includes the song, "Let Me Love You," from Ashento. We head to Kipahulu, Maui for a vacation.

The 'Gaea Star Crystal' songs blaze a shining path, creating a loving musical, with many expressions from spirit.

Maui, Hawaii, home of Pele, the volcano Goddess. It is a priceless gem of powerful fiery energy, a vortex for many of the tribes of light. We are with you in her fiery realms.

February 11

Dear Spirit of Oneness,

Aloha, thank you for the blessing of incarnation this life.
You are grace, love, beauty, order and chaos.
You created Gaea Star, with magnificent oneness, infinite
patience, compassion and gentleness of loving light.
All that I know and care for, is from you.
I feel rays of love from the source of the essence of all. Radiant
one of loving light, you have given hope and joy in the belief of perfection.

I am that I am, grateful from the depth of my heart, as I live surrounded by your belief in the beauty of humanity.

I am happy to be alive, hopeful for this world to learn to serve you, to live in peace, as we dance exuberantly, on your holy ground, seeing joy in all life, all beings and all creatures.

Thank you for Machu Picchu, kittens, butterflies, smiling people, for fruit trees, friends, family, and Goddess and God.

Thank you for male/female energies, harmonizing in unity.
Thank you for wonderful music that expresses so delightfully,
The essence of love. We are blessed at your generosity.

Dear Spiritual Sister, Goddess of the Blue/Violet rays of love, we are pleased you take rest and swim in the sacred waters of love. Thank you for your beautiful songs inspired from the healing vibrations of Mother Gaea, for creatively expressing the light force.

As an emissary of love, you are truly a ray of light.

Bless your life and loves as you open to the will of heaven.

Oh, sparkling star ray of light, as you shine, you receive the gifts of knowledge, the nectar of peace and manna from heaven.

We call you Natinia, Anatohey, Pishana Iska Apuka Alleya. The one who hears the voice of heaven, from deep within her heart. Return to the light of dawn to hear all that is within.

February - Maui

Immerse in the solitude of nature, to look beyond reality into the realms of living light, merging, rising to the beauty.

Now that you are away from your busy life, unwind, opening like a flower, with each petal releasing the material, to sail into the depths of majestic awakening.

Why be bound by the physical? Drop the veils. Stop running, wasting precious moments, when the purpose of ones' path is to unite with loving light.

Go into pure lands, alone, to burn away all that cloaks your full

soul-expression, to find your way to heal yourselves.

Heaven is within reach. Tune into the music from above, celebrate divinity with harmonic heavenly music.

Wear light colors to reflect the light, all that you are.

Stand in your power, to express loving light with joyful wonder. The awakening of your soul's true expression will lead you homeward.

All life is exquisite to witness and to learn from.

I am not a captive of your imagination. I float at whim wherever my energies flow, although you're writing always calls.

Thank you for the soothing wisdom from my twin flame. I hear the gentle voice of a master, singing through me.

May I be a divine emissary of love, like you, every day, grasping more fully what I came to do.

May I be free, full of peaceful love and light.

February 21

Dream: movie scenes of cars, changing into horses, charging up hills, reflecting life before the technological aspects that disconnected us from the natural cycles of life.

We showed old ways using nature's elements, to build stagecoaches, buggies, sailboats and ships, powered by wind, animals or people rowing, before technology overran the ways.

Is it too late to restore nature, to return to simplicity?

April 14

The code of life is inherent within the language of love.

It is the connection of light that creates a golden thread, a link manifesting spirit into matter in a peaceful, harmonious loving way.

June

Dream -Visions of humanity, washed in waves of loving light, merging into oneness, into a new era with peace, beauty and stillness, while also activating the Earth's crystalline grid.

July 23

There is a presence in all of Creation called "Vital body energy," measurable, discernible, unique, reflecting the pattern of the soul's blueprint, which can be renewed, through breath and pure water.

Everyone is consumed by the veils of reality, missing their connection to Divine Spirit. Humans are vastly different, yet underneath the surface is the same essence of spirit.

Now is the moment to commit to expressing your loving self.

Strive to maintain connection with Spirit, to reconnect with the healing force of eternal love, especially in unfortunate circumstances.

Everything is part of the game of life, just move the players.

Even if you falter or slip just get up, dust off, fly again, love life, each other, yourself and return to the light within, that's it.

You are energetic expressions between universal forces of light. Celebrate the treasure of life in joyful songs, in circles, with arms held high.

When the circle is broken, the union is disconnected and forgotten.

Through love, the forces of nature are balanced, and creative expression is perfected.

Sharing life in partnership is never meant to be a struggle.

It's joyful to remember why you are here, to commune and realign in the deepest sense with the essence of Spirit.

Enjoy the fruit of loves, the gift of light, of grace, touch and sensuality.

It awakens the heart to embrace the sacred ground of Gaea Star, to arouse the fires of desire, to climb the mountains of passion, to honor the beauty of the treasure of pleasure.

Life is to keep moving like rivers flowing, along the journey, to

the light, with realization, simplicity, wisdom, peace, acceptance.

It is the learning one does daily, that is a blessing of light.

October 3 - 15 - 21 - 22

Make a temple to expand your spiritual light body.

Practice joyful prayers of thanksgiving, affirmations and yoga.

Laugh, play, resist always working. Embrace a holy life again.

Each day brings renewal and hope, an honoring of all that you are, as daughters and sons of the great sun, source of love.

Sunshine reflects the source of light everywhere.

Always embrace this radiance of divine loving light.

To enter the void of creation, awaken to this holy place.

It is merely a flash away from your physical life.

Refresh by communing with nature, to become aligned.

Greet the day with a smile, a sparkle in your heart. Blessings.

Divine love shines every moment in both heaven and earth.

Within these realms, are rainbows, with beautiful colorful reflections in full visionary emanations of loving light filled essences.

November 11

May I reflect love in all moments of this beautiful journey. I surrender to the powerful energetic vortex of creativity.

Celebrate past, present, future – It is all your destiny, sung sweetly, never forgotten by her star travelers.

Our connection is a powerful expression of this same essence. We see you striving for balance, to establish intentions for peace.

Moving and healing stagnation in forgotten places, is what matters.

November 20 - 27 - 30

How does one film the Gaea Star Crystal movie?

Create the Genesis, the prelude, as the temple doors open into crystalline magnificence and sacred geometry. Look to celestial beauty to feel renewed.

Dress as if you are from the stars, with reflective light.

Always direct your attention inward. Follow leads as you gather the tribe.

Your expanding light reaches into the realms of omnipresence.

Gathering in celebration to spirit, heals the raiment, the fabric of life. The veils drop, as the light rises in a circle of beautiful love.

Be one, as you follow the truth with visionary commitment.

Within the depth of your soul, is the source of loving, radiant light.

It is all within the crystalline temple that dwells deep inside your soul.

Dash across the universe like courageous, lightning, experiencing life with unbridled passion, the true reason for being.

Opportunity is a graceful growing to the source of oneness.

Keep your hearts singing as all desires are fulfilled.

Being one with the light is removing all distractions.

Be discerning in what you ingest and engage in for well- being.

Maintain the bridge between Heaven and Earth, to stay connected to the source of light, love and divine awareness.

Be a beacon of love by extending your antenna to receive the signal, that is constantly present from Source.

To love freely, reach high as if walking in both realms.

What is above, is below, united in the heart of love, the mandala of life. Keep the light of truth on, have faith.

There is no waiting, or turning away, from the importance of remembering why all of you came to live on Gaea Star.

Any difficulties are illusions of walls of emotional distancing

that obscure visions and the essence of life, living with love.

To walk with the breath of life, is to be aware and present, in union with all spirit and truth, with companions and no separation.

All is as it should be, wherever you are, whomever you're with.

Your mission is complete, when you co-create, harmoniously together. What else is there, but to gracefully live with unified love?

December 1 - Full Moon

Dream: We are in a circle, praying, naming things we want to change, like poverty. We feel the angst of the negatives spoken, realizing its' better to pray in the positive, to sing of the light of the goodness, that we desire for the world around us.

Awakened by the bright full moon. Her luminous soul peers into my soul, reminding me of the power of heaven.

Blessed By Light-filled Love

Be active and aware of the full moons' qualities and mystical powers, as she reflects the sunlight, in her passage around Gaea Star.

It is the first of two full moons in December, so seek through introspection, the impact of each, upon your depths within.

The moon energies are so different each month and season.

The new day beckons as the gorgeous dawn rises. I am grateful to open to my destiny, to what I came to do. I am touched by writing Ashento's teachings. I surrender releasing what no longer serves me, asking for courage, to transform, to stand strong, to deeply connect to the source of love.

I communicate when you are receptive to hear my whispering.

Every moment that you follow your divine expression, brings you the pleasure of Earth's paradise.

Gaea Star provides elemental wonders, to enrich all lives.

You are all blessed to receive love, gratitude and goodness, as it is your divine right, to be surrounded with total love and healing.

Walk the path of peaceful star travelers, as spiritual warriors, by transcending, releasing, and celebrating each chapter of life.

Truth rings free, within the soft realms of the soul.

Just as dawn appears, after night, so does transformation always come to help fulfill your purpose at any time.

There is no choice for those who align with Archangel Michael, but to also carry his sword of discernment, power and wisdom.

Wash away doubts by believing that all is, as it is.

Trust what happens every day to be perfect, even if you do not understand why, for one always learn from every instance.

December 4

I love your sayings, Ashento. Thank you for the images, for helping me to tap into my power. I am one with you.

I await your total understanding, so you may also revel in the magnificence of this realm that I frequent.

Deep everlasting love only befalls those who dive into love's deep waters with passion, courage and the willingness to surrender to the will of heaven.

To enter into unfamiliar or unsafe waters, without a known secure outcome is the first step as a spiritual warrior, for one does not always know the way or where they may end up.

Just show up in trust when spirit calls you.

When asked to enter into co-creation on a deep level, we merge into a force of unity, of two polarities into oneness, the unique sum of the two opposites.

True love is royal, pure, and warm, knows no boundaries, and is healing, regardless of the outcome.

One cannot expect love to be predictable or long lasting, as love is unconditional, with living, breathing acceptance.

Pure love warms your soul and heals deeply.

To love is to know God, Goddess, all that there is.

All boundaries are transcended, merged into with joyful enthusiasm and the willingness to forge, full steam ahead.

Love grows when you plant the seed and water it, with consideration, compassion, caring and nurturing.

You and I are here to serve, dance and sing in the light of love. Be good to yourself, love each other and it will set you free.

December 5

In the passage of time as you know it, there is a moment at one point where all that you have focused on for years, appears in front of you. Now you are face to face with your divine aspirations.

Embrace it as the hour of truth. You have arrived, as this is what you prayed for. Your deepest longing has manifested.

Think carefully before you walk away from the opportunity to merge with the manifestations of your desire, of your soul's longing.

All that comes before you lead you onward. All are lessons of love, of life, of the truth.

Follow your heart. It will lead you toward the light.

December 6 - 9 - 12 - 16

It's Never Too Late

It's never too late to be who you want to be to change your life, to manifest your destiny. There's no such thing as being too old,

For doing new feats, of being bold.

So, play upon the stage of life.

It's never too late to climb the tallest mountain

Or write like an eternal fountain,

Or plant an herb and flower garden.

Look to the sky as you fly, fly, fly.

It's never too late, to try, try, try.

We are reflections of each other, where we go is not important.

It is how we move through life.

Is it with grace and love, aware of the impact on each other?

Are we remembering that life is a group effort, a large web of interrelated dynamic beings, all helping to focus the beauty of spirituality in human form?

It is a composite of previous lives, a melting pot of experiences, that may have touched on the true reason for incarnating, with many evolving challenges in each stage.

Choosing the path of least resistance is easy, if you attune to your beating heart, as it flows with vital life force.

Most of the time, the subtle pulsations are not even noticed, unless one is physically exerted or touches their heart.

Life is a rich, full unique blessing to love, cherish and grow with. Breakthroughs happen when hearts open to all that comes along, believing it is sent by spirit, to enliven, to enrich and nurture.

Dream: Isis with astonishing imagery, healing with gentle, enigmatic power, singing, "Walk with me into the sun, high above the Earth, floating on dreams of creativity into the night."

December 17

At some moment in life, the opportunity to transform appears mysteriously, as if out of nowhere. The inevitable happens, one walks through the portal, easily changed forever with no difficulty.

The power and force of the new change, pulls the soul forward in the fashion of calling home, the lost pieces of a puzzle.

Many times, the message for change, of reaching deeper towards the light, presents itself as sayings in a book, an article or photo, a friend speaking or a stranger passing by, all weaving the same message from spirit, calling you toward the wisdom of the new experience, of a deeper connection to Source, to the brilliant light of your creative self.

Realizing oneness, then becomes a painless mission of connecting all the missing pieces, unifying the body, mind and spirit.

Each unique being or soul, is striving to reintegrate all of these parts, which is the subconscious mission of returning to the light.

Most have forgotten this path of knowing, due to their so-called misfortunes of life, which are merely lessons along the journey.

There are now many awakening souls, who are flying smoothly onward in unity, singing, celebrating peace, breaking free of dysfunctional, patterns of disharmony.

This pathos is dissipating rapidly, due to the wondrous strides and efforts of many beings, gathering the force of love everywhere.

Gather Together

Gather together in oneness, gather together in peace.

Let the feelings of love arise, let the feelings of love release.

May the light within continue to shine,

May the force of compassion begin to align.

Beings of light return to your center.

Beings of light, reenter, unity of pure light, unity of pure love,

Pure light, pure love, divine source, divine light.

December 22 - 23

Completion. Stretch beyond concepts. Reach past mortal mentality. Dive deep until you reach the power and presence of the distant waves of the swirling expressions of truth.

You know the feeling when you arrive; it is clear, concise and gentle. You relinquish all previous expectations.

Imagine diving into a pool, where you see a room at the bottom, that calls you to enter. You swim excitedly, propelling yourself into this intriguing cavern, which at first, is a narrow passage, then opens into a canyon of exquisite crystalline formations.

Light is gleaming in from somewhere else. You are in spacious serenity, in this wonder, beneath the surface, yet how can this be?

Where am I? Is this Heaven or Earth? Serene music plays softly. A gentle breeze flows. The water disappears as the moisture on your skin is slowly absorbed. An angelic choir sings a haunting song:

You Are at Peace

You are at peace, you are at peace, you are at peace.

Within your heart, within your heart, a gentle way to release

All is well, all is at peace. Love yourself, open like a shell.

Release love, release. Be at peace, just like a dove.

You are love within your heart.

Now is the time to start. You are peace.

It's only a moment in your perception, that you hear me, in whatever you are in the midst of.

Discipline comes by maintaining an ever-present connection with your higher self by reaching deeper within often.

Cultivate all things relevant for well-being, rather than blindly tending the ego with gratification. Place attention where important.

Diamonds sparkle in the night sky, with stars illuminating the passage of night. How little we understand the vastness of space.

Where do humans fit, in the symphony of life, in the universe?

There are many aspects of reality in this realm.

From the minutest to the grandest of light or dark, some are visible to the beholder, some are not.

Each person is ultimately called to stand strong for their ever-evolving awareness, some never heed the call, remaining fixed within their own limited perception of reality.

There is no other planet like Gaea Star. She stands alone.

Trail of Light

Follow the trail of light, keeping your dreams in sight.

Revel in the mystery of whom you came to be.

Dance in the mystery of the grass and the sea.

Oh, the sun brings warmth and light,

Oh, the moon, bathes us in the night.

Dive deep into the fountain of love, so sweet.

Open like a butterfly emerging from the chrysalis of a cocoon.

Shine your holy light just like the radiant moon

Let your spirit sail high, keeping your dreams in sight

Along the trail of light, along the trail of light.

December 30

As I received this, I typed into the computer, instead of writing.

Once I am drawn into physical reality, I manifest even stronger to those that seek direct communion, within the realms I frequent.

I do not spend all my time here, as there is always a new action, a request from spirit to flow to, a different aspect of universal consciousness, to occupy my energy. I assist with the healing forces wherever needed.

All of my actions, express love for everyone, from the realms above, for we hold the universal intention, to realign humanity with the highest vision of love.

There is renewed fervor in what all of you are doing now.

It is the willingness to express what flows on the deep level.

You are awakening, stretching beyond limits of physical life.

A gentle reminder to all who follow the path of loving light, know that all is well and flowing, despite the shadowy grip of chaos.

In every aspect of human life, there are choices that may not seem easy or pleasant to move toward, because of the loss that is perceived to be greater than the path that lies in front of you.

The illusions are more powerful than realized.

Rise above the drama, that is habitually perceived, to let the winds of change, remove all that no longer serves.

Move toward the new direction, to the essence of all that sings, from the silence within your true heart's desire.

Ask yourself in the quiet moments of peaceful places in nature,

"How many times have I been at this same juncture?"

Did you not survive, escaping from the shadows of difficult choices that no longer allowed you to bloom, develop and emerge from within, as a fuller expression?

Come, my sweetness, to the table of abundant love, the fruit is here, piled high with the colors of the rainbow.

Bless you and all that flows to you, as you dance in pure joyfullove, light, healing and union.

Your Divine Spirit is within, let her sing to the great one, to the Crystala, that awaits your returning in graceful poetic love.

Blessings as you celebrate the procession of the Full Moon, ending this year of great change.

January 2, 2010 - The New Year

The new decade begins with a powerful Full Moon, with prayers for hope, peace and joyous union with all sentient beings.

Everyone feels the promise within their challenging lives, unraveling every moment, a little more of their true nature, as they access the great depths of their spiritual hearts.

Joyful ecstatic union of the body with the spirit within: is the only reason one incarnates to holy Mother Gaea.

She brings out the best and the worst in souls, as they learn to love and do battles with the demons, they think they encounter on their journey home.

Call forth her healing, guiding light that is always there.

Nature is pure majesty swirling in the ether. Breathe it in to recover when you are overwhelmed from the heat and cold winter.

Renew with water and rest. Absorb her resources, that give what is needed, to fully regain power, strength, and creativity.

Love flows strongly from the heart - the soul's home.

Be one with beauty as it rises from the depths within.

The delightful New Year is what we make of it, what we bring home. So, let go, believe everything was and is created perfectly.

If you allow fearful doubts to creep in, then you do not believe the light is always shining within. The reason you are not aware, is that you do not see what is right before you. Know there is only love.

A friend calls, "You're blessed to receive the abundance of divine inspiration. Be aware that the ego does not grow as you cultivate these gifts. As are a steward of the All-ness of God, you must remain impeccable in all that you do."

Snow falls gently making deep piles of white, with fierce cold and ice, creating a winter of indoor creativity.

Prayer: Thank You

Thank you for life, for the visitation rights granted, for all that comes along, every moment, to open wide, to the way, to shine deeply as we peel the layers away.

Thank you for the brilliant sun shining, for green grass blooming, for the fluffy snow, for the healing from the quiet countryside, for the pure flowing tasty water to quench our thirst.

Thank you for delicious plants and fruits that nurture us.

Thank you for exuberant, exhilaration and creative expressions.

Thank you for hope, for dreams, for all the blessings that flow, for helping us to know the way, to find what we seek, to discover why we're here, what we're doing.

As we sail in our small boats, sometimes we feel like we're floundering, having lost our way.

Thank you for guiding us to stay on course, to follow the path, laid before us, for your patience, for letting us make our own mistakes.

Thank you for inspiring respect for Mother Earth.

May we continue to nurture, support and help each other.

Thank you for what flows, as we learn to get it right again, for another day, full of wonderful awe for the magnificence.

Thank you for our families, for each other.

Thank you, holy Mother. Thank you, holy Father.

May we live in peace and harmony, soon for everyone.

Thank you for giving your abiding sweet love.

Blessed By Light-filled Love

Into the evening, you release your consciousness, to renew your body. Listen to hear the stillness and the softness of the night.

If you remain awake, you will assimilate the stars, generating a refreshing awareness of the mysteries of celestial oneness.

Pray with me then, my sweetness. Share with me as you awaken, for we are one in the early light.

Yes, in communion, I breathe with you, for the veils of illusion, the curtains of darkness, the shadows of forgetfulness, dissipate and disappear the moment, when one reaches deep into their dreamtime, to reconnect, to merge with Spirit, to carry it forward, to understand the force of love made manifest.

When Lightworkers seek the depths within, they activate their love core, sending, reflecting, receiving and affirming light.

The sun and the stars are a constant barometer of Creation manifested. To feel this flow is to be in alignment with Source.

Believe that all is one, that you are progressing toward the light, to illuminate your way home, to integrate what has separated humanity from the source of love.

You'll remember your star past, as you wake to Divine essence.

These realizations are not difficult, they occur through direct communion with Creator and the acceptance of light and love.

Recognizing these aspects, reworks life into an expression of devotion, assimilation and reflecting the light.

You and I are one constant stream of blessings of eternal love. Finding your way to Source is always my pleasure to witness.

It matters not what I look like. Thank you for reflecting me, for giving love and attention, to connect to our Divine essence.

Bless your light and oneness. We are always in sweet union.

January 3

Dameron and I meet other loves, conflicting our relationship.

To reach deep into the heart, to shed ways of relating, may be difficult in love. Making room for others, within the inner sanctum, requires sacrifice. Release the familiar and comfortable.

Losing a lover for another love opportunity, may bring deeper spiritual growth. When you look back on what has gone on, you will see how great changes, nurture our soul for the better.

Pursuing the souls' expression within, assert its' true destiny.

The soul says, "I am here to reckon with, so listen to my lingering wishes, for yes, it will bring you greater happiness."

I am the window of the soul, brightly showing the glory of your true path, to reflect the light, like a beacon in the night, forging through, shining a clear way to the source of love.

I am your guide, steering you through the dark choppy waters, through the tunnel of love. I am your companion, celestial flame, and dynamic partner, here to nurture and remind you, that all is well.

Trust me, allow the magic of a new gentle spiritual voice to evolve. When left by a lover, you are never really alone. All is well.

Seeking change within, brings you to a higher realization, to honor your commitment as a spiritual warrior, to share messages of love and healing for the world. Walk that path as you breathe in and do yoga to nurture the physical.

Your soul knows the way to the depths of your fullest expression.

Bless you, my sweetness, you are loved, so open your radiant heart to the joy within, then love will flow deeply.

Connect with the mystery of self-expression, for everything will relax into place, refreshed. Great change means great shifts.

Everyone is blessed. Trust that what flows to you is the next lesson, to help you align even more with your spiritual path.

The Goddess appears to help everyone to stand strong through the coming change.

Gathering the family of love is all that matters, as you awaken, to merge into the path of light, love and communion with the Divine.

January 6

Misunderstandings arise due to complexities of personalities. Each soul carries a unique destiny on their path of life. Understand that whatever occurs, brings lessons of learning, that may go deep into previous lives and prearranged encounters.

Always maintaining a loving heart, requires great strength and courage in the face of adversity.

If you believe you are guided, then ask for help, to raise each situation to the highest realm of loving awareness.

When one denies all that is unseen, they feel alone and discouraged, wondering if one dimensional living is all there is.

In the realms of spirit, there are many souls that seek fulfillment.

Dwelling in despair is not an option here, there or anywhere.

Every lesson is a blessing, a new knowing, another layer peeled away to reveal the core of the true essence, returning to love.

Where is the medicine of the moment? Who we are is not what we do or make, but how we relate to each other. Is the enemy a shadow of disillusion or lack of love?

Reunite your fragments to rebuild trust, forging ahead, in all that you do for the sake of peaceful, loving light.

Accept the mystery of life, as a treasure of healing medicine.

I am surrounded by happy people, eager to create with harmonious love. May we shine the torch of light for all less fortunate.

January 8

Dream: A festive performance of the 'Gaea Star Crystal' with enthusiastic passion, fabulous musicians, fantastic costumes, a choir of angels, arial silk dancers and fire jugglers.

The Portal is Opening

The portal is opening, you can see the way.

The light is shining for this new day

Awaken, awaken, let your melodies arise.

Sing it out, sing it loud, oh holy ones stand proud.

Ohay yahay, ohay yahay, ohay yahay, yahay

Carry the message for this wondrous season,

For healing in the light of love and compassion

Now is the time to purify, to call in the blessings of attraction.

To spread the petals of love as far as one can see

To dance, play, sing and enjoy the mystery.

January 10

The new year is a time of renewal. The air, charged with radiant love is beaming everywhere with the increasing visibility of the magnificent Divine Feminine, as she touches humanity.

Let anything that no longer serves or is of benefit, disappear

without regret.

We're happy to see you release what no longer serves you as you strive to make positive change.

Returning to a space of love, is essential for you and the others, as you embrace this powerful moment, in the evolution of Earth.

Many hear angelic guidance during these pressing times, in dreams, children's words or elsewhere. One never knows where these important messages may come from.

Cultivate acts of love and kindness for each other.

Yes, the media is presenting distorted news to incite fear.

Their grip on the minds of unsuspecting people, is a dilemma, for it is the conqueror causing fear before the takeover is complete.

January 13 - 17

It is the ending of cycles that is difficult for so many to accept.

You can walk away with remorse or be happy for the valuable lessons learned from the intense experiences.

There are several approaches to understand which way to proceed. Each is a unique blessing, as the soul knows no limits.

The easier choice flows with ease and is lined with warmth and light. Usually other signs around you, also point to that choice.

It is an aha moment, when you finally realize your true purpose, an epiphany, as if a light is suddenly turned on in a dark room, and now you are never in the dark again.

One realizes their liberated soul is flying on the carpet of newly released desires, into the realms of vibrant expression, on a powerful roll, on fire, with no stopping the creative floodgate of love.

To open to the will of spirit, is to see the light within, shining ever brightly, showing you the way, like a homing pigeon returning to their original family of love.

Each mission began with magnitude, with similar beings, listening to the goals set before them. They agreed to travel with the speed of light to complete their missions without looking back.

It is a lengthy passage for some, while others have returned and may have even already embarked on another mission.

Be at peace with all that you encounter, for it is part of the whole.

Relaxing, is the art of believing you are a being of light, guided by love, spirit and free will, always returning to source, to love.

Saying goodbye to a partner, is to bless the next phase, with loving intentions, for friendship to evolve.

Feeling the hope for a new way, to restore, redirect and open your heart, mind and body to the new love waiting to be with you.

Yes, there is potential for a union of great significance for it is

truly a blessing as your souls weaves high magic.

Revel in your co-creative partnership, as you sing and play together. Open the floodgates of love, celebrating and sharing the message of harmonious love, with light, laughter and joy.

January 19 - 17 - 21

Bask in the radiance of love as you praise and cherish life. There is a moment before passing from the Earth to heaven, that one may feel sad or lost, for the change from the physical to the spirit, appears final, especially to those who remain behind.

All life is temporary; some do come and go quite quickly.

My llama Nina had a baby on the coldest day of the winter. He died later. We named him Mira Coco.

Mira Coco gave the lesson of caring, bringing your family together into oneness, realizing how precious life is, even if temporary.

There is no right or wrong, as everyone lives within boundaries of time, love and relationships, for their own soul's destiny.

Prepare for the illusions of life becoming more transparent.

Now is the time for Light Workers to act for Gaea Star, by forming groups, organizing events, focusing on manifesting change. Spontaneity is the key!

Begin with live improv theater, using artistic themes of discontent, disillusionment with governments and world leaders. Brilliant performance art overcomes the shadows by reflecting love.

January 24 - 25

As one opens to the light within, they welcome the grace of Source, by entering into a pure harmonious space, thus changing the downward spiral of life's conditions.

You are each responsible for raising the essence of love to where you affect change, for humanity is at a critical phase.

Every positive vibration adds to itself, to create a feeling of love, excitement, and power, with hope and joyful exuberance for life.

Begin every day with acts of love. Think, how may I serve? Who may I help, to feel loving inspiration by my goodness and caring?

May your smile inspire contentment, and peaceful happiness.

Shine like the brilliant sun, for even when it's cloudy, you feel the light behind the clouds, always warm, giving and fully present.

Reflect your joy and truth with courage and power.

No matter what is going on, remain in a loving space, helping others to cultivate love even more.

If you see what I see, outlooks will change, as love heals.

Everything negative falls, as both cannot exist in the same place.

Light filled love dissolves shadows, diminishing the darkness.

As my new love played the piano, I saw Ashento. He asked to play through his hands. It was a magical moment of beautiful music. The Hermit of the Tarot was shining, like a mantle over the Earth.

Life moves onward, with twists and turns, regardless of what one does. Each leaves an imprint on your soul and consciousness within, to be utilized whenever possible.

Sometimes memories of previous lifetimes are activated by unconscious acts that excite you.

Every aspect of being, is learning and growing in the moment.

The willingness to change, to merge softly with life's conditions, is very important to maintain calmness and inner peace.

The dance of intimacy is based on trust, a willingness to serve, to surrender, to the grace of love, like a flower opening petal by petal.

January 28

Every moment is a treasure of pleasure, a blessing, a victory of manifestation. All is well and flowing.

To rise in the dawn of a fresh morning, is to breathe, see, feel and hear life, as a spirit in human form. Honor that important part.

Life is a desired position in the universe, a pristine privilege.

Awaken my sweetness, with a loving heart, with beauty abounding for a new day, in the splendor of paradise.

Appreciate the magnificence of Gaea Star, by creating joyful harmonies in all that you do.

I have a staph infection on my wrist, passed on from Maui.

The condition reflects your life, indicating something not right. Use your healing herbal and clay poultices. Bless with sunshine. Do not let negativity fester. Respect the sacredness of your body.

Love you, my sweetness, I am off to a galaxy to answer the call.

The full moon casts brilliant light on the snow. A heavy rainstorm flooded, making icy roads. Despite the restless energy, the Earth still blesses with radiance every day.

Healing energy sweeping the Earth, is heralding the thousand years of peace. We are grateful to be in the homestretch, to see the light dawning. There is no stopping now, nothing to fear, as we feel the love vibrations.

January 29 - 30

Into the bliss of knowingness, you ascend a little more every day, returning and reconnecting with me, your celestial partner.

Yes, I am far away from you, however, look deeply into your heart. See and feel me as the one who nurtures and loves you always.

Ride the waves of our divine union, aligning as our blue and purple rays transform into swirling magenta majesty.

Come my sweetness, sail into my light filled wonder, release the density of Earth life, to, traverse briefly, in your rainbow light body, with wings opened wide. Come sail with me, forever and a day.

Wherever you are, feel royalty from the path of your most high home. Imagine wearing celestial gowns with Moonstones, Crystals and Turquoise, reflecting sparkly sunshine and the stars above.

Yes, combining earth and sea energies, develops your power as a radiant sky priestess, a Queen of the Sun and the Moon.

Wear star crowns to open third eye or crown energies.

February 1 - 2

The magical Full Moon on the snow, is exceptional. She is the pearl of the night, shining with vital life force, refreshing with her magnificent phases, maiden, mother, crone.

We love when you look up into the starry night, greeting us, as we are always listening.

To remember your connection to spirit, to the source of love and light, is to delve deeply into awakening, for every moment you accept spirit, releases the veils ever more.

Yes, that seems like a good idea, I shall dream on it.

February 3

Dream: In a room, meeting with business reps. I turned lights on that faced East and watered the plants, as people came in. I said, "I'm done with their services." A few left, rather than discuss it. The space was to be my new music studio instead.

Each day is another chance to get it right, to feel love, to breathe in pure air and to work or play upon Gaea Star. Everything everywhere is connected through love and beauty. One is healed, by merely merging with the Sun or Moon energy.

The rhythm of life is full of blessings, ever flowing love, deepening connections, embracing the light, discovering new ideas, and creating and developing one's talents.

Breathe deeply. Sit in stillness. Walk in nature. Slow down. Relax. Release stress. Everything brings love, lessons, knowledge, and happiness.

Nothing is wasted if one stays focused on loving light within. Appreciate the blessing of life, the moment you awaken.

Dance, sing and share your zest, by gracefully helping each other. Keep sharing our songs, for healing the world.

My love is always there. I feel your encompassing deep sweetness. Instead of writing, sing, pray, rest or commune together.

I will always take you to the higher realms. Feel our union as you fly with me through celestial realms of serene purification and attunement.

Please stop grasping for and after love. It will flow, when the right person is in front of you. Often, we connect for only a moment.

I am undecided about taking a shamanic journey to Peru.

February 5

It is good to go to Peru, as the sacred energy is building there. The change of scenery and working with spiritual shamans, from the ancient path of light, is powerfully rewarding and healing.

Remaining is also an option, for it will provide much needed time to clear, to move ahead, to release all that no longer serves.

Use the time to focus within, to foster creativity further. Every day, declutter, to invite in healing rays of star energy.

Water your plants with conscious prayers, think or say, "How can I bring in the light even more?" Remain peacefully loving.

Meditate in the morning stillness, to seek the sacred within. We await all who join us. You are always with me, with Source.

Celebrate creativity, by being aware, joyfully connecting to Spirit. Wait for no one, to create acts of beauty, upon the stage of life.

Say, "I am radiantly alive in paradise." You are whole within.

Everyone chooses their path, so let them go.

There is no other way to walk the path of divine star priestess, except toward the light, that grows stronger within and around you.

Breathe in sunlight to restore, when feeling alone or confused. Immerse in nature to connect to the source of love and light.

February 8

Bless the changes. Find a quiet spot where your soul sings in ecstatic expression, to help you realize your deepest longings.

How can I serve the divine aspect of my life even more?

Pay attention to the blessings of each moment. All flows to you in love, drawn by your actions, now or from the past.

To bless your life with wonderful beauty; exercise, serve others, pray for you and for the world.

Release negativity as you monitor words and actions, for everything matters.

Be at peace with what comes along, like logs in the river, flowing downstream with the current, always sailing onward.

Each day develop a ritual of connecting in nature, to release, to relax, to relieve the chaos of the material density of life.

Arrange space as a symbol of what you want to call to you.

Seek stillness to foster the awareness of the sweet pleasures of the brilliant light, that is always shining within.

Remember the choice to serve the light, may be difficult at times. Step into it with courageous understanding, for it is a golden opportunity to accelerate rapidly, to accept this unique opportunity, to do exactly what you came here to do, as a spirit in human form.

Thank you for singing our sweet songs. My love, warmth and peaceful light flows to you forever.

I am love. You are love. We are love. Trust in Spirit.

Our Divine loving union has no boundaries, it is pure bliss.

February 12

Restore balance between work, home and spiritual life.

Blessed By Light-filled Love

Clear your past, to heal the strands of your light body. Rework the auric configuration by surrounding yourself with love, joyful actions, compassion, hope and pleasure.

Serving humanity is more important than watching senseless movies or TV, which disconnects anyone from the source of love.

When you experience negative perceptions regarding actions, send that person love and forgiveness, for their un-centered energy is judgmental, lacking love and respect.

Rework nothing because of anyone else's opinion, for you never have to defend or explain why you do anything as long as it does no harm.

You have the courage and strength to overcome anything that does not flow from the source of love.

Every day you are in the presence of the divinity of Gaea Star. Acknowledge, pray and work with her as a living treasure. Many humans are unaware that there is no other reason to be amidst all her radiance, so smile, relax and celebrate her blessings.

Sing praises to Spirit and revel in the mysteries of all life.

Anything that does not feel, look or sound right, is just an illusion, a malfunction that can be fixed by sending the love brigade to reconnect the circuitry in the proper alignment.

It truly is that easy to find blissful, peace once again.

All we ask is for everyone to carry on with love, strength and light, to believe that what flows in, supports all that you came to be.

Focus on healing the world, as a path of love, sacrifice and inspiration.

Please sing or say, these words, "I only serve the light, the source of love, that brings me joy, peace, happiness and healing. I never have to defend my position as a human being to anyone, as we are equal in connections, duties and ways of serving Spirit."

Everything is always in balance. Bless the shining peaceful light.

February 14 -16

As a carrier of light, affirm there is more to life than what one sees. Release the veils, to feel the healing, nurturing force of the sweet energy of love. It is a sacred journey, from the stars above, blessed with the breath, sight, touch and sounds of human existence.

Give all you can, whether it's a song, smile, warm gesture, touch or kind word. The light shines for everyone you encounter.

Remember to think every day, "How may I serve the light?"

Who is here that my grace can touch? How may I be more loving? Bless everyone on their way home, to the source of light.

Have fun creating the journey, as you awaken to the sacredness of your missions, for there is no other action more important than serving. You will all find the way soon.

February 26

The new loves that came between Dameron and I, did not work out for either of us.

Always accept what Divine Spirit brings.

Allow your partner what they want as long as no one is hurt.

The point is to surrender, to receive with no agenda or ego issues. Acceptance, love, forgiveness and compassion, come from trusting in the universe.

I am saddened as he still moves out, leaving his studio empty. I have experienced this raw deep sadness in my heart before.

Yes, life is ruthless when familiar patterns are broken.

Blessed By Light-filled Love

Reach deep into the core of inner knowing, to redistribute love, when you want more caring and nurturing.

Refocus what you need to remain at peace.

Use this time to reassess your Star Medicine Priestess path. Who you are now, is significant to your own loving expression. Remain in your center, despite the outer veils of illusion.

Wash away despair by receiving the love, beaming from heaven, surrounding you completely. You are blessed and beautiful.

Waste no time in discussing these things.

Be at peace, in love with all that you are and will be, for the future, past and present are all one and fully within you right now.

Feel the magnificence of nature. Love for the sake of love.

Let yourself heal. Trust that all will change for the best soon.

As you experience love challenges, stay connected to life's essence. You are blessed by the paths you have chosen to walk on, in the face of comfort and familiarity. Remain open to Spirit.

To love is to take a chance, to say good-bye is often difficult, however, life always flows onward. There will be others to love.

All is well when we pray and accept the mysteries of love.

March 12 - 17

True love feels like a devoted harmonious friendship, a pure, powerful and blissful balanced union.

To know love, is to experience all the ups, downs, aspects and lessons that you agreed to learn on Gaea Star.

Integrate whatever comes, as it brings great strength.

Writing, meditation, exercise and patience, help release angst. Devote yourself to forgiveness, letting go, accepting ones' self. Hold fast to your vision for change, clarity and purpose.

Keep releasing, let it flow into the rivers of life.

Watch it float away as you return to your happy place within. Develop your arts and music. Set a goal to write a song daily. Teach what inspires you. It will attract those who attune to it. Sharing musical messages, is your gift to awaken humanity.

March 20 *My son, Jesse's Birthday.*

As a messenger of spirit, a carrier and servant, be the hands, the voice, the touch, the example to shine, to reflect the deep abiding love, that flows eternally from spirit into life, to heal and spread light even more.

As you walk the path of a peaceful messenger, the goal is to release negativity, which enlarges the capacity to receive and share love, now that you are free of self-imposed burdens.

Everyone forgets that all life is created from the union of opposites, the masculine and the feminine.

Many are caught in the illusion within the material realm, of these deeply ingrained, perceived differences, with the false belief, that this is where all is gained or lost.

Compassion, forgiveness, understanding and acceptance, are nurturing aspects evolved from the foundation of love.

When one is fully present, regardless of one's circumstances, they may be overflowing with these qualities, constantly connecting with love, no matter what is going on, growing stronger in communion with Spirit, every day.

Appreciate every morning, by immersing in the beautiful bliss of breathing, the sweet air of life and treasuring the magnificent blessing of nature.

Love flows endlessly from the wellspring of your heart.

Follow your path home to the sacred place within, to your celestial origin, to your holy family of love.

March 25

When love abruptly goes, the sudden loss, distracts one from accepting that everything that flows to you is meant to bring joy, softness and compassion, if it does not, then it is not meant to be.

Envision a special one to embrace your love in a direct, honest and non-collapsed way. You offer a richness on many different levels.

There is much to miss by not receiving your gift of love.

Just keep clearing your life and restoring order in your home which helps to resolve emotional loss.

Everyone notices, the great strides you undertake.

Thank you, Star Queen, for as you transform, the Earth does.

As a daughter of the light, you are blessed by the universe, the source of eternal wonder.

We help to shine the light brightly through all of you.

Keep sharing your unique uplifting, healing musical messages.

March 29

Rhiannon

Rhiannon, heyo wayyo heyo

Oya, nahey noway yo heyo

To you oh Goddess, we feel your light,

To you Rhiannon, we feel your love

Pele, heyo way yo heyo

Humaya heyno wayway yohey

(Use other Goddess names for more verses.)

Oh sweetness, steeped in creative power, you make it happen.

May you manifest what you seek, drawing love in.

Let it embrace you joyfully, to receive the Goddess energy.

Keep clearing, accepting, moving toward the light within.

Be blessed by being single, for you are one within.

April 5 - Easter   On This Holy Day

On this holy day, on this holy day
Golden light, golden rays, healing light
Breathe in light, breathe in love, oh beauty of sight.
Birds are singing, sweet wonders of life.
Yahay, Yahay, Yahay, Yahay heyya, heyya
I greet the sweetness of this holy day
I thank you for this holy way,
for the warm sunshine, on this lovely morning
As the winds dance and the rivers flow
Oh, thank you, source of light, we love you so

April 10

You and I are one, no matter how long the separation of thoughts, are of me, for I am always within and you within me.

Life is remarkably challenging with ups, downs and hard work.

Reach deep to be grounded, to release control, fear or pressure.

Breeze through, blessed by spirit, full of light, from the stars, as

Blessed By Light-filled Love

you accept everything that flows your way.

The Way Home

You and I are one, on the way home

Bless life with love, as we breathe in light.

Back to the source. Aho na hay

On the way home, on the way home

She's Alive

She's alive, I'm alive in the beauty of the Earth.

I feel the brilliant sun, rising warm.

She's alive, I'm alive in the wonders of the Earth.

I see tall trees rising in the blue sky.

She's alive, I'm alive, listening to the melody of the Earth.

I hear gentle birds singing, celebrating life. She's alive, I'm alive on the healing green Earth.

I feel peace, away hey Nia, Nia, Nia, Nia,

Hiyana heyya, nahey, hey hey ho

May 14

I return from another trek on the Peruvian Inca trail, with fifteen goddesses on a Sierra Bender retreat. I received a song with Alicia DiGiovanni, a soul sister, in the village of Aguas Caliente, at the base of Machu Picchu, on my birthday, May 7.

Mariam Massaro

I Only Want to Serve

I only want to serve in the light My Lord,

I only want to live for you.

When I wake in the morning, all my thoughts are of you.

I only want to live for you.

I'm a daughter of the light, I am humble,

to serve you day and night,

I only want to live for you,

I only want to serve in the light my

Lord, I only want to live for you.

How sweet your light shines. Thank you for hiking in the Andes, following inspirations, and opening to all that is.

You and I are so connected between Heaven and Earth.

May we share our peaceful love, with humanity, illuminating

happiness for those who seek clarity and filling their lives with light.

May 16 - 17 - 19

I release my distractions to become a creatress in all ways. A businessman is asking to buy Wise Ways Herbals.
Have no fear, as you relax the controls, for it may free you to emerge as a peaceful, abundant, flowing, visionary priestess.
Every so often, be still. Do nothing. Pet purring cats.
Stand in the full moonlight. Swim naked in the rivers.
Sweep the stones in the path. Play the harmonica.

Blessed By Light-filled Love

Greet the morning with a love song to the sun.
Sing to the forest and the faeries.
Do yoga in the warm sunlight on the grass.
Learn bird songs. Mow around wildflowers.
Go to the ocean with friends for the day, with toys and a picnic.
Walk barefoot and naked deep in the forest.
Grow delicious organic vegetables, berries
and medicinal herbs to make healing teas and salves.
Sing to the sunflowers, to the rivers, to the stars.

In this new spring season of growth, for fertile Gaea Star, celebrate the fresh energy to create positive change.

I hear you singing joyfully, with a deeper spiritual expression, now that you released the encumbrances of working so hard.

The time nears, for Gaea Star to ascend into another dimension, bringing her to new majesty, with great changes for humanity.

The teachings of the Light, are revealed to the ones who listen. The shadow forces are desperate to keep their darkness from

being dissipated, by the loving light that grows stronger every day.

June 1 - 3 - 4 - 14

Thank you, Ashento. I release what binds my spirit. May I open

my wings ever more, to fly high with you.

My sweetness, you are blessed by my flowing love. I hear you

singing in heaven. Your lovely prayers are sweet. I long to grow old with you, until then we are one in spirit.

Ana, my housemate, dreamed the 'Gaea Star Crystal' story was performed with fantastic costumes in a beautiful outdoor theater.

(In October 2011, the Gaea Star Goddess show, performed at the Three Sisters Sanctuary, a stone amphitheater in Goshen, Ma.)

To reconfigure your livelihood, imagine what you want to manifest, by writing every day at the same time. For example, I am a musician, singer, writer, performer, costumer, healer, teacher, band leader, filmmaker and herbal farmer.

There is always so much going on at Singing Brook Farm, let some go, to free your life even more, to focus on deeper inner growth.

I feel the Great Shift. This may be the time to evaluate selling my herb business.

Yes, there are many factors. Each are unique to consider.low to without the demands of the business?

Why let go, however, of what you created, based on your love for the Earth, if it is successful?

WiseWays Herbals will always use your guidance. Turn it over to a competent staff, let the business prosper and evolve that way.

You and I are one essence, created eons ago, from the spark, of

the passions of fire within. What a blessed moment of creation.

So, my beautiful, sail into a new life, free, content, confident, full

of wonder at the miracle of creation.

Strive to breeze through great changes proudly, for there is no regret, or feeling that you lost something.

It is never a loss, when we choose to honor our soul's true expression, to go on in truth, to fulfill your mission, to take the opportunity, to develop even more creativity now.

Each chapter in life, is a lesson learned, an honoring of the contracts, the pre-birth commitments, before coming to Gaea Star.

Letting go of whatever you desire, is an option, as a very different life may evolve by becoming freer.

When you release things, the space that remains fills with love.

June 16 - 17 - 20

The filming of Gaea Star Crystal is coming together.

All dreams find true expression if one becomes a conduit of inspiration, like William Shakespeare, who wrote with a quill pen.

One can do anything they desire to, if led by their convictions. Believe you are just as inventive as the creator of the starry night, for you are guided by the shining light, the Source of love.

I want to sing to the ocean, where the oil well is gushing, black crude oil into her waters, every day. How can we stop it?

Believing you can, through prayer to rework her energy.

The oil gushing is like an artery that has burst from an attack, a wound, to be repaired. Weave a web of compassion and love, imagining a mesh of healing, a cover over the fountain of oil.

Dream - A friend printed Ashento's book with Dameron's photos of nature. We compiled it together.

To begin the process of what one desires to do, one must first feel the pull, the passion to give, to create from a feeling, an idea. Then take that inspiration, to work it into a visible creation.

Focus your attention, to complete projects and writings, to be published, even if only one copy. Write even for an hour, to achieve the prosperity that you have the talent for.

Dream: Creating a video broadcast of live improv music, singing beautiful songs on the Internet, with musicians jamming.

Note - In 2012, Mariam recorded the Gaea Star Crystal Radio Hour in her studio with Bob Sherwood, through a web podcast on the Dream Visions7 Network.

Ashento, I feel the power of the stars, awakening me with the beauty of nature outside. Life on Mother Gaea is sweet.

We are so parallel. I too, am swept by my spirit floating in the silvery realms of magnificent celestial wonders, where I dwell.

Alaya, Anahitohay, I find my way through the many layers to you, whenever I sense you calling. I am happy to see you such beauty.

July 15

Thank you for manifesting, even when not sure what to do.

August 1 -10 - 17

I am with you in all aspects, to embrace you from the realms of knowing. Thank you for the prayers from your medicine circles.

Fly with me to the stars, whenever you desire to.

Many positive experiences are filling Light Workers' lives.

More are coming to gather as forces of truth, love and serenity.

Look at the magnificence of Gaea, she is truly a star.

To creatively share the message of the movie with those who are ready, is happening soon.

A new wave of love is flowing everywhere.

This is the moment of reunification with the celestial ones. They have waited for all of you to awaken, for a long time. Waste no more precious moments.

It is only an illusion that humanity has hidden behind, forgetting their true missions. For some, it requires a great sacrifice that many are not willing to do, since life in the fast lane is so pleasurable.

So why not get going, to really express yourselves?

Lighten loads, as changes are arising that one may not control.

Listen to the eternal language of all that is dancing in the wind,

in the flowers, in the birds, in the beauty of the richness.

We are one, there is no separation as "above" or "below."

We are all connected to the divine essence of life.

August 19 - 22

Dream: In a house, going through doorways. The last one opens into a pretty, panoramic green, hilly view. Wearing a running outfit, I fly into the blue sky. I fly far, laughing. It is powerful to have perfect control. I am ecstatic to be so free. I think, "Why not do this for my career? People will love it and support me."

Take This Day

Take this day to seek the light, to what is calling you.

Stay with truth and peace, by opening to love,

as you climb the mountains of your visions

From that deep place within your heart,

where your soul resides.

Honor all who are drawn with gratitude.

Gather the forces of light, weaving strands of love.

The rainbow is arching, from heaven to sweet Gaea Star,

The Planet of Blue waters, where humanity strayed so far.

Rise and feel the oneness of all.

Center yourselves, accept your power.

Keep walking toward the light.

She's calling. She's rising, as you feel her might,

Into the center of your being, into the depth of your soul.

August 23

Thank you Ashento, for the song and beautiful words.

You're welcome, my sweetness as love flows freely.

Be succinct as you journey deep into the well of experiences.

All debts are forgiven in heaven. Do your best to release them.

Keep manifesting, for the real film is about to begin.

Bring magical creations to life. Call on celestials for their help.

Weave together joyful creations to awaken the Star Beings.

Develop the children and your friends as the characters.

August 26

Be strong in your visions to benefit everyone by nurturing creativity, with expressive prayers, exuberant celebrations, and dancing in the beauty of Gaea Star.

Stay serene, in love, light, peace and healing to your very core. I hold you close. Thank you for singing songs of light.

Full moon late. Is going to Peru advantageous?

Yes, you are being led to facilitate filming the original elders, from the celestial realm that never forgot who why they came.

Release fear as everything is taken care of with finances. Trust the universe as you reinvent your right livelihood. The butterflies are faeries, gathering around you.

As one winds in life, they freely choose the path of expression.

Blessed By Light-filled Love

Note: White butterflies fluttered in clusters on my dirt road. We had to stop driving to not run over them. Singing Brook Farm. Photo Credit: Mariam

Tell me your story, Ashento, oh holy being of light. You and I have known each other through the millennia, when our original crystalline magnificent connection grew.

Yes, my sweetness, from our first spark, we flew in unison, with golden wings through the galaxy of the seventh realm, to the silver Golden Star Palace, with our light beaming, like beacons in the night.

September 3

Life flows, despite setbacks, so remain in the present moment, renewed by rest, natural foods, love and hope.

Surrender to the promise of the new day, to the peaceful morning, to the dynamic breath of life, purity of Mother Gaea, soft bird melodies, gentle breezes and puffy clouds.

You are always blessed by this powerful life.

Express gratitude, even when you are working hard, or missing someone, dear.

Reflect purity by smiling, touching, speaking kindly, giving love out every day.

September 5 - Simply Be

Connect to the most essential aspect of life, your breath, by breathing in deeply, to help awaken, to feel alive and aware. This is your prayer, for you are the altar and the temple.

Yes, one can practice religions developed for centuries on Gaea Star. However, thinking these are relevant and important, in order to pray, is not the truth, they are illusions.

Religions are comfortable and familiar, giving a sense of spirituality and a feeling of home, but they are not necessary for existence, for you are the creators of your own lives.

Religions exist because humanity created them, not because of the non-denominational spiritual realm, that exists around, above, below and within.

Practice simply being aware of breathing, to feel the deep connection of prayer and spirituality, with the loving family of light.

You will not need to follow a church or statues, or anyone, or wear anything special, or be with a director, for you are the leaders, the followers. You, and I, are all one, that is the truth, oneness.

Train yourselves as the priest, priestess, shaman, teacher, counselor or whomever, to lead in peaceful healing places.

Simply be with the breath, communing with the oneness, opening to receive and give love, shining as a being of light, always connected to the source of love.

Recognize the Divine everywhere, by feeling the presence of love. This activates the soul's longing to reconnect with the master.

The master being the source of light that energizes and nurtures you.

A light bulb has the ability to shine light, but only when it is screwed into a socket, plugged in and turned on, using Earth's electrical power, yet it is still a light bulb.

Think of your soul this way, that it lives and breathes but it also needs to be turned on, to connect to the master, to the power generator of spirituality, to reunite with the wholeness.

Place yourself in the receptacle, so you may shine brightly.

There is no other reason to be. Simply be aware. As you feel this, you gain strength as a being of light.

Be attentive to this energy flow, to receive what you need.

Listen to spirit singing through nature, to awaken your DNA. When you sit quietly, attuning - you soothe, heal and nurture the deeper essence of your pure, perfect soul.

The physical form, which includes the mental, and emotional bodies, often clouds the soul's presence, so intensely, that one forgets who they truly are.

Awakening releases your soul to bubble up from your core.

When you take the lid off a wine bottle, sometimes it bursts out, if the cork is released too fast.

You can suddenly explode with life or come out very slowly, as

if something is blocking, holding back the flow. It all depends on how quickly you want to find yourself.

Yes, you search, going here, there, but not reaching anywhere just treading in the waterways of life.

The most important human aspect is to simply be, grateful, thankful, loving, compassionate, caring and forgiving of all that comes along, realizing they are only bubbles bubbling up through the surface of illusions.

Remember when young, holding a wand, to blow bubbles as they popped, or floated away? How sweet, the joy and laughter.

This is life, bubbles, some land, while others, float, drifting on. You create the aspects, manifest dreams, and visions, into magnificent actions, through caring, loving touch, sweet voices, gentle looks, and open hearts. Simply be. Love is the answer.

Dameron and Mariam, first day of filming the Gaea Star Crystal.

Blessed By Light-filled Love

Dane Lee, Selena Goldberg, Mariam and Andray Lee filming.

September 9 -15 -19

I am excited to film the Gaea Star Crystal story after years of writing and gathering the people. Ashento, you were right, it is coming to life with lovely costumes, faeries and inspired music.

Yes, it is a blessing that you utilize your manifesting powers.

Each aspect of life is remarkably in balance, once you release and shift all that needs to. The passing of one phase to another is quite easy, when you ask Spirit to co-create and direct with you.

Power flows when you meld energies with one's higher self.

Film in the beautiful splendor of nature.

Every moment is an expression, like a feather floating.

Quick, catch it in the breeze, before it sails away, to share your, ever shining, loving, healing light to the world.

Expressing your inner longing, heals and nourishes you, like the loving presence of a child. Smile. Resolution is coming.

Have faith in the angelic ones' guidance. Shine the way.

Be the strong one, to fearlessly lead on, sweet sister of the light.

September 21-23-29

Release colorful creativity, as you channel the wisdom from the stars, liberating yourself to shine, like the brilliant full moon light.

Follow your inner voice, as you unravel the creative complexities.

Slow down to appreciate the elemental wonder of Mother Gaea, especially the passage of the heavenly stars.

I prayed at a sweat lodge, playing the flute to the four directions. I felt wings on my back, unfurl for the first time. They held sacred space, as I spoke from that winged spirit's perspective, leading a few rounds, "We are here, with nothing to fear. The circle of life flows to the light, even difficult challenges, cannot deter its' passage. Life is led by courageous strength, and the belief, there is a higher purpose than just daily material existence."

Slow down, relax, listen, appreciate the surroundings.

Reground after busyness to simpleness, cats, babbling brook, clothes drying in the sunshine, gardens of food and crickets chanting.

Return to this serenity often to gain energy to sail through life.

October 2

Louise Finn is leaving after ten years as a WiseWays Herbals employee. I wonder about the transition after her absence.

Be content as life is on to a new chapter, to a different melody. Cherish each moment, as the treasures from spirit that they are.

Follow your heart, as the soul whispers to reclaim what you love, to connect to your true expression, to serve Spirit.

It is your mission, to be a kind, compassionate, forgiving being, while fostering a spiritual connection, with loving waves, emanating from your heart, like ripples in a pool when something touches it.

Send out currents of loving intentions and healing thoughts.

Each soul has their own unique, self-realized journey, leading to different places, but always toward the light of love.

Wherever you go, whatever you do, it flows as a golden circle of

love with the intention of peaceful union with Spirit.

October 5 - 7- 8 - 9 - 11

Dream - Winter, monks on horseback, are gathered around me on an unknown journey. A handsome male with long dark hair and piercing dark eyes, filled with deep spiritual power, says, "Hello, Saloka" to me. I knew him from an ancient time.

Love is the answer, as inspiration arrives through prayer, acceptance and surrender to that blissful place within.

May the healing force of love always be with you.

Stars, twinkle, I wonder is it time to tell our love story?

My sweetness, the world is ready for share our powerful love that spans centuries and different realms. Bless our love from afar.

May you guide me on my adventure to Peru. I am blessed to feel your love. Hugs. Yes, let's keep singing.

I sail into the light with you, Ashento. We are forever linked as carriers of love and light. May we dance in delightful union as one guidance and the abundant universe.

Colca Canyon, Peru, among the deepest canyons in the world. We hiked down and up to the top to see amazing ruins like Machu Pichu.

As you go about your busy life, pause to listen to the wisdom of the trees, as they release their beautiful leaves, beginning their passage into the inner realms, deep within for the winter.

Wherever you are, accept the moment, to sail through the veils of illusion, to reconnect with your higher self, your loving essence, that remained in your divine ancestral home.

The Earth is a radiant star, with perfect love, as she revolves in splendor, moving into the next dimension.

Prepare to reflect your light, to shine brightly for all to see.

Every moment is a treasure, giving gifts of colorful golden, red and oranges leaves, fading out in full glory.

Spirit, source of eternal bliss, from our celestial home, may we return to love, filled with intentions to heal all we meet anywhere.

May I surrender to love within, uniting in Spirit, as a being of light.

November 5 -11

All is well in this beautiful realm. As you evolve from one life to the next, you'll learn of many different ways of existence.

Which do you prefer, that which requires alignment on so many levels, or that which flows endlessly like the river?

The only aspect of life that actually matters, is to be true to oneself. Simply be, who you are deep inside your core.

Sunlight shining. Sunny, Puffy and Sparky nestle in.

Upon rising, breathe in the mystery of the miracle of life, to experience one more day as a human, giving and receiving life, nurturing compassionate awareness, and remembering and reconnecting to the essence of your core.

Arise, It's a New Day

Arise, arise it's a beautiful morning.
Open your eyes, to the new day dawning.
Arise, arise to the new life unfolding
Open to the light of love emerging
Oh, the divine doorway of heaven and earth
Arise, arise, yaweh, yaweh, yaweh, yaweh
Arise, arise, sing a song
that's never been sung before
Sing it out from deep within your core
Arise, arise, may the melody of spirit help you heal
Oh, the divine doorway of heaven and earth
'Vision Quest' CD, 2014 - Spirits of the Sun Music

Thank you for another day to open the portal between spirit and matter, for serving as a conduit, between Heaven and Earth.

May I remember the path to access my mission here, illuminating the way with wonder-filled appreciation for the miracle of life.

I welcome opportunities with an open mind and heart, as I consciously become an emissary of Divine loving essence.

May we tap into our unique potential, that waits patiently, for recognition, to be given the controls, to direct our lives, as we whole heartedly, breathe it all in, surrendering to the essence of who we are.

May we accept the differences in each other's journey, to begin each beautiful day with love and patience.

11/11/11 at 11 a.m.

I'm sitting on the bridge with the Singing Brook flowing beneath, glistening in the sunlight. Sparky, Puffy, Tommy, Inka and Nia followed me. They are so excited to play here. I open to hear Ashento.

Hello, my sweetness, I am pleased to see you watch the waters that fall from the skies, unimpeded, nurturing the Earth, meandering past rocks, reflecting purity as it flows to the sea.

Just as easily, the mystery of life, cascades like rays from Heaven, into the body, returning to the light, eventually, as all life flows home, to the vast ocean of Divine love.

Peace fosters love and compassion, which develops the heart to beat with love just as the vibrant Earth pulsates with natures' soothing sunshine, blue skies, animals, love and unity.

Watch the seasons evolve, changing from seed to flower, to plants, to leaves, to expressions as plants dancing in the wind, reaching high as they grow.

All life changes, moving on, eventually transforming into death.

Blessed By Light-filled Love

Today is a day of renewal, of finding the way, even deeper into your hearts, to breathe in the colors that surround you, tranquil blue, serene green and the warmth of golden light.

Find a moment to sit quietly and attune, to the soothing melodies of the rushing, rippling waters.

Breathe in pure air, feel the wind breeze and tickle your skin.

All life just flows, evolves and realigns.

Every day is a good day to pray, to thank Spirit for existence. Appreciate natures' beauty, as you absorb her healing Earth

energy by laying upon her magnificent, throbbing, pulsating ground.

Let her feel you. Play like kittens, expressing joy to be alive. Thank each other for being in your lives.

All is. Is this all? There is no other place, no other, just be. You and I, spirit and human.

We unify ourselves, as we remember our loved ones.

We honor those who have gone, sacrificing precious lives as

soldiers, to do something they believe in.

Who are we to judge? Once we replace war with love, where will the soldiers go?

Perhaps to places that build positive support, like communities that need pure water flowing, or building homes for the needy.

Why not transform what we do for each other, replacing war with nurturing compassion, forgiveness and acceptance, severing all ties to the old ways of aggression?

Release what impedes our progress as living, dynamic beings.

Walk away, on toward the path of light filled love.

The way of the peaceful worker is the way of the gardener, the dancer, the singer, the creative one, the builder, the healer, those who serve humanity, by doing only good things, God things, nurturing, lovingly and peacefully.

As we open our hearts, they pulsate with love.

We become beacons of light, love beings, Buddha beings, Jesus beings, happy radiant sun-beings of all ethnicities.

Shine your light, reflecting warm love from deep within, flowing to all you encounter, as you evolve as radiant stars of light in human form. May all feel the blessings of love.

November 18- - Hold on to your dreams

In the morning when the sun is brilliantly shining, breaking through, you feel the radiance of light on your skin.

You awaken your consciousness, to return to this realm.

You open your eyes to see nature, clouds drifting, cats purring, happy to be near you. This is life, alive and breathing.

Hold on to your dreams, seek the wisdom from those experiences. Each night you travel on a different journey, sometimes far away, sometimes close. Awaken with consciousness, fully aware.

Say in the evening, "I am going to remember my dreams."

In the morning say, "Ah, the sun feels warm. It's a beautiful day." Unwind and stretch as the sun begins its steady climb in the sky.

You hear the birds, also radiantly happy from the warmth.

Now you remember your dream, you flew above the buildings

watching life. Make sense of dreams, to put the pieces together.

November 25

Thanksgiving. I ask for a message about life.

It may seem that we are waiting to connect, but we are busy here in the higher realms as you are.

It is a pleasurable experience, to exist in spirit form, released from bodily incarnation a long time ago.

I am blessed to live a unique existence.

We heed the call of the universe wherever we are led to, putting aside our needs, to promote, heal and nurture all souls in spirit, while they are manifesting lightness of being.

Let us begin with the journey, to the essence of who we are.

As individuals having spent lifetimes on Earth, we are conscious of how to communicate with those left behind on Gaea Star.

It is important that we connect as celestials to earth beings, even though it is between two different realms, we still remain in contact with our own realms. We are many in this presence, some are called to commune, while others remain distant and quiet.

What is above, is also below, what is within, is also without. It is the shadow and the light.

You and I are unique due to maintaining celestial connections.

November 26

Can't sleep. Cold. Kitties on my bed, as I receive the shining light of the half-moon. I ask her healing rays to enter my body, to help relax and listen to the wisdom of the universe.

In the one-ness of life, there's a presence, a stillness, a quiet pool where one feels the essence of Spirit, of all there is.

The soul has many layers: compassion, love, gentleness and sweetness, feelings of one-ness, memories, flashbacks and longings. Where do they lead?

How does one walk the best path on Gaea Star?

To find the way home, sit still, listen to the voice within, to the whisper in the wind, the song in the shower, the hum as you drive.

The melodies of love, joy and happiness arise in every moment when you are in alignment with their essence.

When you feel the deep connection between Spirit, God, or Goddess, then all flows free in love, light, warmth and balance.

The disharmonies of life, release as you weave your way home. Returning to the essence of peace within is a gentle process of shedding layers of confusion, of letting light, shine deep into the recesses of all the uncomfortable places within.

Cultivate stillness, slow down, just breathe.

Be content with where you are, what you have, do or create. Strive, to realize that this light from within, releases all that binds you, to rediscover the depths of your essence.

Shine your light within. Ask who you are? Where are you going? What do you want to be? Take a moment, listen to the melody within, to know that you are a unique form of divine spiritual substance. Surrender to this presence that you seek.

Thank you for listening, for letting us flow from here into yours, to touch your soul with love.

Relax, stay home, nurture and heal. All comes in good time.

November 28

Thank you Ashento for your love and teachings.

From a distant star, I open the way of love in peaceful gratitude. As I remain here and you there, our connection is forever united, right from our humble beginning, as two sparks from the same flame.

Bless you and your divine Earthly path.

May you open to the loving force of self-less devotion within.

I send pure blissful unending love, with loving attention.

Feel love unifying your connection to Source, for it always sparks the illumination of the highest expression of your soul.

November 29

Sunshine. Frosty. Cats nearby. Peaceful, radiant light. Blue skies. Ireceive Great Spirit every day.

Yes, in the morning, one feels the clearing and nurturing, healing from the restful stillness of the night.

As you drift through realms of spirit, you may see, feel or hear experiences that may not make sense upon awakening.

Sometimes you remember where you've gone, but often the dreams, just fade away, unless you piece the fragments together, which may help to realize an important aspect of life.

Gaea Star constantly blesses, as you wind through life, with her tall trees, anchored in alignment with the sun, moon and stars.

Open to the love, which permeates Air, Water, Earth and Fire. Bring these natural elements in, for balanced healing harmony.

Start your morning with sunshine flooding over you, exercising,

drinking pure water, nourishing vital fruits and centering meditation.

This will help you to focus, to be healthy, in tune with spirit.

Be courageous, to stand strong, marching forward, while joyfully expressing your soul's deep longing. It is whispering,

"Now is time to follow the path of spiritual wisdom."

Listen to what sings through you in harmonious blessings. Lift up your soul by supporting and nurturing it.

Pay attention when you are overexerting or doing too much.

How can you follow your mission if life is so engrossing that you can't feel or notice the sparks that ignite your soul's fire with the passion of joy that sings ecstatically inside?

There comes a time when you must set yourselves free, believing that you're always supported, in all that you do.

Whatever form or path you choose is the lesson.

Walk away with courage, grateful for all that you have and do. Do not hold on for dear life, as if there's nothing else that will come along, to sustain you, perhaps even better.

Release, ask, "May I open to the abundance of the universe, to hear and receive the next movement of my Divine path."

I genuinely seek to satisfy my soul's desire within.

May I be guided by my mission in fullness and expression.

Thank you, life, for what I have, for all my experiences.

Thank you, Spirit, for beautiful days on my peaceful farm, where I have a sense of home, a place of love, of Earth.

Thank you for the tasty food grown in this rich soil, for the animals that roam through, for the cats that feel protected and happy, for the trees, the flowing brook, the flowers, the bees, for all of it.

I'm grateful for the magnificent power, for the presence of mind to liberate my life, so I sail on the wings of light, on the wings of love.

Oh, my sweetness, you and I are one. Forever we are linked in the unity of divine love, merged into one-ness and peace.

November 30 - *Inside the Turtle*

The turtle carries her home on her back. In native cultures, the Turtle represents vibrant Mother Earth. All life, human or animal, is born from her living vitality. Every human has a distinct life path, a unique expression of their soul's mission. So, sharing this vision, this multi-dimensional path with others, creates the history of humanity.

Take the shell on the turtle's back. Is that what makes a turtle? What happens if she loses her shell? What is it then, a creature? Is it a turtle without a shell?

When the human soul leaves the body, what is the soul then?

It remains a soul regardless, of whether it wears a body or not. The soul, upon leaving Earth, returns to Divine Source, perhaps

wiser from the lessons they agreed to undertake on Earth.

Let's begin with the fork in the road, where someone takes the left fork, and someone takes the right fork.

What about people, who stand not knowing which way to go? They wait for a sign, a visible clue, as to which direction to choose.

Is evil good? Is good evil? Evil is good for those who play that role. Evil is bad for those who experience that which deters them from feeling good.

Bless either way. Bless left, bless right, up and down. The key to the mystery, is that there is no evil. Is there just left or right then?

No, there is neither, it just is, life, good, bad, right, left, up, down, inside out, right side up.

Follow the balance point, to where the truth lives deep within.

Knowing that what is within, is also without, is the certainty.

Earth is a multidimensional reality. So, go deeper within, to the beginning, to self-realization. Help each other open to love.

December 4

Early, stars sparkle, difficult to sleep. I open to receive.

Your rainbow bridge, arching in the beautiful, colorful vibration of the celestial realm, creates a passageway of radiant colors:

Oh, the fiery passion of red, all the way through the colors, to white.

Each reflects a vibration of gentle love, flowing from different sources of patterns of light, sweet magical rays, an unlimited phenomenon, of creative, elemental funnels of fountains of love.

Shamiyaya

Shamiyaya, Shamiyaya, Shami Shamiyaya,

And the river knows who you are,

Show me the way, weaving ribbons of light

Turquoise ribbons of lovely light

Open your hands to receive my light

Shamiyaya, Shamiyaya, Shami Shamiyaya,

She's showing me the way

She's asking to stand in her waters

To hear what she has to say

And the rivers know who you are,

She's calling you, for she knows you're a shining star

She's holding sacred all along

She's shining, she's shining just for you

She's radiant, she's radiant,

She's full of pure, pure, pure light

Blessed By Light-filled Love

And the rivers know who you are,

Oh, the moon, priestess of the stars,

she's rising with beautiful light shimmering on the waters,

Reflecting rainbows of light

Shamiyaya, Shamiyaya, Shami Shamiyaya,

And the rivers know who you are,

She's asking us to receive all of her love

To hold her in your embrace

To know, to know, to know, the river, the river

And the river knows who we are

Shamiyaya, Shamiyaya, Shami Shamiyaya

'Release,' CD January 2021 Spirits of the Sun Music

Thank you Ashento for refusing to give up on us, for holding the door open, for guiding, nurturing and supporting humanity.

December 6 - 8

Gather the tribes, dress as if you are from the stars.

Cultivate being the positive one for a new way is coming. Promote, seek, create. Do what is right. Reward readers with your beautiful utilization of the elements of life, this is the teaching.

Wind howls. Nestled with purring Pawny and Nia. Winter came fast, freezing the earth before carrots and beets were dug up.

We search for ways to express light, radiance and serenity from our sweet place, to feel productive, in tune with our higher self and the spirit of the Universe.

May we find peaceful acceptance as we go inward, and inside, due to the cold, winding our way home to light filled love, surrendering and releasing what blocks the way.

Where are we, as we give a little and receive a lot?

May we choose what is good and wise as we surrender to a simple life, that supports and nurtures our lives with love.

May we ask "Do I surrender, to let go, to allow my higher self to step in, or do I keep on directing the vision, or give permission to share the vision, to let their energy move with me?

Return to the beginning, to the spiral within. Listen to the Universe singing, announcing, what catches your attention. Choices and opportunities may lead us down an unfamiliar path, even though it is viable. As soon as you withdraw from the old path, the new one may lead in a different but positive track. Or it may remain the same.

How many have never tried to break free, to seek the freedom to change their unhappy lives? Many are afraid to leave, even if they know they need to.

Rail Train to Heaven

Oh, oh, take the rail train to Heaven.
Oh, oh, follow the path all the way around.
Let the music guide you on.
Return your soul to the peaceful place
Winding along the rail train to Heaven
Following the path around
Listen to the voice of spirit
Guiding you home, home, home
Oh, oh, dare to dream, to love, to sing

Blessed By Light-filled Love

Come celebrate the light, shining through the trees
Always shining so bright, with sweet delight.
Dance along the river of life,
flowing to the mystery
Oh, oh let the music guide you home, home, home.

I am still unclear about selling my company. I cannot see the other side yet. I realize great changes require leaps of faith.

To release the essence of truth, relax, praise life, feel the power of the universe emanating from your light. As you learn this important aspect, it propels your desire to evolve.

May the New Year bring hope, grace, beauty, awakening of power and the ability to manifest change. I am amazed by our deep connection, Ashento.

All is well in the realms of heaven. We are fortunate to commune as other spirit beings do. Telepathy is wondrous, is it not?

Each critical moment used, expresses the essential aspect of being present.

Relaxing at home realigns your Divine star matrix.

December 13 - 17 -19

It is a gentle renewal as you travel nightly to the stars, free of the body. People are so concerned with daily material aspects, they forget to seek the higher realms, especially during dreamtime.

To reconnect to Divine Source, pray to be happy, to return to graceful harmony. It is a long-lasting benefit to begin with meditation and yoga.

I am right there with you when you write. So creatively play being an author with loving warmth and wise words to say.

Gaea Star's mighty quartz crystals are constantly emanating radiant light and energetic resonance. Placed at sacred energetic portals in nature or anywhere relevant, help to rebalance humanity.

Wisdom whispers, as I open to the morning air, feeling the wind, the presence of spirit everywhere. Cats appreciate our love as we let the miracles of the day, unfold with love.

At Solstice, when daylight dims, you feel the light within, even stronger, as families and friends, celebrate with food, gifts and rituals.

Love is the fullness, the source of light, the expression that binds, to hold close, to be at peace, in unity on Gaea Star.

You can always find the way home to spirit, even if surrounded by darkness, by reaching within to feel this light, to the connection to Source, which never disappears or changes, always helping you to become the portals of light that you came here to be.

Reach Out

Reach out, reach out, when you need someone to care,

Reach out, reach out to feel love in the air.

Wrap your arms around a friend, with love to share.

Peace is within, oh, oh, just open your eyes

To see the wind dancing in the trees, under bright blue skies.

Reach out, reach out to show you care

with love and peace, that you freely share,

Reach out, reach out, to share. 2x

December 20 - 21 - 22 - *My father's birthday*

Dream: Awakened by moonlight streaming with powerful brilliance stillness and peace. I see, Ashento and I, being born from the same flame, our faces rising from oneness, separating into bodies, a perfect union of co-creation, a beautiful image of love dividing, of becoming twin flames from the same beginning. I drew this very special wonderful lovers' vision.

I open my eyes, oh, brilliant golden sun, as you rise, over the trees, surrounded by soft clouds, in the southeastern sky.

I am proud to be alive on Gaea Star, learning, absorbing, creating wonder, beauty and inspirations.

May we walk in bountiful abundance, in happiness, called by loving light to share who we are regardless. As we age, we are more relaxed and willing to give.

Melody filmed me as the Ice Queen, in the freezing cold, in Ice Gulch, Stockbridge. I wore sparkling white in the majesty of winter.

May I always sing praises to Divine creation, whose spirit is visible everywhere. I am so blessed for my breath of life.

I have an idea to create a Goddess show with beautiful Goddesses from aspects of life on Gaea Star. I ask dynamic women who know their true essence within, to join with me in creating Goddess costumes, to perform colorful acts with lively music, singing and honoring dances.

We reflect the vibrant essence of the Divine Feminine, by bringing

Goddesses to life; from the past and present. These are the goddesses that came to me in dreams or inspired me in my life.

Isis, Egyptian mother, healer, teacher of esoteric mysteries.

Vajrayogini, Tibetan Dakini of transformation, dispels illusions.

Diana, fierce, independent priestess of the forest.

Crystal Ice Queen, with her stark winter beauty.

Pele, Volcano Fire Goddess on the big island of Hawaii.

Oya, Thunder queen and **Chango**, Thunder King.

Pacha Mama, South American Earth Goddess.

Inanna, Sumerian Rainbow Goddess

Yemanja, Yoruba ocean goddess and others.

May I focus on sharing my art filled essence, changing in midlife, to a new career, a different pathway. It is like peeling the layers of an onion, one by one, to reveal the true sweet core, as one's expression.

As light workers, you agreed to come to Gaea Star, to help humanity by utilizing your specific talents and healing ways. Follow through on what sustains you energetically.

Listen, to your dreams, insights, friends and all connections, to the messages that flow from your heart's desire. They are meant to assist, in expressing your souls' deepest knowing.

We await requests to work with you as supportive spirit guides.

December 25 - 26

Use stars, designs and medallions on the shields, staffs and costumes that you make, to use in ceremonies and musical events.

Create an artistic sacred space, to honor your life pursuits. Seek what you sent out, to return to you ten times. Organize with cohesive focus, to return to powerful place.

Even the llamas will work in a gentle and loving manner. They too, are from the stars.

Blessed By Light-filled Love

What one does daily, reflects the choices made prior to arriving from the stars. Just before incarnation, there was a review, a process to choose the learning, giving and receiving aspects, one was to encounter on Gaea Star.

As life unfolds, these prearranged contracts are revealed. At times, they are forgotten, as material density, creates a detour, so long that one forgets how to find their way to the original main path.

Spirituality is the first step to awaken to the truth of being. Honor what feeds your spirit, such as creating art, pleasing music and sharing teachings.

Transforming into radiant, fully aware starry selves, requires courage to follow right livelihoods, for they may be unique to each individual and not approved by the mainstream.

Many of you forgot the key to spiritual transformation is inside, for to know oneself, is to feel the essence of your spirit within.

I awaken to my talents and essential parts of my spirit. May I assimilate the changes, openings and insights.

I release anything that no longer serves my highest good.

I free my spirit to soar higher than before, as I express my passion for performing peaceful, powerful music.

December 28 - 29 - 30

May I follow the way, illuminated by the stars, in peaceful awareness, to co-create this unique story, with the angelic ones. I enjoy scouting for items to fashion beautiful costumes with.

Marisa Gesaldi is excited to edit the 'Gaea Star Crystal' movie clips into a film trailer. Quaglia, from the spiritual artistic community of Damanhur, Italy is helping me to make arrangements to go in March, to film as celestials meeting on the crisis on Gaea Star.

You have lovingly created the story, designs and music, all the while surrounded by your home's positive energies.

Surrender to the intention, to be with the fire, with love, prayers, healing medicines and pageantry.

We circle as beings of light, all around the universe, to help humanity experience this great moment of change.

I live at peace, when I relax into healing light.

I am always in the presence of loving intention and in constant awareness of Divine vision, flowing and creating the 'The Celestial Teachings of Ashento.'

Keep singing, no matter who or what comes and goes, with songs from the ceremonies. Get the sign from the closed business at the building at Eagle Bay sanctuary in upstate NY.

Note - the following March the barns burned down at Eagle Bay. Thanks to Ashento, we saved the sign.

I ask 2011 to open a clear path to abundance.

Oh, sensuous love star, so like the moon you shine, in the early dawning, waking me with your brilliance.

Such a sweet morning, serene peach-colored clouds as I hear a voice within, "To pray, to honor all that I see."

I'm grateful for New England life, with tall evergreen trees, reaching in solitude to heaven.

As the sun bears light, I'm beginning to understand life.

I love celebrating the beauty here, to cherish who we are and where we are led too. Love blooms our souls wide open.

Arise, freely sail into the realms of joyful expressions of grace, hope, compassion, wonder, acceptance and trust.

January 4 – 5, 2011

Thank you for breathing in love, for nurturing rituals and songs, for believing in each other and trying to remember the ancient ways, for seeking the source of light, for letting it wrap a warm mantle of love around you, for the glimmering light in your hearts and for sharing goodness in your lives. Blessings, we love you.

It's beautiful. I woke to see brilliant Venus, the Morning Star, shining brightly, illuminating the night sky.

Oh, heavenly stars as you reflect above, sparkling light, we feel deep, delightful healing, before dawn.

I am thankful for creation, singing, dancing, being free. I offer myself to love, as Nia purrs, lying on me.

Yes, my sweetness, you taste the nourishment that Gaea Star provides, the magnificent gift of creator's life. Enjoy and rejuvenate.

We are here in truth and love. We too, share in the exhilaration of creation, of divine vision, with no expectation.

Only in oneness, in divine supplication, to all that is, was and ever shall be, aligning with truth, harmony, compassion and light.

Come my child, open into my heart, flowing into mine, like a river into the sea.

Let's dance upon this mystery of pure love, light and serenity, like a fountain of flame, arising from one, spewing forth, as if from the volcano of love.

May we be fortunate to listen to the melodies of the universe.

For even, as the sun rises every morning, so too, does beauty

from these higher realms, reflect light, love and peace.

Difficult as it is to remain awake, it is a healing blessing to witness the magnificent power of the night sky.

O thank you, great source of light, for bringing us together, for weaving Heaven and Earth, for completion of this union.

To all who seek understanding and compassion, keep opening to light. Feel hope for the coming years, for there is nothing to fear.

Life is a blessing, wherever and whenever it is. All are protected to continue their missions. No one shall take it away.

We encourage truth, calmness, forgiveness and compassion. Return to the simple ways of life, honor each other.

January 6 - Manifesting Visions

Dream - In a women's group to affirm, nurture and heal, a powerful council to teach, empower and enliven, to be strong, centered, clear to make positive decisions. Every inspiration, I want to act upon, especially at this awakening time.

Note - In January 2013, Mariam and Robin Rooney host medicine women circles in Western Mass and Vermont. Seven women move on for positive reasons within the year.

To hear and acknowledge your soul's longing has far reaching effects. When you expand into your true expression, you feel Spirit.

Let the sun flow in your heart and radiant light in your soul.

Feel the blessings of sight, touch- all that guides your existence.

It is a powerful experience now, life, and well worth the effort.

So, pay attention at sunrise, feel your body, listen to the silence.

Be joyous, attuned and inspired to create with celebration.

Nurture each other, the children, and the mothers.

Unify resources. Gather power, in strength, you'll do anything.

I now draw to me all that I seek as a creatress, singer songstress and musician with a spiritual message. I affirm to live within a budget, "Enough is good enough."

To make an agreement about spending, is to believe in your energetic force of manifestation of material abundance.

As long as you keep calling it from Source, there is no reason to doubt, it will continue to flow to you, for Source is unlimited.

Yes, it is good to be moderate, but do not have guilt over spending. As you pay attention, you will let go of unnecessary things as they accumulate, clutter and confuse energies.

Ask do I need this? Does it serve me? Does it have an end in sight? What are my long-term goals? Can I live without it?

Keep flowing, as you create and draw to you. Return to simplicity as you consciously feed your heart's desire.

January 9

I feel you deep within, Ashento. We breathe as one.

Yes, it is only time that keeps us apart, so make the best of your wondrous experience on Gaea Star. All of this bliss will expand, enhance and open you to the Divine. You and I are one.

Be consciously attuned to spirit within and around. To be blessed by this awareness daily, is to remain in communion with love, with creation, with the source of light.

One then moves toward being of service on the highest level. We await the moment when all of humanity opens in this way.

Honor the highest in each other in conscious ways through prayer and commitment, to settling differences peacefully.

Whenever you are not in alignment with these aspects, move away from whatever is creating disharmony, whether it is in relationship, a job or anything uncomfortable, as soon as you realize.

Everyone knows what this refers to. At some point the soul will rise up and make a move by causing the change to happen suddenly.

This may not always be the smoothest path, but it is necessary.

Each day is a blank page in your journal, unique in its own. Take the time to paint a rosy picture of life, by consciously working as if you are the artist.

Create, do, paint, make the pictures as lovely as possible, as memorable to each day.

In all that you do, honor and respect, the precious moment of life as you breathe, as you live, as you love.

Flow on knowing this, weaving a peaceful, loving, giving web of beauty, creativity and sweetness.

Life is to learn, prosper, and know the truth of the soul within.

January 14

It's a clear starry night. Moonlight is shining crystalline, sparkling on the snow. Making music for Wise Ways Herbals' 25-year anniversary on 1-29-2011. Five ones, reflect change, adventure, love and creativity. We share art, music, food and dance. Grateful for the years, for the abundance of helping humanity with herbal products.

My life is blessed from the mother and the father, gently growing in this womb of life, as high as the tall trees reaching for the light. Returning home, returning love, on the journey home.

Spirit says thank you, for your majestic voice, words and inspiration, for the teachings you share, for respecting above, below and within and for remembering the compassionate ways of the ancient wise ones, and for trusting, hoping and believing in the holy.

Thank you for helping nurture and support the beauty of Mother Gaea, for appreciating her flowing waters, the whiteness of snow, and for her cleansing, fertilizing ability to cover with warmth.

Thank you for having fun, for trying to live peacefully, for devoting time to nurture, love, being kind, for listening, for opening the way and to seek to know goodness and truth.

Thank you for putting down all that no longer serves, for peeling away the layers, to allow your hearts to sing and dance.

Thank you for returning to the light, for following the journey of love, to surrender to what flows through.

Thank you for acknowledging the higher realms, by looking up and feeling us looking down, for nurturing your souls with wisdom from these wondrous avenues of love.

We send you light, compassion, songs and inspiration.

Thank you for seeking truth, for discovering the way home, to the source, to what wraps you in a warm mantle of loving light.

Thank you for expressing beauty, for the light that shines, as you raise the vibration of love, through uplifting songs of devotion.

Thank you for bringing love home. In blessings, we love you.

January 18

Rain drips. An ice storm after six inches of snow, cold, stillness. Few cars drove by. Roofs are ice encrusted, dripping. Staying home.

All is well in the celestial realms. We await the homecoming of Gaea Star, with her beautiful transformation, as old ways are dissolving, and memories of nurturing and healing, resurface.

Embrace your heart songs, to peel away the many layers, revealing the pearl, the fruit, the gem, and the flower, bursting from the garden of love.

You are unique, wondrous creations, sparks of light, from the highest spiritual foundation, the Source of love.

It is no longer possible, to not feel a connection to all life.

Muster the courage, to wind your way through the labyrinth of the illusions of life, to re-connect, to know love and light, with no doubt, or sadness, to feel trust in the beauty and purity of love, with the intention to raise your vibration to the highest.

Always project loving positive energy toward humanity.

Cultivate the garden of love, fertilize with joy and sprinkle goodness. Seek what nourishes your soul and accept differences.

Following the path of love, leads to a happy reunion with your spiritual origins, revealing why you chose this incarnation. Expand in awareness that all life matters and exists all for important reasons.

As you follow the way home, you release each layer, giving all that you can, as you heal the separations and difficulties, for you are connected to Source and to Source, you shall return.

January 20 - 25

Baby-blue sky. Sparky meows. Sun rising through southeastern clouds, soon to shine on snow-laden trees. I am joyous in seeing, hearing, and walking, on this glorious winter day.

I am grateful for the surprises and blessings, that teach me to be courageous, dynamic, and strong, empowered by the light that I constantly seek to shine ever brighter.

I cultivate awareness and compassion, to change what I can with loving respect. As we strive to satisfy our goals, we see how easier it is, to combine with others, to live with spirit flowing, in goodness.

Let's move on into graceful forgiveness to fulfill our destinies, to live in harmony, love, and peace.

There's nothing more powerful, than when your time has come.

I seek the wisdom to activate, to look within, to know how to evolve as beings of light, showering each other with radiant nurturing.

I feel an opening to keep going, to let it unfold, to be the best, to realize each moment brings rewards, when I cultivate peaceful actions and do it well.

What you accomplish in a day, is all up to you, to rekindle your ideas into action and make do with what you have.

February 4 - Star Priestess, Birth

Dream - A show with a birth/ regeneration theme. I gathered people and costumes. I wore a black, beaded star- dress. I helped a woman put on a star dress. We went to meet someone, people stared, astonished. The person wasn't there, so we turned and came back.

An earlier dream - I entered a cavernous room, to see a woman giving birth on the floor alone. I went to help with twins she had just birthed. I ran to look for something to wrap around the babies and found only wet towels. As I was returning, I said, "She's given birth." People replied, "We know. Soon." "She already did it." No time to explain since they didn't believe me.

She was a proud, primal, priestess of birth, carrying on, for she knew what to do, for her babies' safety. She had them tucked in her arms, on her belly, to keep warm. I wrapped each one, with the damp towels. They were small, yet healthy. It was a beautiful birth scene.

February 7 -11

I dream about sexuality in relationships.

Opening the portal of sexual expression, invigorates, nurtures and awakens the life force, prana, or the breath of life, causing happiness, and inspiration to flow from the healing force of love.

Find the Way

Find the way, find the way to show your love

Find the way, in all that you do, in all that you say

Find the way, find the way, to spread your love

To give a little love in every day, in every way.

I wonder about my long-time employees leaving, for new horizons.

Bless the company with guiding wisdom, to grow into a productive company, even in a new location. At some point in life, there comes a moment to have faith, to let Spirit, be the director, the moving force, as you head courageously into the winds of change.

Focusing on your passion is recognizing the true essence of your path. When it is poised in front of you, that is the perfect opportunity to act on it, to let it unfold with swift and true creativity.

Surrender, releasing fear, reconnecting, heading home to peace.

I accept my destiny, setting myself free in a positive new way, to make art, music, costumes and the 'Gaea Star Crystal' story, to inspire humanity. Thank you, Isis, for your creative inspiration.

February 12

Morning stillness, dawn coming, the moon shines through the clouds. Nia purrs softly. I put anxious thoughts in order, releasing what keeps me from my mission. I give it the opportunity to do that.

I say, thank you, for showing me the path of love and light.

My sweetness, there are great changes coming, nothing to fear. Embrace all of what you do. It is helpful, sustaining and nurturing.

To manifest your divine essence in all its glory, take time to create, to find that calm, joyful place, to allow other things to flow in.

Of course, this new space may be unfamiliar, after the many years of working, but think of the arts as a new beginning, to become even more the Creatress, by diving in fully to share your wisdom.

In January 2013, Ben Tobin from Williamsburg Ma, releases a film documentary on Mariam - Creatress of the Hilltown's.

It is time to birth the powerful, active, joyful expressions of the teachings of Gaea Star.

We appreciate what all of you, are striving to manifest, working with love and peace, reaching across boundaries, dissolving into oneness, as a family of love. Look for the beauty in everything.

The changing energies are moving quickly now. Each of you, can tap into the Universal consciousness of love, through breathing, teaching, and leading in profound, peaceful ways. Thank you.

I decline to sell WiseWays Herbals. It was not the right offer. I free myself, by turning over daily operations to my willing staff.

February 14 -18 -19 - 24

Dream, I hear, "You are a recording star." I'm finishing recording the 'Gaea Star Goddess' CD with Bob Sherwood, Dameron and Diana Noble, as vocal back up. It is an upbeat, musical compilation with many diverse instruments. The Goddess in her many forms moves me, to turn my inspiration into songs.

Being in the body is just a temporary experience, while the spirit seeks to manifest its' true self.

May we reflect our powerful love, bringing out the best within our soul's light through the passion of creation. Our twin flame love is rich and not diminished, even as we exist in different realms, bridging Heaven and Earth. I reside, amidst brilliant stars, shining through mystical hazes of light. Love to you, as I drift in and out.

Bring in the Beauty

Bring in the beauty, bring in the love
Sing in the beauty, sing in the love
. Oh, so sweetly, bring in the love,
Oh, so sweetly, sing in the love.
To find your light within, within,
Tenderly loving your light,
Like a new moon in the night,
Oh, your heart holds beauty and love,
Within, within, within.
Hold true to your vision,
Walk on, walk on, in the beauty of love

Mariam Massaro

I am Love Unfolding

In the morning, when I open my eyes,
I face the east, to watch the sun rise.
I hear a voice singing within my mind,
To love everyone, to always be kind.
I am love unfolding,
like a petal of the rose.
Opening to share my perfume with those,
To whom I meet and whom I greet, I share my light.
Every moment of my life, I release pure love
Pure light to whom I meet, whom I greet.
I share my light, every moment of my life.
I release pure light, pure light, pure light.

March 2

What a blessing to open your eyes in the morning, to see the glorious wind, dancing wildly in the trees, under the blue sky. As you notice familiar things in your peaceful room, you feel the power of breath, your beating heart and the sun's soft rays, so warm on your skin. You are alive for one more day.

Let yourself love this new dance of life, to feel holy passion. It's all good, for every breath is a blessing.

Jay Lynch, who helped film the 'Gaea Star Crystal' and played a wizard, is coming to Damanhur with three new friends, Kristen Grella, Corina Miller, and Joanne Gabler. Corina contacted me after she saw a news article, about the WiseWays Herbals, 25-year anniversary party where I dressed as Isis in honor of her inspiration to start the company.

Blessed By Light-filled Love

Ashento, you are my special light even from far away. I feel strong in my mission. Bless you.

A silvery crescent moon appears with Venus, the brilliant morning star, as the brook gurgles and wind whistles. I remain relaxed with the tremendous Earth changes happening, opening to the unfolding mystery, to all that I attract.

May I be loving, positive and focused on my Divine essence.

Into the void of knowingness, we leap like a grasshopper, happily-hoppity, carefree, exuberant. Little do we realize when we call in our heart's desire, it may arrive in moderate terms, or in grandiose expressions. One never knows. Let's celebrate it all, as gifts from the universe, as fulfillment of our deep longings.

Thank you for those who guide, through our confusion in the realm of materiality. Some remain invisible but are still felt.

It is fulfilling as you hear messages from spirit. Savor the magnificence of nature, the Sun, Moon, Fire, Water, Earth, Air.

Make it easy, simplify. Walk to work. Drink pure water. Eat well. Exercise. Cultivate joy. The happy factor is how you keep going.

How does one remain peaceful, while supporting their heart's desire? Trust, positivity, opening and letting loving selves emerge.

You will be remembered as ones who brighten with love.

March 15 - 17

A nuclear meltdown in Japan, releases toxicity into the ocean.

Unify as a family of light, for it is time to reassess. The dramatic Earth changes are coming to the vulnerable areas of the continents. A visible network of the safe areas is being created.

Meditate, eat live food, immerse in nature. Trust that all will unfold in peaceful loving vibrations. Nurture, as you gather in the light. Gaea is ascending and releasing what longer serves her.

Early morning, my fire man brother, Steve calls, from a massive fire at Eagle Bay Sanctuary! I hear sirens. "Oh, no." All the barns with everything, along with my favorite sheep, and her newborn lambs are gone. I'm shocked at the loss of the one -hundred-year-old grandpa barn, along with my handmade tipis, retreat items and other things. I ask to be at peace, to let it go. I'm grateful we brought the lovely handmade colorful WiseWays Herbals sign here months ago.

Do not hold onto anything, for as you move into the deeper expression of your Divine path, you will understand why the fire took it away. So many responsibilities now gone, to help you break free of the chains of material density, to follow a new path.

Open to a new reality, with willingness to unfold, gracefully.

Despite the pain of the great loss, remain poised for what is next. Deep within is the love of spirit, overriding the loss. You'll find the way to return to your peaceful life of love filled light.

After seeing the results of the fire, we return to leave for Damanhur, the artistic community in Italy, to hopefully film there. They honor the essence of humanity in fantastic art forms through their magnificent underground temples. I have visionary experiences, everywhere we visit. We are awed by the communities, especially the treehouse one, where one of the members was inspired to create a device to record the trees, singing haunting and harmonious melodies. We bought one of the mechanical devices to use for creating music here with my plants.

The Damanhur community only allow us to film in the outdoor ritual temples, partly due to the Italian Catholic church, not approving of their controversial art and community living, that advocates self-discovery, time travel and other progressive thinking.

We dressed as celestial star beings, meeting, dancing and healing together. It was natural and spontaneous, to improvise there, joined by members who loved us. Flying home from Damanhur, I hear the same words from New Year's Eve 2007. "Begin before the beginning."

Blessed By Light-filled Love

Yes, you see the value of creating the story as you live it. Look at your changes these years, how you perceive alternate realities, as you fly high above, in pressurized air, feeling closer to the realm of spirit, sensing the invisible, yet visible within.

It is easy to return to precious communion with the enlightened presences of brilliant love, as a celestial priestess of glory and beauty.

Everything that is before, behind and within, is one inspiring moment of creativity, all is one.

You are here, there and everywhere, as your consciousness, harmoniously meanders, through all experiences.

Just go deeper within, into the vortex of inspiration and creativity, to discover one's true purpose of existence.

You are always evolving as spiritual beings, learning from every event and experience.

The ultimate goal is to accept living as radiant, emissaries of light. Welcome in love, every moment through joyful music.

Imagine communing with stars, from stage, screen, Share the limelight with them as helpful guides to assist your goals.

You are a Creatress for the Emerald Gold Queen of Heaven. She awaits your expression of her visible presence on Gaea Star. Weave her and other Goddesses into a circle of loving light, to offer to the world, everywhere. Take on the task.

Lead on to realms of inspiration. I am your guiding lover of light.

You're at the threshold of a new life, immersed in the elements.

Let fears dissipate for anything that does not feel of the highest source. Release anxiety over the New York building and loss of the barns. How does that serve you? Compose a new vision for Eagle Bay as it recycles into something else now, free of your concerns. I sail off in celestial wonder, into a parallel realm of natural blue light.

March 20 - Jesse's birthday

Dream, we are conducting a ritual in a temple, holding sacred space for this land and Eagle Bay, celebrating their existence with the elemental energies of Gaea Star. I am a high priestess, wearing fantastic jewelry, a headdress and simple clothing. We invited the Divine in all beings, to be expressed.

Awaken the creative force within. Gather for rituals, prayer and community. Create temples to honor the flowing waters, the forest, the four directions and always singing to the sacred trees.

I resume life with awakened creativity after visiting Damanhur. I'm inspired with new music flowing and playing the melodies in different ways.

April 1

Dream: Surfing on the waters of life. Beauty is within and around. I am a Queen, sailing into my daily dilemmas, pulling me into this alternate reality, back from the feeling of supreme power, of connection to the oneness of all.

I think of the Lady of the Lake statue, that gazes across the water, of the Black River Bay, at Eagle Bay with shore birds, flying by. As she calmly faces what comes with silence, surrounded by stately Birch trees, even as stormy winds blow, holding her power.

I accept every moment of life with joy, peace, and a willingness to connect with the Source of love. Through contemplation and nurturing, the physician within, heals itself.

We weave the web of life, with a gossamer string of golden white light, full of vitality and pleasure at the sight of its own beauty.

April 3 - 8 -12

The path you chose to illuminate your way, is always the easy one, full of inspiration, excitement, direction, passion and deep feelings. You know to fully connect, is to celebrate your truth within, to flow deeply with certainty, for the dawning light always comes.

Blessed By Light-filled Love

Darkness then light, light then darkness, as above then below. Continue to play, to set the movement, for all that you came to do.

Be at peace, at one with life, as it flows in love and light.

Thank you. The songs for the "Gaea Star Goddesses" CD, are taking harmonious shape, with inspired messages of creativity.

You and I feel each other as one, wherever we are. The Goddesses are pleased for presenting the messages of feminine expressions in beauty in song, costume, and dance.

Reveal your soul's song in sweet poetic beauty each day. Cultivate inspired expressions that nurture creativity and joy.

Be like the sun, bring in light and warmth, as you let the winds, of creation, flow through.

Feel the blessings of light - filled love, while fostering your soul's longing, singing praises to a beautiful existence.

Yes, life is good, pure and powerful. Celebrate all that you are right now, in great colorful, authentic aliveness.

Breathe in the beauty, as you see the dawning of the new day.

Joyful positivism encourages abundance to flow.

To live, is to honor love. Yes, to be alive, is to live in peace.

The creativity, inspired from Damanhur, demonstrates how bastions of spiritual creativity, have harmonizing, beneficial effects. WiseWays Herbals nurtures humanity in the same way.

Bless the world with your healing spirit filled music.

April 24 -27

I am thankfully happy for this lovely day. Good morning to Ashento. I see you proud, handsome, ageless, a powerful memory from long ago. I hold you close within.

We are always a cohesive force of light, even in our own realities. We remain connected, no matter where we are or what we are doing.

It's the middle of the night. The toads are singing after a rain and thundering lightning storm, for the first time this spring.

It is a pleasure to commune any time, as it joyfully expresses our oneness in love despite our separation.

To look through your eyes, hear through your ears and speak through your voice, is soothing. I too, love the toads singing, waters flowing in the night, mingled with the hue of the starry sky. Yes, the pleasure of being alive is a very special experience.

All the work, all the songs, great power flows as you connect to creativity. It is truly a pleasure, is it not? When you put aside all that distracts your flow, you open the door, to learning more. It's like a fire: when you feed it, it grows warmer, brighter, and powerful.

The Earth is transforming, shedding the skin of illusions. Be not alarmed, she is changing for the better.

Becoming one, is to simply live in peaceful, harmony. Develop this realization. There is no other choice but to remove all blockages. We are all one. There is no separation or "other." This is the truth, to function as humans, as spirits in human form. All is well. To remember this takes great commitment.

Thank you for delving in, to see, to know, to produce great work, to develop momentum and appreciation for the radiance of your light. Be blessed, healed, and nurtured by my love.

April 28

I have a nightmare about the upcoming show.

Set your intention. The Divine Feminine is creativity in progress. All is perfect. Begin with an invocation of peace. Use Isis and her song to set the tone, with the element of air, to express the power of your vision. This beautiful show will shine on.

May 6   Memories

Memories, are you making memories with someone you love?

Memories, are you making memories as a family,

with people you hold dear?

Are you yearning for a special one, to warm your heart?

To fill you with blissful union, with loving smiles,

happiness and peaceful walks?

Memories, over and over again.

Are you calling your true love, to enter in?

to fill your life with memories, sweet loving memories?

May 11 - 14 - 25

Release everything that no longer serves you. Express yourself as a leader of expansive, pure, flowing, healing light.

'Goddess' CD is done, now I am developing the Goddess show and will resume writing, Ashentos' teachings, for the world needs his inspiring wisdom.

I understand your dedication to releasing my messages, however the Goddesses are also the teachings, so it is already done. You and I share the beauty of life, through the music. Be confident for your performance, on auspicious May 22, to bring this work to light, to inspire and enjoy all that flows.

Thank you Ashento, we send greetings today.

To dance upon the Earth in creative ways, is an expression of your divine essence. As above, so below, spirit to human. Life is wonder and achievement, bliss and bless are the same.

Awakening to your missions is the first step. Abundance flows if you believe everything is good. Receive and give with kindness.

June 5 - 8

Listen to the messages in the melodies of spirit, to share your musical gifts in celebration of the beauty, of a joyful abundant life.

To breathe, see and feel love is gratifying when united with all that calls you to a spirit filled existence. Mother Gaea releases intensity from nuclear disturbances and other actions of disregard for her beautiful natural resources. She is a force to reckon with in a positive, proactive, respectful way.

I surrender to the will of Heaven.

Your creative force within, is emerging as a butterfly from the cocoon, transforming into a dynamic being of light, adoring of all life.

I didn't remember writing the following lyrics when I found them under the couch.

Filled with Love

Every day, every moment of your life

I feel your beating heart right within me,

Deep within, my soul.

You and I are one in the holy light,

Beneath the Stars, the Suns, and the Moons.

Fly with me to my celestial home

Beyond your galaxy of life,

You and I can find the glorious way

To share our love every day.

I've always held you within my heart

From the moment of our eternal spark.

Oh, my sweetness, we are one in the same,

My divine twin flame

Blessed By Light-filled Love

Third CD, "Smooth Sailing Love Songs." March 2013

Spirit of the Sun Music.

June 11 - 13 - 15 -16

It is essential to open to inspiration daily. You know what to do, to manifest your soul's purpose. Follow your bliss, as you focus, to let creativity emerge. Unravel the knots of busyness, of rushing around. Stay grounded, firmly planted, for then you make a difference.

Ask before you go in the car. Do I need to do this? Stay in tune, to the essence of all, to the central power of life, like a tree growing, as long as its' roots tap into water and energy.

The more you connect to the vital, alive, powerful essence of spirit, the more it nurtures your presence.

Thank you for life on this farm, where I hear birds, the singing brook and watch drifting clouds sail by, all under the brilliant blue.

To listen to what guides us, is to dance with pure wonder, to create even more, as we shed the layers of illusion, becoming free, simpler, softer, open, loving and grateful.

May we nurture our soul's longing, the dynamic essence that whispers softly, to manifest our dreams, to face the truth of our heart's desire. Standing for what sings inside, following the path of light, to shelter us, from the stormy sides of love, so we may celebrate life in joy.

My sweetness, you found the way for our work to flourish, through your songs, bless your heart and life, from my soul to yours.

Ashento, you guide, nurture and love me. When we sang and prayed, during a healing ceremony, he spoke through me. I wonder if that's alright.

Thank you for concern of voicing my message. It is an appropriate place for my words. You do not pull me in from anywhere, as we are one. You and I, may accomplish great work together, now that you are realizing your true potential, serving in the highest realm.

The river of life flows home to the source, to the soul's origin.

The Akashic Records, the Encyclopedia of life, holds everything from many lifetimes. All pieces can be accessed easily, to read like a book. Past, present and future occur in symphony simultaneously. Each chapter is already written.

June 29

It is valuable to present our wisdom, for together, we have the potential to create sweet loving words, weaving Heaven and Earth.

Your accomplishments reflect your beautiful radiant light. Complete projects for positive and powerful responses. There are many who will appreciate our messages that flow so freely.

Thank you for receiving these inspirations of heavenly origin.

Gentle wind blow, away my cares, as I begin this new day, returning to peaceful balance, free of restraints and strife.

May I appreciate each moment, aware, in complete unison with Source, with each breath, nurturing, my body, mind and spirit, to express joyful love, to all I encounter.

May I walk as a radiant being of light, remembering each day is another wondrous opportunity to create something special on Gaea Star, a gift, a treasure, a part of myself to leave behind.

July 1

Each day is a new blessing, a clean slate, bursting with sunshine, clouds and pure rivers flowing to the sea.

I heard a Fox calling for a mate, while a rambunctious family of four raccoons, played with the crystals on my deck.

I'm dreaming melodies, until a song sparrow, singing in the Oak tree awakens me. The Catalpa's, pretty, white blossoms float everywhere, like Faeries, dancing. Fragrant roses beckon to gather their colorful petals while Puffy brings snakes and frogs under the bed.

To receive the gifts of the universe, take in the serene flowing abundant love from the air, water, sunshine and healing plants.

Let your love flow as rays of grace, like the ocean touching the shore with waves of overlapping beauty.

Nurture your body with luscious alive fruit, every day. Take time to appreciate all that you have. Bless your lovely mornings.

July 7

Returning from dreamtime, I thank life for being sweet on this blue-sky morning, for leaves on silent trees, for the golden sun, shining through the window.

Yes, my sweetness, today is good, just like the others. To seek the best outcome, pick from your colorful decks. Let that card be your theme for the day. Place it on an altar visibly. Say, "I begin today with love in my heart, cultivating patience and compassion for all beings, and unraveling difficult situations."

To have a full life, be conscious and aware in all moments, for to be fully present, is to share your loving light, vibration and peaceful healing, with everyone you connect with.

So spread your love, by reaching within, expressing by singing, and sharing your serene, compassionate and nurturing music.

I commune with a variety of guardians from the higher realms who are willing to help those who seek our healing ways.

July 8 - 11 - 14

Dream: performing in beautiful costumes with fantastic sets. I awake with inspiration from Ashento.

Your dreams reveal truths, their glimpses guide you within, to view these multiple realities, to connect to your life's work.

My sweetness, every moment is a precious jewel, a treasure of existence, a breath to praise creation, to do, be, sing or create a work of art.

Imagine yourselves, growing tall and strong as the trees, from the nourishing elements, developing with wondrous rings of age.

Reach deep into your loving heart, to tap the sweet essence of pure love, to radiate freely to all you encounter, with no judgment.

Your show is lovely. Let it develop as you focus attention. You know what it takes for a dynamic show. Be the principal but gather resources. Create the Gaea Star Goddess Troupe. Ask for support for projects with loving energy. Change is afoot.

Water flows sweetly. Frogs croaking. Moon shines bright.

The goal is to express the truth of existence, by manifesting, nurturing, healing and taking loving care of yourselves.

Before birth on Earth and after passing, there are distinct passages, phases and momentous instances. Each brings an "Aha!" moment if we allow, choose, or surrender.

All is well, in whichever realm we reside. Abundant, healing blessings are showered upon you now.

May you stand at the precipice, seeing the vast expansiveness, realizing one needs only to open their wings, to fly into all experiences by releasing all fear.

Trust that the journey is the ride, the flight, the all- embracing adventure you chose for the lessons to learn, for the creations to manifest on the golden path of peace, the final destination.

Yes, all flows as you move forward, looking deeper within.

You are building the temple, based on the crystalline structure of the magical, mystical Mother Gaea, the planet you reside on.

She revolves in loving creative effort, holding humanity firmly, for she knows she is in a vulnerable position.

We wrap Mother Gaea in celestial raiment's of beauty, as you are a Priestess of purple, wearing golden and blue robes of light.

May the colors of her angelic presence become visible as you seek, pray and surrender to her goodness.

She is flying ever deeper, to sustain and support you. Bless your lives and each other in gratitude. Hold strong. She will manifest a life like no other, very soon.

July 18 - 20

After enjoying a spectacular waterfall in Savoy Forest, I dreamed I met a man with dancers and singers at a California festival. I offered to help the troupe with costumes, breathing and singing advice. He agreed. I said, "I'm returning to the West soon." I talked to a couple about their Isis company. I showed my Isis logo, described her rainbow flamboyant costume and Gaea Star Goddess shows. They were excited for me to return there.

I record the brook and bullfrogs singing, beneath the shining moon. I am one with you, Ashento, I feel your presence within.

What we do, benefits ourselves and others of like minds, on Gaea Star. Surround yourself with colors that you feel drawn to.

Re-do your sacred spaces to restore clarity, to recharge the auric-field and to renew connection to spirit.

The universe showers you with loving essence, through your hands, eyes, ears and feet touching the Earth.

Float gently along the river of life, shining light and wisdom, sharing creativity and expressing courageous, pure vision.

Reconnect, with your tribe. Speak with kindness and truth, refrain from talking too much.

Kindle friendships with all animals, as you peacefully immerse in the inspiring wonder of nature.

Use your body as a temple. Stay connected to the energetic vortex flowing from the center of Earth. Take your shoes off, ground to the Earth with bare feet as you enjoy her living vitality.

Release everything that distracts from the essence of love. This is what resides within your luminous fiber and nurtures your core.

To reconnect, breathe in, say, "I am filled with the essence of light. I carry light. I am light. I am love. I am everything and everything am I. I completely relax. I only eat when my body wants to eat. I enjoy being connected to all that serves my higher contentment."

July 25 – 26

I am inspired to complete the 'Celestial Teachings of Ashento.' Dream, Wearing a silvery costume, with sparkling stars on it.

I am one with you, in the midst of all that you do. Hold me close within your heart, breathing, feeling alive, vital and joyful.

Together we beam a unified beacon of healing love and light.

Create music even when others are near you.

You are an excellent channel of light flowing from Source.

July 27 - 28

May the universe bless everyone with light and love, today. My love flows to you, Ashento.

Life flows on, like brilliant light shining at the end of a tunnel. When you express what you love, your soul sings with joyful warmth. Spirit supports manifesting dreams, so go ahead, let them fly.

Do you have birds and flowers like Gaea Star has?

Yes, there are multitudes of colorfully, opulent, winged birds of heaven. They fly in between the starry realms in beautiful splendor.

Each moment is a prayerful celebration, a creation of wonderful beauty with an awareness, that to be alive, is an essence of the reflection of love, a visible manifestation of the masculine and feminine polarity, united in passion and love.

Now is the moment for humanity to wake to their true calling.

We pray for my baby llama Miracle who is falling from an illness. She is so sweet. She can't follow the herd.

All life grows or contracts. One hopes for the best outcome, however she is deeply damaged, so there may be nothing more to do. Through prayer, there is peaceful acceptance.

July 30

Move through daily challenges by remaining unattached, as if they are feathers floating on the breeze.

Reward yourself for living in aware spirituality, moving ahead of the debris that flows along the river of life.

August 12 - 21

There comes a moment, when you can reconfigure life into exactly what you seek, to manifest what you want to do with passion.

So never give up focusing on all levels, as you take the steps to free yourself even more.

Life flows swiftly, then slows, becoming still like a lake, with no wind.

See how you cause ripples upon the water, as you use creative energy to create a costume, rehearse music, or make a connection.

Dreams manifest with active intention, no one else can do it.

There are opportunities to grow with, sometimes, they are insignificant in magnitude and others are pivotal for great change.

This is the moment now, to disperse what no longer serves you.

Seize the chance, to accept what comes as a gift of divine light, inspiring you to move with grace into even higher consciousness as a spiritual being in human form.

The options of life that were previously selected to occur, prior to coming to Gaea Star, although only possibilities, are not always what one chooses to do now in this lifetime.

For the older one is, the farther away from the memory of Divine Source, making it difficult to re-awaken the original connection. There are ways to rekindle, to "shake the wire," in case it's not a good one, as the message may be cloudy, or be off - kilter.

But in your case, you knew, sensed, longed, and envisioned, it to rise up, powerfully, wonderfully, bubbling up, from within.

Thank you for singing, for relating, for your devotion, for all the words that flow. We create beautiful songs together.

The more you practice, the more aware, insightful and comfortable, you are as a performer, as a leader to foster change, to express celebrating life with a song in your heart for every moment.

I ask for blessings for my brother Steve, who is in the Middle East, and for my aging parents who are separated in nursing homes. We pray they are united for their last years together.

August 22.   Every Moment

May I be guided by love, truth and light.

Every moment of my day, every moment of my night,

Every moment of my life.

I'll sing in the morning. I'll sing in the night.

I'll sing all day with my wings in flight.

September 4

Smile as you look into the stars, for I'm way up here, singing to you, loving your spirit, longing to play with you, as you hear, night birds cheeping, letting life unfold in serene beauty.

May I follow the will of heaven, flying on the wings of Isis, guiding me to connect with her Goddess energy, dancing everywhere, even on the leaves of tall trees, in joyful abandon.

The constancy of air sustains life without conscious effort. Unconsciously, we breathe in and out the energy around us. There is enough for everyone to have what they need to survive freely.

It is good to be grateful for love and for Earth's bountiful life.

When one goes through a difficult choice or transition, the path clears, the logjam is freed in the river, allowing momentum to build, for what is coming next, full speed ahead.

Trust that you'll navigate, where your hearts' desire wants to go.

May each moment be conscious, aware and guided by love.

Always shine your radiant light for everyone who may need it.

September 15 - 25

No matter how dark the shadows of life are, the inner light always shines bright within, like the sun hidden by the clouds, but all along the glory of its' radiance is always there.

Every moment on the journey, there is a choice, to return even closer to the loving Spirit within.

I'm reading Moriah's book, channeled from a spiritual being, called 'The Tibetan.' I open to Ashento to his wisdom.

The singing brook rearranged recently, with sweeping changes from Hurricane Irene, causing a big pool at the bend, a new course through the rocks and nearly destroying the wood bridge as she flowed wildly even into the woods.

Fascinating how I find something new when I go there. I place rocks across the water for Puffy to cross and a week later, they've moved, sometimes totally downstream.

It's a time of momentous change. Nothing remains the same. Nature, is beautiful, destroying and transforming.

Thank you for calling me to see the sun's golden beauty peeking above the clouds, high upon the ridge, as I stopped to watch the glorious view.

I hear Ashento flowing in my heart, in the depths of my soul, from the glory above.

Thank you, my sweetness. Yes, it is a while since the waters overflowed in New England, wiping away years of illusions.

It is the dawning of the Awakening, the moment of the Great

Shift, the time to be aware and reconnect with clarity. The veils are lifting as the light is shining brighter.

Your intuition is tapping into the resources of all knowing.

Connect to your missions, which dwell warmly within the soul.

You are beacons in the gardens of love, flowers of peaceful manifestations of the plantings, that you willingly participated in.

The stem of the flower is sustained by the vitality, power and presence of the Source of life.

Remember, you are always connected to the Source of healing, in the presence of oneness, even if one has not opened.

Many Seeds Have Fallen

Many seeds have fallen, many seeds have fallen

To the Earth, to the Earth

Some will grow tall some will grow strong

Some will grow thin. Some will never open.

We are all seeds from the same source

On and on we learn, on and on we grow,

on this journey we flow,

Divine light, divine love, divine truth, divine peace

Many seeds have fallen,

Many seeds have fallen to the Earth

Blessed By Light-filled Love

"Many Seeds Have Fallen," 6th Cd, Vision Quest, 2014, Spirit of the Sun Music.

Yes, it is good to visit the forest regularly, to pray, to find the way, to fine-tune your radio antenna.

Everyone has a unique way of receiving information.

You tap into powerful depths, by sitting, listening and observing, far from busy-ness, inspired by the solitude of nature.

As you seek the way, you'll find the courage to change, to find the resources to form a new life.

Each journey is a movement of transformation, of awakening, of surrender and allegiance to the higher forces of destiny.

Just keep releasing all that no longer serves you. Believe in the capacity to grow and enlighten your life.

Thank you for seeking me, for holding sacred space, for moving through the challenges, for being proudly courageous, as you stand transfixed, full of light. Create exactly as you believe.

You power your life, as the Creatress, a holy Goddess of love. Thank you, sweetness, for all that you are blessed to do.

September 28

Dream, Showing the Gaea Star Crystal movie trailer. Another dream; I'm riding an ornately decorated Star Faery bike in a parade.

October 14 -15 - 21

As we work together, we are one endless flame of light.

Touch this essence of knowing as you connect.

In every yoga session you heal and sustain that nurturing place within.

Be well with all the love and light that flows eternally from me to you.

Thank you, night for my restful journey. I feel the cool breeze. Dawn is bringing another lovely peaceful day ahead. I stay home to ground in, being creative for the upcoming show. The moon is softly glowing above the trees in the south, as the river rumbles in the dark. Sleepless, I hear the voice within.

Moonlight maiden, stargazer, you inhabit the Earth with the others. We await your success and even your failures, each has its balance point. All is well. We have spent lifetimes as one, bonded. Thank you for living, for breathing deep within me.

I am grateful, for all that you have given me. I see the way forward now in truth and passion for my dreams.

November 2 - Prayer to Mother Gaea

What a beautiful month, water flowing, stars glowing in the night. Thank you for guiding me to manifest the show into reality.

Such a good process to believe in myself, to venture onto the thin branches, to have the courage to take the opportunity to create and all that I am. It feels good, to gather people, to produce music, and now the homestretch for publicity. Whew, a lot of work.

I see the Earth's changes, with her destruction from massive snowfall, the ice covering the trees, causing outages. The desperate, without food or heat, the weakness it stirs in humanity, having lost the connection, the trust that Spirit has everything under control.

Thank you for the reminder: to understand the way of life, is to believe in you Spirit, to know that this is a sacred time, that the Earth is ascending, shedding, assuming her new form.

She is willing to take us along, but only if we adhere to living in love and being one. We are messengers of light.

November 3

What an amazing day: touring the Academy of Music theater for the premier of Gaea Star Goddesses, on their beautiful stage.

Blessed By Light-filled Love

I'm grateful for the chance to dream big, for the courage to perform this dynamic show, in such a regal theater.

Thank you, Ashento and Ganesh, Lakshmi, Saraswathi, Isis and all the divine beings that have touched me. Your healing presence is felt and seen through the performances of the Goddesses, as we share songs, poetic words, and fantastic costumes. I'm thrilled to play and sing at the piano, as Yemanja, Goddess of the Ocean.

Less than a week ago was the huge snowstorm, many are still barely recovered, without power.

May we find our way, utilizing what supports us.

I feel the mystery and the magic within. Thank you for the grace of love, for the breath of life. Ode to the beauty of the constant glow of the stars. What worlds and universes do you shine from?

The vastness of the sky touches deep. Sometimes it awakens us, with the glow of the moon, or the Pleiades, the seven-star sisters, all dancing together.

Life flows from you Holy Mother, Holy Father.

I hear melodies in the water, mesmerizing me into sleep.

Maka hey

Maka hey, 4 x
Oh, yana heyai, nitoway, 2x. ay, ay, ay.
I am the Rainbow Queen,
I share joyful exuberance with all beings
Oo hoo muny, 2x Papeo 2x
I am truly one with Divine Light.
Yes, it is so.

May I receive you, Archangels, beings of light. I follow you from here, homeward bound.

I open my heart and soul to remember the path. As the darkness heals the day, I nurture with rest and feel alive.

Thank you for giving humanity a chance, for the gifts of Gaea Star, for my llamas. So many blessings. I send prayers to all beings.

May my heart keep opening like a glowing rainbow, lingering in the bright blue sky.

November 11 (11/11/11)

We release our second CD, "Gaea Star Goddesses" produced by Bob Sherwood, on my Spirit of the Sun Music, label. Sixteen songs with assistance from Dameron and Diana Noble, backing vocals, that inspired our dynamic Gaea Star Goddess show and the evolution of the Gaea Star Band.

Isis, Full Moon, Pele, Pacha Mama, Amaru Machay, Queen of Love, Ladies of the Lake, Queen of Heaven, Crystal Ice Queen, Aja, Yemanja, Ganesh, Lotus Queen, Oya Thunder queen, and Dancing as a Faery

Note - Review "**The Valley Advocate**," a weekly news magazine in Northampton Massachusetts. January 5, 2012

Mariam Massaro/ Gaea Goddesses/ Spirits of the Sun

"Looking at the cover of this overtly New Age-y recording, I fully anticipated tearing it to pieces with my cynical claws of critical evisceration. While I appreciate that music is a deeply spiritual thing, releasing "devotional music" is generally a bad idea.

Even so, Gaea Goddesses takes varieties of music from Indian, African, Peruvian, and Hawaiian traditions and effectively combines them with a George Harrison meets Stevie Nicks musical piety.

Production/arrangement that includes banjos, tablas, ukuleles, flutes, gorgeous string parts and sound effects really adds value and texture and vocals, well executed, with pleasing melodies and harmonies."

Tom Strum

There is nothing you can ever do to turn my love away from you. Wonders never cease as we integrate new energies, experiences and difficult challenges.

These may be difficult for people that have emotional issues.

The only solution is to trust in the spirit that rings true within each moment of life.

The challenges are meant to teach, heal and awaken.

If you slip or experience an unfavorable response, just keep going, gliding through the best you can. Everyone can do it.

Eventually you'll find balance again, to restore your energy to sweep it away with a renewed commitment to growth, to just be.

Clearly accept anything that comes along, for every moment blesses, whatever it is or does, all is perfect.

Life is short, so shed your leaves each season, renew within, without shame or guilt.

Be loving and peaceful, for if you remember Spirit at all times, nothing disturbs your center. Be of service to yourself, be love.

The Full Moon

The Full moon beaming high
beckons to gaze into the sky.
Oh, oh to slip through the portal of reality
To travel along her moonbeams, so silvery.
She's a constant reminder of the dance of Heaven
with her co-creator of light, the Great Sun.
Goddess of mysterious magical light,
floating in the night,
whispering silently her loving inspiration.

Luring you from dreams, to rise, to sing, to stay up late.
So, slip away, take a chance on romance.
Dance in the wind, in the night, radiant, alive, full of pure light,
just like the Moon, oh, just like the full moon.

November 14 -Yemanja

The beautiful Goddess Yemanja sang this song all night to me.
Yemanja, Yemanja, Yemanja ahey
I surround your human light, with my loving waters,
with my healing force of love, from the holy source of light.
My loving waters surround Mother Earth.
Every moment, I flow from the source of creation
Yemanja, Yemanja, Yemanja, ahey
Goddess of serenity, from the depths of the sea
Oh, holy waters of life rising, rising,
full of life, full of love, full of life, full of love.
Walk upon my shore
Feel the sand beneath your feet, touching your core.
Hear my waves singing, feel my love, feel my life
Yemanja, Blue Goddess of the Sea
There is nothing you can ever do
There is nothing you can ever say
To turn my love away from you
Because I love you. I love you

Life is a mystery, as it beckons us to pay attention, to correct all that is in disarray, on our journey.

Many wake up thinking, "I have to go to work," forgetting to say, "Thank you Spirit for life, for the sun shining rays of love."

May I begin today with beauty, love and a commitment to listening, sharing and being in one-ness with you.

Then if we encounter challenges in the day, we'll remember, we are created with love and with love, we're going home.

There's always forgiveness and compassion in our hearts. Try to release the blame or shame, replacing with only joy.

As we encounter dense material issues, that damage our tissues, casting shadows and illusions, we forget the prayers of love.

When the Goddess sings, "There is nothing you can ever do to turn my love away from you," be joyful, celebratory, grateful.

Say, "Yay! Let's go to the ocean and enjoy our life today!"

November 20 – 27 Mighty are the Wings of Love

Mighty are the wings of love
As they weave together from above.
Swirling together patterns of communion.
Distant places flowing deeply into spirals of union
Blessed by rays of warm sunshine and the breath of life.
Oh, how union thrills the bodies, mind and hearts.
With joy and peaceful expression,
Healing the world with loving communication.
Mighty are the wings of love
As they weave together from above.

Academy of Music theater, Northampton, Mass. 2011

Dameron Midgett, Mariam, Ezell Floranina

Finale to Gaea Star Goddess show, November 22, 2011

After a stormy night, the brook is gushing. Water droplets cling to the Oak branches. Hello to the spirit above.

We are here in spirit, vastly different from humans.

Each of you selected your path before entering your mother's womb, with the goal to eventually unify all the essential components to manifest your chosen mission.

Some believe the law of attraction brings unfavorable things because the mind, full of negative thoughts, may draw them in.

Really? All experiences are meant to teach ways in helping to fulfill your purpose. Before coming to Gaea Star, you met with a guide to help select the best choices for your upcoming life.

No one just leaps onto Earth without a "guiding counselor," to prepare you. That being remains energetically with you and is always willing to assist in your further development.

When one meditates in the soothing sounds of nature, you'll hear their guidance. Foster that awareness to develop the connection.

No one says life is easy. Yes, it has challenges, especially the crucial aspects of existence. All will balance itself soon. Peace and nurturing love will arrive easily within the next twenty years

Gaea Star is a living being, with her own evolution process.

The changes predicted in 2012 is looming in everyone's minds. Yes, they are coming, but it's not to say, "These things will occur."

We don't see destruction, instead, there is a spiritual opening to accept the present and all that is still yet to come. It is a time of new beginnings, with hope, for the thousand years of peace to blossom for humanity. It is a blessing to be alive, to hold strong the goodness in your hearts.

January 6, 2012

Sunny golden rays, greet this peaceful morning, rising silent yet radiantly warm, over the treetops. Snow glistens on frozen earth. Nature forms beautiful ice sculptures on the brook. May I be filled with inspiration as I attune with Ashento.

Soul travelers, we await your return to these heavenly realms, with missions completed, and renewed enthusiasm for the next assignment. There is no rush.

The pace you set is directed by your motivation to weather through life's many challenges. Acceptance and understanding of these, enables you to flow in a positive manner despite setbacks.

Be at peace with all that you encounter. Cherish every moment.

January 18 -19

Bring it All Back

Bring it all back, to the happy peaceful way.

    Let it wash away, to set us free every day

Let life surround with warm serenity all around

with glowing love. Yeah, yeah love

May we remember our true spirit, full of joy and light.

To take care, to heal our lives, oh let's climb so high

Blessed By Light-filled Love

The mountains of this new way, oh peace and love.

Bring it all back, bring it all back, to the happy peaceful way

Oh, light filled love, healing from above, bring it all back

If one is busily entrenched in life, they may miss important opportunities to connect with their higher, creative self.

Let your spirits flow like the river to the sea, toward the source of eternal love, no matter what comes.

Float painlessly through, without grasping too tight.

Breathe in the air, feel the warm sun and pure Earth, to heal and motivate you every day.

As you walk the path of a peaceful being of light and love, accept with gratitude, the blessings of transformation that grace you.

Gaea Star, Emerald Queen, ripples with magnificent changes.

Music is an intimate expression of my soul having journeyed here. In winter, when the trees are bare, you see the shape of the Earth. She is such a round planet with her passengers sailing in the galaxy.

Surrender to your vision that shines clearly within, staying purely happy, resonating with the highest vibration of love, as you express with joyful passion, your unique glowing soul.

It is the perfect opportunity to sift through illusions of material existence. Choose wisely the best path to complete your mission.

Be a light emissary of love, truth, compassion and forgiveness.

January 22 -31

I feel the presence of spirit as stars silently twinkle, opening the view to eternity, to the past and future.

I breathe in wonder, hopeful to manifest beauty as I sing, pray, love, listen, dance, walk, touch, allow, learn, connect, commune, transform, surrender and choose happiness.

Wherever you are, create a vision of love, service and compassion.

February - Full Moon

The powerful moon energizes. So much recently, selling NY property, Goddess shows, recording CD's. I love to play music for kids, wearing a wild zany costume. 'Sparkle, the Starfish' is a song on the children's album that we dress up and sing.

Every day is a treasure to behold, a mystery unfolding, a blessing to inspire, to flourish, to remember my spirit.

March 3

Snow, clouds, birds, cats purring, peaceful moments.

I sense your call, when you beckon, as I traverse these celestial realms. After many earthly lives, I arrived here, where the sounds of universal awareness are detailed with vibrant colors in wondrous swirling patterns, in beautiful arrays of serenading musical tones.

It's like a choir of angelic beings, that celebrate existence in harmonious union, singing in wonderful light tones, a collage of gracious loving sounds.

That is poetic, thank you. May I always hear your delightful messages, prayers and music.

I feel you preciously honoring me when you look at the stars.

From the depths of my soul, love flows, on a golden ray of light.

Take charge of everything. Many positive changes are in store.

I eat fruit and nuts in the morning, for vitality, health, feeling light. I am grateful to enjoy the power of raw food to keep my weight stable, as well as doing yoga daily down by the river when I can.

March 6 – 17 - 19   Holy Medicine of Light

> As you walk on the path of love, you carry the light
> in your heart, in your mind, in your soul, so bright.

Blessed By Light-filled Love

Open wide the door, to all that you know,
Let your truth unfold, as your love flows
You are the holy medicine of light
Let your spirit always shine, from deep within, so bright
Yati dada, imana yana hey hey hey
Oya Oya Oya, hey hey hey
Imana, imana, Oya Oya Oya, hey hey hey
Mahia maheya, hey hey, namahiya mahey hey
I am loved, nurtured, and healed by Gaea Star's beautiful birds, land, rivers, and animals. Songs of inspiration always flow freely.

River of Light

River of light, river of light,
Let it flow, let it flow, from the East,
River of love, let it flow from the South
River of truth, let it flow from the West
River of peace, let it flow from the North
Flowing river of peace, flowing river of truth
Flowing river of love, flowing river all around
The circle of light, on this sacred ground,
River of light, river of light, let it flow, let it flow.
I am running. I am changing,
as I flow along the river of life
I am well, I am well. I am happy to be free.

Mariam Massaro

April   **The Presence of the Almighty**

Oh, I feel the presence of the almighty,
in the swirling wind,
Whispering, honor mother nature,
Oh, listen to the almighty, in the dancing trees,
in the birds, in the bees, in peaceful serenity
Whay heya, heya, heya ho
So many ways we live our lives, all morning, all night
Always in the presence of the almighty, of the almighty

Perhaps

Perhaps on this glorious morning,
on this beautiful new day, under the blue sky, yay
with birds sweetly singing, sunshine calling
Come sail like the wind so free
Perhaps we'll heal the world with prayers for peace
with forgiveness, love, and gentle compassion,
Perhaps we'll build a bridge from heaven to earth,
of love and peace, perhaps

May - A Spring Day

We played faery music for the radio show. Sunshine radiance. What a glorious way to awaken. How peaceful and clean solar energy is. The silent warmth. I love how sunflowers grow facing the sun. Why don't all houses face the sun to collect the energy all day? Its' renewable, easy to harness power, so simple and non-destructive for the Earth. Thank you sun for your powerful warm daylight, and for teaching us to honor your radiance.

Blessed By Light-filled Love

Note - In 2013 Singing Brook Farm had a solar hot water and electrical system installed by Gary Tuttle of Sun is Solar. How nice.

June 11 - 12

I rest as I say goodbye to the majestic beauty of Eagle Bay farm after ten years. I loved your spectacular waterfront beauty, friendly Eagles, Hawks, Turkeys, limestone caves, oak and pine trees and the peaceful good times. I release you to sail away free.

I'll cherish the songs that were inspired by your splendor, Reborn, You're the One, Wind over the Water, Ladies of the Lake, I was wondering and All my Life.

Music heals me as I sing the melodies of life. I open to the magical treasure in the abundance of every day. Yoga beckons as a white hawk, flies by, calling. I ask for a song for the end when all is at rest.

Night is Here

Night is near, rest is here, rain is falling
Oh, you can hear the drops on the roof
Close your eyes, rest your weary body
Sail away on your magic carpet,
riding the pony of your dreams
Oh, sail away, sail away into your dream time
into your dreams tonight, goodnight

"Songs for the Children," 5th CD, Spirit of the Sun Music, 2014

Thank you for the rivers always knowing where to go. Thank you for roses blooming, in all the fragrant gardens.

I appreciate all this loving beauty. I'm grateful, happy, peaceful, sharing, doing and unifying myself into one.

June 24

Yes, it's momentous as you align with your higher purpose. May peace express itself especially in the music. Rewriting the story into a musical is a good way to share the message.

Keep on Coming Around

Just keep coming, coming around, dancing the
path of love, on this holy ground, celebrating
as beings of light, standing strong Never give
up, always forge ahead, in all ways.
Wherever you go, whatever you do, is the circle of life
. Under the starlight, the shining sun and heavens gaze

July 6

Beautiful morning, awakening from peaceful rest as the sun casts golden light. The frogs sang all night, now it's a Chipping Sparrow.

Thank you for the invitation, to be close, hearing the birds.

Oh, so many blessings on Gaea Star. Her astonishing beauty is unrivaled with the great powerful Sun, illuminating the day.

Your radio show is a dynamic expression of wonderful talent.

Blessed By Light-filled Love

Mariam rehearsing in her studio.

Into Your Heart

Into your heart, into your soul

Rays of light, to make you whole.

Into your heart, into your soul,

To know, to know, to know.

The path of radiance is to let it flow.

Oh, oh, to bless with life.

To bless with love, to bless with beauty.

Rays of light, to make you whole.

Into your heart, into your soul

Maya nakahay who hay

Dameron and Mariam, Singing Brook Studio, Photo Kim Iacono.

Mariam and Nia at the harp at Singing Brook Studio

Thank you for patience in selling the NY land. You showed courageous strength, to see the task through to resolution. You made it happen by being firm, grounded and connecting with spirit.

July 17   Happy I Am

Happy I am, grateful I am, joyful I am,
peaceful I am, to be alive, here in this wonderful life
Awake, aware, happy I am, to be here
Under the blue sky, with puffy clouds drifting by,
To hear birds sweetly singing in the morning sunshine.
To see green leaves dancing in the gentle breeze.
Happy I am, grateful I am, joyful I am, peaceful I am
To play in the gardens, with the flowers, roses, healing herbs
The carrots, the greens, oh, life is so good.
Happy I Am
Songs for the Children - 5th CD, Spirits of the Sun Music. 2014

August 5 -17-24 -29

At some point in life, there is a choice, a crossroads, an action that one can chose that is clearly a significant option to change and move on to the next phase of life.

Life is good even as you encounter challenging aspects.

Little by little, you weave a new path of least resistance, to fully express what you came to do, to bring it back home, to gather the dynamic momentum to set your life free.

Dream: I'm performing a snake song, with a media landscape back drop, illuminating the dancers. Someone waves their hand, casting a shadow on the curtain behind, to look like a snake. There were photos, clouds, misty, quiet, peaceful.

The music we played, was uplifting and inspiring.

I had another incredible dream, where I was a visionary storyteller, creating a story in a group setting. As I looked at the audience, I sensed which ones I would fall in love, or have experiences with.

The leader came to say, "Make up a story about yourselves. Have fun, don't take life so seriously. Remember the good things you're bringing with you." I made up a new story before the people.

When I returned to Earth, I saw how I've woven my story as a visionary songstress, a priestess from beyond the sun, on lovely earth with blue skies, singing birds, and grateful for life.

I hear, "Come on! Get up! Arise, dreamtime is fading, be one with life, a bringer-of-light, now. Do yoga on the bridge. Use the radiant Earth's tools to create with beautiful light. Wake up, the sun is like a pep-talk, come on, get up, do it!"

The sun's rays shine through the trees. Evening moisture dissipates as cool autumn air is coming on as the summer is waning.

Thank you, sun for teaching me to gather your energy in. Do what you love, your money will follow. I love that.

May we get it right. Creation is beautiful in every way.

One More Day

May I be one with the beauty of the morning sun

May I be one with the wind dancing in the trees

May I see the majesty of the green leaves

    One more day, one more day

    To breath in life, to see hummingbirds, beneath the blue sky

    for another chance to be or do, anything you want to

    A fresh new start, to feel love in your heart

One more day, one more day

To be alive, barefoot on fresh grass,

to heal your life, to get it right

To feel spirit everywhere, breathing in fresh clear air,

One more day, one more day

To grow gardens, beautiful flowers, to share with the birds,

frogs and crickets, to hear the rivers flow endlessly.

It's so fine to sing songs celebrating life

For one more day, one more day

Release, 8th Cd, Spirits of the Sun Music, 2021

August 30

Cool days, still beautiful with green leaves. A mourning dove coos as I hear flowing waters and wise words. Last night, I smelled skunk in the barn, as I fed the llamas. While canoeing, we saw a Merganser on the glorious sunny day on the water.

Thank you for co-creating such a wonderful book together, weaving in my spirit after carrying it in your heart for years.

All is well, while you finish the loose ends. As you reflect back, you will see the wisdom of skillfully melding the raw materials into a positive message, expressing our spiritual connection while nurturing our twin flame union.

Your spirit within, gains insights when encouraged to seek its deep core essence. Yes, it is good to rest. Since we are always connected, it does not matter when we attune to each other.

Our oneness is part of creation. There's no need to be constantly in communication. Our Divine Essence is woven with a ribbon of light from the source of love, beyond the physical capacity of thoughts in a deeper balanced perspective.

Very few allow themselves too just be. Rarely is the mind not thinking of a being, place, object, or endeavor that requires alignment of focus.

Each mission is unique. Some may find their way, being clear with where they want to go, leaving their family behind, choosing a path that no one expects them too.

When people mature, they find a different home, seeking new experiences away from the familiar, but it does not change their connection to their family of origin. When you left home, did you say, "Good-bye," energetically, physically and mentally?

How can anyone be aligned to their soul's expression, if they are disconnected, far from the source of light and love?

September 6

Moon shines. Insights, flow. I am grounded, present, light, flowing like the wind, content to follow the path of love, to reach deep within. I feel the shifting energies and the moment at hand.

I want to sing with grace, beauty and a strong voice.

I seek understanding to flow with everything I encounter, to release all that no longer serves our highest good.

Just give them away, to bring clarity, to discover the treasure within, that's waiting like an empty vessel to be filled.

What about our minds that contain the seeds of ideas?

We tap into more wisdom when we open, to new ways to grow and flow, learning to prosper, accept, heal and nurture all.

Thank You

Thank you for life.
May I be at peace, one with the light,
as I lie beneath the golden sun, listening,

Blessed By Light-filled Love

learning in every way,
Oh life, how sweet you are today
Oh, the love, oh the light, shining in my window tonight
Thank you, life, for the healing starry night,
for the rain, for the succulent green Earth
. For all the days, thank you, life. Thank you.

September 8 -10

May I be of value, remembering my dreams, completing what I came here for. I love your messages, Ashento.

Thank you for listening to spirit, for writing all the time.

May we continue to co-create, with messages that fill you with anticipation. Everything is perfection.

Your new relaxed way of living, singing and doing Yoga daily is developing and enhancing your body, mind and spirit connections.

A smile for you, as the brook flows and the frogs, chatter.

There is exciting celebration now, for all that is to come.

It is interesting one does not see the whole picture as we do.

Trust that everything you need will flow to you with ease.

There's plenty that isn't right, however even though not positive, negative is valid, as it helps you to grow, motivate, learn, and choose wisely the next time you encounter a similar situation.

Try to think things through, before you make a decision that's in the best interest of your heart, mind and soul.

Life rewards you with abiding love, even though it is complex and often challenging. There's nothing to be afraid of.

September 26 - 29

Your Own Divinity

Nurture every moment of every day.

As you open to your divinity, you will know the way.

As you stand at the helm, of your journey of life,

Oh, the journey of life, let it take you home.

Hold on, hold on as you journey along

Just in case the wind gets a little strong,

Just hold on, oh let it take you home. Oh, oh, hu, hu, hu

Open to the sweetness that is all around

Open so you may hear, so you may do, so you may be.

Nurture every moment of every day.

So, rise and sing praises, oh yay, oh yay.

Thank you for the melodies of life, for the waters that flow.

Healing everyone, in their divinity in every way.

Nurture every moment of every day, that is truly the way

I hear the call of my Divine essence. It is a moment with radiant light energy surging deep inside. Singing Brook meanders through the forest in the darkness. The moon's rays are so healing and beautiful.

As I rested from overworking for the Goddess Show, I asked for healing. Blue and gold rays flowed over me with sweet nurturing vibrations. A brilliant star with silver purple rays filled with light filled love, swirled from the center of my heart. Refreshed, I went on to rehearse for hours. Thank you for strength and clarity.

I am blessed to hear celestial music in my soul's songs.

October 4

Sun rays heal. I am inspired to sing "Every moment is a treasure. Every moment is your pleasure, on Earth."

Thank you for a powerful waking-up, to feel my radiant Star self.

I celebrate life, standing straight, as a mystical priestess with starry silver purple rays flowing from my heart.

Blessings on my mother, who's releasing her Earth walk. I wish I lived near to see her and my father. I'll miss her. The infinite energy of the universe feeds my body and soul.

I love moving things around to change the energy.

October 7 - 15 - 24

I'm excited to dress in dynamic costumes and perform powerful music all about the Divine Goddesses of Gaea Star.

Academy of Music Finale, October 12, 2012
Sula, Mikhul Henderson, Mariam, Maya Apfelbaum, Corine Miller, Amy, Helene Aninos, Opeyemi Parham, Robin Rooney, Diana Noble and faery

We send love as you tap the essence of your artistic expression. Deep within the depths of everyone's heart, there is a powerful epicenter of creativity, with flourishing rays of golden flowing love.

It is the holy beginning before life, the second dwelling place of the origin of Divine essence, the home of the soul. Move to that sacred center, to know the comfort of where to go or what to do.

Hold the lantern of light in front, for those who are lost, who need direction, helping to shine the way, for their true path of light.

As it shines brighter, the soul sees the way, to take the next positive step and fear and stagnation dissipate.

As you stand in your place of power, you help others to shine, to easily cast aside their darkness, through the magic of just being, simply light. Nothing else is required or necessary.

Light arrives as easily as dawn comes every morning.

All moments balance between light and dark, day and night.

To be at peace, rest, recharge, to achieve for spirit and yourself.

I attend a spiritual messenger conference in California. I sang with my ukulele, sharing Ashento's messages. I connect with my priestess self in a meditation.

Wealth flows as abundant energy.

By simply being, all types of energy are conducted.

Through a powerful drive to succeed, you find the way to make the pieces align to satisfy physical desires.

Contemplation helps to understand all that one chooses to do. Now is the time to rein yourself in, to come home, to slow down, just like the horse that grazes after galloping around the pasture.

Release worry about finances. Respond to all calls.

Money flows as needs grow. I believe in what I do. I am fortunate to progress to where I am. Everything I need is here.

The Aha moment is within your mind and heart.

Yes, you can learn a great deal from powerful connections.

Nebi Wabo is the native prayer for the flowing waters. It is a ceremonial song that makes the serene waters, run pure. Wherever rain falls peacefully, that is cascading heavenly love.

October 26 - 27

I focus to finish this, to receive what flows with grace, and love as a messenger of inspiration, truth, beauty, awareness, and gentleness.

Oh, my sweetness, you shine as a sweet healing singer of love, filled gentle words and calming music.

Release tensions, to align with the healing energies of love.

Thank you, I am healed by the singing waters, constantly moving to the sea with purpose.

Dream - I saw photos of me, on a web site, changing, as a different vital, expressive, entertainer and costume designer.

January 2013 – I launch **mariammassaro.com**, *with colorful photos in costumes.*

October 28

There is much ahead to create and participate in.

Each chapter of your journey brings powerful lessons.

You have progressed in improving your skills. Are you not happier when you are singing, creating and simply in peace at home?

Yes, there is always more to long for and connect with.

Shine like a beacon in the fog, even when it is thick or stormy. Someone will be grateful for small acts of kindness or love.

All is in balance. To simply be, let go even more, as you reduce the need for so many avenues of expression. An answer to your dreams, the recognition of your talents is coming.

I receive the infinite abundance of the Universe, guided by inspiration, intuition and loving light.

November 6

Election Day. Obama, I hope. He will benefit us more.

Dream - I am writing a spiritual adventure, about seekers who go between the worlds. I placed Ashento's manuscript on my pillow, the night before. I often sleep with a musical instrument to know their essence, ukuleles, harp, guitars, kalimba, sitar and even a violin.

There is a message yearning to express in exquisite creation, within the complexity of you. Through writing, art, or music this realization of self is expressed in the present moment.

Each of you has potential, to stand firmly rooted, tapping into the deep molten core within the Earth, fully in your power, connected to the Source of Love.

Blessed By Light-filled Love

Pele, the Hawaiian Volcano Goddess, represents the spirit of the Earth, with her fiery foundation, deeply connecting the energy lines and charka centers to the Earth's magnetic pulsation.

These powerful energies help to become grounded as the trees.

The vital waters of life, course around the Earth, with her precious blood, which is composed of the bodies' same substance. Drinking water, releases water.

Everything you ingest, is processed into usefulness for the body. As long as it is not too much or too little to maintain balance.

How does one receive all the information that flows?

Where you live, there is an energy core, a crystalline vibrational source of power that teaches, heals and nurtures. You gain wisdom from that particular quadrant's energetic resonance.

For example, New England, has a vibrational vortex of prismatic minerals, attuned, magnetized, and empowered to heal and preserve the vitality of those who walk upon on her.

The chaotic nature that humanity has lived with for years, has engrained many negative beliefs about money.

The most prevalent, being that money is pursued to buy what you think you need, but once you have it, you spend; once you don't have, you long, or go hungry, until earning more, to fit into norms.

This is the inherent problem with modern society, as it has changed from the equalitarian, communal way of life from long ago.

May we help one another, through sharing compassion, for those who have so little, or are unable to navigate the way.

May the circle of light shine in the dark caverns of Creation.

May we find peace through meditation, yoga, simple living and acceptance.

May we understand life is a committed state of healing, nurturing and fostering love, to generate the transformation of humanity.

May we usher the Divine Feminine into balance with the masculine, to stand firmly, in expressing dynamic, unified majesty, in recognition of all that we are as one family in peace.

May we simply listen to our hearts, to connect with our spiritual self, who is always there ready to reunite with us.

When we came to Gaea Star, we left a part of our higher self, anchored to that place of origin, to never disconnect from the Source of love and light. May we align together, into dynamic Star Beings.

May we empower and change all that is uncertain or impure within, which keeps us from being, totally in our power.

We open to light and love by looking within, to discover our true essence, to celebrate Spirit, with joyful exuberance.

May we express fully what our inherent aura radiates. Can we surrender more to the presence of spirit within? May we listen to truth, like the burning bush of Moses.

May we reconnect to our starry origins, by being loving, shining beacons of light, for all to feel, casting out the dark shadows of illusion.

May we remember the path home, going around obstacles with grace, through the rivers, lakes and seas of life.

May we admire the success of other's and give to the needy. May we share and protect Gaea Star's resources.

Oh Spirit, may you guide us, to always connect to the source of love, to weave together, as one holy family of light.

November 12

A vision: A fantastic stage, with dancing star faeries and sparkling angels, spiraling, and swirling around on colorful silks with rainbows arching over the dancers. Rays of light were shining from the stars as the spiral kept expanding into oneness. Wow, a brilliant finale to the Gaea Star Goddess show, with this celestial song that came also.

Rays of Light

Rays of light sweeping, rays of light swirling,
Sailing from the starry realms, sweeping to the holy ground
as the stars are shining, and the people are circling around,
dancing, happy, celebrating peace throughout the land.
Rays of light are shining, as the people are dancing
in a circle, alive with the breath of life
Singing in a spiral of light, in a spiral of light,
as all the people are dancing around,
Spiraling in light, in rainbows of spiraling light
I choose this day to make a silver, sparkly Star Queen costume.

November 13 -15

An email from the Hollywood and Vine Film Festival, listing winners for their independent film festival on December 7th. I looked, curious to see the winners, but assuming the film trailer I submitted in July was not selected. I scanned the names until I saw number 19.

What, how can this be? My name is next to the 'Gaea Star Crystal' trailer, listed. Startled, I checked out the site. Yes, it is indeed real, our trailer is a finalist. After years of dreaming the story into a movie or musical someday, it may be coming true.

Someone in Hollywood liked our humble creation of this timely story. I never let go of feeling it deserved to be born, although it was overdue inside. With friends and local actors, we brought the story to life by filming it here and in Peru, with colorful costumes and live music. The five-minute trailer from the filming, was wonderful even if only reflecting a segment of the story, not even the whole theme.

The song, "Let's Sail to the Realms," from the "Gaea Star Crystal" CD, was the soundtrack.

I played Isis, and Shalaya, who gathers the faeries, and the crystal seekers to unify Gaea Star to restore harmonious balance even if there were thieves after us.

Either option is rewarding, to go where you love, the Andes, or to see your trailer showing in Hollywood. Going there is a good choice. It is a strong avenue to present your work, and a unique opportunity to be with other like-minded people. Follow your heart's desire with exuberance to manifest the Gaea Star Crystal Story into a movie. Now is the time to go for it.

I canceled my planned hiking trip to Peru, which was for the same week and made plans to go with Dameron to Hollywood, to attend the showing of the 'Gaea Star Crystal,' trailer at the festival.

Energies are swiftly helping to clarify goals faster than ever.

May we help you to sail your ship on the river of life, although, you always do what you believe is the best.

When you go into a dark room, at first, it's hard to see, but then eyes adjust, enabling you to see better. Now is the time to look into the darkness, until you clearly see the way that serves your dreams.

Present your powerful star self, shining, radiant and proud, expressing a powerful message with bold clarity. It is fascinating to the others who will remember a similar mission.

Apply the Laws of Attraction to manifest the desired outcome. When you meet beings from other lifetimes and recognize each other, all the time in between fades quickly, as if there was no space at all, the connection is instantaneous and never forgotten.

The soul always remembers, as the heart responds with deep feelings, rekindling loving, warm sensations, recognizing the previous love bond, that familiar, totally encompassing light.

It is hard to walk away from connection, even if involved with someone else, for when souls remember, they strive to overcome all boundaries, regardless of the situation.

One may choose to ignore the recognition, but the soul rekindles the feelings, every time they think of that person, no matter where they are or who they are with.

Do you see how memories of love connections transcends time?

So be open to receive, to feel the power of the ancient love and the inevitable commitment to meet again in this life.

November 15 - 22

I awake with a brilliant star shining in the west and Pleiades twinkling bright. It is twelve years since my inspiration to write the play, "The Rainbow Crystals of the Earth".

Bliss

Oh, oh, oh, oh, the bliss of life
Is pure pleasure, oh, oh, pure pleasure.
Oh, oh, oh, oh, the bliss of life
Is a delightful treasure. Oh, oh, a pure treasure.
Every moment be grateful, every moment, be thankful
For the new day, for the golden rays,
Painting the treetops against the blue sky.
Oh, oh, oh, and the clouds drifting by,
Oh, and the mountains rising high.
Oh, oh, oh, oh, the bliss of life
Is pure pleasure, oh, oh, pure pleasure.
A delightful treasure, oh, oh, a pure treasure.
Every moment be grateful, every moment be thankful.

I saw a film about channeling spiritual beings. Ashento, "Thank you for sharing your wisdom, so easily and gently in the same manner. I am blessed by your presence flowing and touched by our connection."

We are unified of masculine/feminine Divinity, communing easily. It is not necessary to be in any form as the power and presence of our love from our light-filled words and feelings, heals and nurtures, allowing one to relax in moments of conscious expression.

All is as it needs to be. When you find the time to celebrate your art and music, your life will change. The insights and inspirations gained as you move toward the lightness of being, will bring you joy.

November 26 - 28

After years, I am grateful to overcome my blocks to keep going, despite distractions, to finish writing. I fly with powerful revelations as my spirit is rising. Magical moonlight on snow. Her powerful illumination lures me outside.

Mariam as the Star Queen

*I seek resolution with Eagle Bay Sanctuary. It is beautiful yet far away and drains my energy. The sale did not go thru. *

You are fixing it for the next family to enjoy. Hold on, things will get better soon. Remember there's nothing you can ever do to turn your life away from you. Practice music and release a song daily.

The world loves your tender singing and heart felt inspirations.

Thank you for the music that flows through me.

*On January 15, 2014, Mariam sold Eagle Bay Sanctuary with plans to purchase an 1800's building to create the Singing Bridge Performing Arts Lodge in West Cummington, Massachusetts.

December 1 - 2

Galactic Alignments on December 3rd, three planets align with the Pyramids of Giza, others on December 12 and 21. I feel a strong connection to the Earth at this powerful moment.

Yes, you attend to life's details. The aspects take on important attributes, even though the illusions of reality are apparent.

What remains when life disappears? Each soul sustains their connection to Divine Source, throughout their incarnations.

It is a blessing that nothing severs you from the connection, like trees standing in the wind, laden with heavy snow, deeply rooted into the Earth, always tapping into the source of their life force.

Winter settles in. Gaea Star is silent in soft snow. Singing Brook flows endlessly. I awake, feeling like I am surfing the waves of life. Steady, riding the big one, with wings outstretched, coasting gracefully. I open to Ashento.

It is pure bliss when you ask for communion with me, bringing warmth and joy to align our power together, like two flames burning brightly merged into one.

The stars and the planets are in grand alignment now. Many are honoring this moment with prayers and sacred ceremony.

You are the creators of all you came to do. Stay in your circles, leave the gatherings to others, to anchor the power where you are.

You'll feel the power surging while attuning to Spirit.

The keys to unlock this knowing are within, carried like seeds inside, waiting to be united together in fertility.

The mystery is revealed with the support of the stars, the beings of light, the loving guardians of the heavens.

No need to go anywhere, merely stand still, sing praises as you gather to honor each other.

All is well, I salute you for the courageous strength to not give up on your missions, in the midst of such challenging times on Earth.

As you see, the preparations are in place, the stage is set, ready for the curtain to rise, for everyone to dance in a circle of light, smiling in joy at the peace and love that they feel.

The finale of the act of life, is the great awakening, to connect to what you want to be and do, by expressing your purpose or soul mission, beginning a new era of living as all of you were meant too.

Follow your hunches as you impart the teachings and the music, anything that enables peaceful conscious ways to evolve, for there is nothing that cannot be revealed in this expansive way.

So, come together, to feel the awakening of returning home, to the depth of your soul's longing, as all the portals are open now.

Sing to the mystery of the glowing dancing stars of light.

You and I are always together, my Purple Ray Priestess. I honor all that you hold, as you shine your light.

Despite my non-physical aspect and the long distance between us, we find the way to unite, embracing the always burning torch of eternal love deep within our souls.

We are one, filled with Divine spiritual light and a warm loving depth that withstands all separations. Be at peace with life. Love.

December 4 - 5 – 14

Dawn. Clouds sail from south to west. A dream; I'm a musician in the "The Gaea Star Crystal" play, with a wild costume with flowery-looking stars, dancing from my head, like galaxies swirling around.

Blessed By Light-filled Love

We go to California to the film festival. What a pleasure to see the manifestation of my vision, the Gaea Star Crystal Story winning for the Best Trailer. The networking support from other filmmakers, was worth the trip.

Mariam as Star Queen in a promo photo.
Photographer: Bob Doyle, Marina Del Rey, California

Receiving the award for the Best Trailer
at the Hollywood and Vine Film Festival, December 7, 2012

Mariam and Dameron with Angela Hutchinson, founder of the Hollywood and Vine Film Festival.

Thank you Ashento for guiding our path of love, light, and beauty. I flow with graceful acceptance, as surely as the sun rises every day.

Family of light, we bless you with hope, peace and bountiful love. The changes will be revealed soon. Gather together in gratitude, to celebrate in joy, reconnecting to your spiritual starry selves, to thank each other and the realms above, that now, we are all one.

Spontaneity is the key. Dare to be free.

Make the difference in someone's life, by freely giving love. Release negative energies, as you feel the powerful light within growing, becoming one with your higher self.

As the veils lift throughout Earth, awareness is more visible, making it easier to know the way, to not worry and express love.

I open more to the rest of my sojourn on Gaea Star. To the heavens, I send love from the depths of my heart. May we always live as if we never apart from you, Spirit.

December 20 - My Father's Birthday

We are thankful for the Mayan shift after 26,000 years.

We are one with the Divine, with all that we came to be.

We are prayer in action, in goodness, in manifestation.

We are present, pure, alive, aware spiritual beings, within the macrocosm of this planetary body of love made manifest.

Artistic musical expressions are pure intentions of love.

We are one with the force of love that flows eternally from the source of creation. We recognize this treasure here. Thank you for this gracious gift of magnificent change.

We feel this moment, coursing as we begin the next phase, with peace, truth, healing and nurturing from deep within our hearts.

We pray for the families of the Newtown tragedy. How can such violence happen to so many sweet innocent beings?

All lives are precious, so honor the grieving period, expressing dismay and sadness at the total lack of love for human life.

There are no accidents, nothing is random in this reality. All is worked out already, as a prearranged plan of action.

The loss of lives is traumatic for those involved, for the loss of their future gone. The families are deeply affected by their untimely departure however, the victims are home with the Creator.

They are well, happy and understanding now, on the other side. Send healing and purple and yellow colors to the families.

December 21 - 30

Solstice, the great shift, a new birth, a moment awaited. May the celebration begin as we shift from one age to the other. A song of serenity flows. I am one on this holy day. May the fears and shadows disappear forever.

May we hear melodies to restore peaceful rays of love flowing into light filled days.

Oh, let the music sing through our hearts, through the winds, with blessings of love, peace, gifts and children laughing.

Mariam Massaro

The Snow Queen is dancing with puffy flakes. Pine branches stand proudly, carrying her soft beauty.

The wind whips everywhere into swirling, snow faeries. Tall trees shake as the wind whistles in the cracks.

Prayer flags shimmer, as the snow flies past the windows.

A winter wonderland is such a wonderful way to end 2012.

January 2 - 3 2013

Thank you, Ashento, for your new evocative poem/song.

The Love Star

Into the depths of my heart, you and I are one.

Into the depths of my life, we'll never be apart.

Along our celestial journey of light,

Oh, my sweetness, I embrace you in your dreams.

I await your awakening. You can feel me in the morning.

You can feel me in the night.

You can hear my sweet song when the dawn star is in sight.

Arise, Arise. You and I are one

One light, one love when the Love star shines bright.

You and I are one, you and I are one light.

A new year begins. I need to be alone, to collect my energies after a busy fall. I am dealing with two big snowstorms. Thank you, for the strength to correct a difficult block in my relationship.

There is no justification necessary to explain one's need to be alone, to be free within heart, mind and body.

We are only married to spirit in that manner and always in a positive loving expression of perfection.

Anything, person, place or condition that distances or removes you from a positive love connection, is to be released gently.

The first rule is to remain connected to the source of love.

Seek the path of least resistance, it will never be one of discord. That deep knowing within your heart and soul, will ring true

even if it may not, please everyone involved.

You may waver and even question, if what you feel, is the correct path. However, it is only an illusion that controls dependency, as fear of change, keeps one stagnant.

Go ahead, plunge over the cliff. Spread your wings, to fly free of all that binds you from love, happiness, and your heart desires. Sail into the well of your strength, rather than someone else.

If they are truly united to you, they will release their wings and fly free. Each finds their way in surrender to their own melodies.

January 6

Thank you for helping me find peace within, where only the power and presence of the spirit of light is welcome.

To be in the "yes" of all life experiences, is to connect with the

essence of truth, to Source, to all that there is.

Believe in the power of love, light and healing to know Divinity.

It is only you who brings in light filled love, who opens the way

to deeper expression, in connecting to Source.

To go where you feel called, is to walk through the portal of awareness of your deepest truth, where you know, to always cultivate creativity, healing warmth, love, happiness and sharing powerful messages that illuminate with joyful positivity.

There is nothing to stop you now, since you chose to live a full, present, aware and dynamic existence.

Those who willingly strive to always reflect the light that shines within their hearts, will change the lives of all they encounter.

If each space within is filled with hope, love and strength, then all will walk in the powerful grace of Source in dynamic ways.

Trust in all that you do. Commune with your highest essence. Shine with unbridled rays of warm light, as bright as the sun. Be radiant, every moment, be love. Bask in the beauty of life.

This is the end of the first printing in 2014. I revised into an eBook in 2016. How interesting to see my life changes inspired by Ashento. The following is an expanded version with new songs and more teachings of his esoteric guiding wisdom.

March 12, 2013 - Fire Song

Dream, In heaven. I asked Ashento, "Do you have fire?" He laughed, "Yes, it is the source of creation, the spark of life, of power, of fury, the emanating essence of spirit." He gave me this song –

Fire, Fire, Burning Bright

Fire, fire, fire, source of light,

Fire, fire, fire, burning bright,

Oh, the power of the light,

Oh, the spark of life, of spirit within,

with the power of creation, purification,

destruction, transformation,

in the same element at once,

Oh Fire, fire, fire, source of light,

Fire, fire, fire, burning bright

Dream - Veranda, the Indigo Queen

A brilliant indigo queen is radiating indigo rays about her. She heals all by speaking only positive words, helping others to be mindful to always speak kindly. She is a queen of goodness, love, compassion, and blessings. We can easily follow her principles of healing energy and pure intentions. I feel her powerful energy.

We thank her for appearing as the indigo dawn queen, bringing the light of truth and awareness of the spoken word, of pure precise communication of the highest vibration. I am grateful for her divine connection as her name came before her image. I open to bringing her into fullness in expression and her song as well.

December 30, 2013

Diamond Eyes

I woke with a beautiful Goddess, smiling at me.

I just loved her dark blue eyes, pointy, elongated,

Diamond eyes, diamond eyes,

A diamond queen with a sparkling smile.

Do you have a message, I asked?

Oh yes, my sweetness, I am in a different incarnation

Yes, it's really me. It's not a masquerade.

It's an aspect, a fragment, an imaginative creation.

Oh, I like my diamond shape, gracing my dark blue eyes.

I see the expressive way you treasure life,

doing good for humanity, being of service.

It's really, really not a masquerade, oh life.

Why not ask yourselves, what are you all hiding behind?

Mariam Massaro

Are you afraid to reveal secrets about yourselves?

Why not reveal the truth of who you really are?

Every moment of breathing, of waking,

Is full of the gift of life is rich,

important to appreciate,

to fill with positive loving energy.

Just like a balloon, waiting for the breath of air,

to give it life, to give it shape. You see life is like that.

You can be flat, just lying there, but when you are a shape

You are dimensional, ready to be of service,

to share who you are.

Breathing, moving, expressing

. Being full of love and inspiring light.

Like the dawn of the new morning

It's not a masquerade, life. It's all the same.

You can take it down or change it all.

Put it up, swing it around, move it forward, on and on.

It's all about who is really under there, inside it all.

It's really me inside all of you.

It's really not a masquerade.

Remember who is really under there, is who you really are.

Diamond eyes, diamond eyes

It was Ashento. He shapeshifted into the diamond eyed goddess, singing a message with humor. Thank you for reaching from heaven, softly into my heart in this loving, supportive way. I love you.

February 8, 2014

Yeah, we've been here all along, helping, watching, guiding.

When we said goodbye, for your earthly journey, it didn't mean forever, only that you're on your own for a while.

We know that life gets hard, at times, beneath all the shadows.

Keep on feeling love, holding your vision of the light. We've never left. We're always close inside. We're listening, breathing, touching, healing, and seeing inside all of you.

Come on, let's hold hands, walking along the edge of life, where you want to be strong, to know that you're in the flow, growing on.

You'll understand more if you sense or feel the life inside of you, deep within your core. It's the miracle of love, breath, touch, healing, sight, hearing, and knowing.

So, ascend to the top, where you're always growing older, together as one, yes together as one.

February 24, 2016

Come, my sweetness, I'm waiting. The stars are brightly shining, just for you. Sail on the path of the blue ray, it illuminates the way.

Waterfalls are cascading, Satyaloka and emerald crystals are reaching high into the azure sky.

Purple rays swirling into blue rays, into magenta, wherever we go, proudly, we'll sail together in celestial union.

Oh, the night swans are circling in still waters, as the silver winged crystal boat waits.

Enter the celestial beauty with reflections of moonlight on the water, shimmering in her sweet light.

Rays of rain, light mistiness, choirs of angels, singing hallelujah.

Magenta rays abounding, as the stars are brilliantly shining, twinkling one after the other. They are waiting just for you.

March 3 – In the Night

I'm drifting in the glory to a different realm,
with grandeur on high, twinkling stars sailing by.
Oh, my sweetness, I'll sing to you tonight,
when the moon dances in luminous light.
Feel my love, as you open to her brilliant light.
Take my hand to sail with me, to a heavenly realm.
Just open wide your silky wings.
I know you'll find the means, to share your dreams
when the moon is shining bright,
to meander in the glory of heaven above,
illuminating your way home, om, om, with my love.
Sail away, into this new reality, through the temple of the sun,
under star light, rainbows and crystals delight.
Where roses, lilies, and lotus grow abundantly.
I'm happy, I'm with you.
The wind is whispering, "My sweetness, rise and sail with me."
So divine, release, leave it all behind.
Let go of all cares, to sail in the crisp night air.
Love to you, as you sail in the night,
with the full moon, illuminating your flight.
It's only a short moment to rise free, to sail with me,
on silvery moonbeams, with your wings in flight,

Blessed By Light-filled Love

into crystalline realms that I roam, listening to the melodies,
where angels await your sweet tunes.
Share your lovely songs, that you sing in the night,
Oh, let your silent wings take flight.
We'll glide past galaxies, where souls are free to choose
with no need for the keys to unravel life.
Let's sail on flowers of delight, listening to melodies
that lead into crystalline light.
Shed your layers, as the moon travels across the night sky.
Let your love soar high.
Oh yes, so high, as the dawn returns.

March 5 - Lightly Caressing You

I'm thinking about you today, my sweetness, so far away.
Do you feel me in the wind?
I'll run my spirit through your hair, lightly caressing you softly.
Oh yeah, so far away, on this new day.
You're always in my heart, always so deep inside,
just a little bit of me, in you, in my spirit sailing so high.
Anatohay, Myuntelia, our blue and purple rays are one.
I'll touch you in the morning. I'll touch you in the night.
I'll grace you with rays of love, gently, showering all the time.
I'll sweep inside all the parts of you, all my love, sweet divine.

March 28 - The Winds of Change

Steady as we go, my sweetness, here we are, together, with our powerful connections, of ancient ways and creative new days, open and aware of each other's magnetic integration.

No need to see the truth about each other, we know our celestial union, and caring from afar, reaching from here to there, one realm to the next.

Yes, I hear and see the flowing waters, through your ears and eyes. I feel life's sweet breath through your lungs and nostrils, and revel in the sensations of touch on your skin.

I am grateful to know you in these physical ways of Gaea Star.

Each moment is peacefully rewarding. Blossoming from spirit into human is growing, changing, learning, the yoga of life, with bodies merging through their hearts into oneness.

That is the secret of understanding, knowing and realignment,

allowing your inherent gifts to flow through all that you are.

May you remove all the blockages and difficulties that interrupt

divine connections with your true self.

Yes, we repeat many words, to help those who need a reminder, an awakening, a remembering of parts of themselves, to create the composite of high and low, yin yang, above and below.

Yes, to rise above, to separate yourself from the fabric of life, requires tools of compassion, workability, service and giving.

Just sitting not doing, just being clear and free of anxiety.

February 9, 2017 - The Angels are Coming

Oh, the angels are coming, coming around the bend.
Oh, the angels are coming, they heard,
all the prayers that every soul, has ever said.

Oh, the angels are coming, they're hearing our new prayers,
to speak the truth, that we are only made of love,
with the power to overcome.
Oh, the angels are smiling, coming around the bend.
They see us gathering to change the world,
by rising from the depths of our hearts.
The angels are helping us to live in harmony on sacred ground.

March 25

In the morning I feel your presence, Ashento, deeply, as I sit basking in the sun. I'm grounding and healing from yoga and the melodies of the morning, sweetly singing.

I am grateful to see your smiling face within. Yes, your enlightening wisdom is in my treasure filled place with lingering love vibrations.

I wonder when our paths will cross again. Whispers from the whistling wind. Echoes of fluttering ghosts and fairies, dancing in billowy white curtains. We have sweet softness and serene spiritual similarities.

Do you feel like me? Yes, you do. I surrender to the truth. You are my Shiva, more wondrous, powerful, and fantastic than I imagined. I'm happy to say as my twin soul, King, or lover, I remember we agreed to recognize one another immediately. Hail to the voice that whispered, soft and powerful, calling me to love at a moment's notice.

May 1, 2017 - Sea of Love

Dream – A Mermaid Song

Mermaids unfurling out of the sea,
fires flaming in frothy surf in an air of victory.
What a sight, unified people, singing down the walls,
celebrating lovely peace.

Rise, to sing the glory of our eyes and ears,
to open our hearts, to the visions we hold dear,
to walk with the ancient ways,
with mermaids, merman's,
and angels, flying and crawling ones,
who hold our hands.

We know those stealing the preciousness of Gaea Star,
Little, do they realize the power of awakening
humanity as one family of loving light, on fire.
Ready to take on what we know is right,
to stand strong, no matter what, together, shining bright.
Everyone is singing, gathering as one force of love.
Oh, what a sight, as we rise above, into victory,
full of love, rising from within, full of love.
Listen to the river flowing, down to the sea,
into the ocean of compassionate love.
Just keep flowing through the sea of love,
Oh, yes, the sea of love.

May 14

Climb the mountains of your dreams, to never walk away, to be your own best friend, every day.

Hold yourself in your heart, no matter who you are, you'll always be there for you.

Friends, how they come and go, yet deep inside is you, forever etched within, grateful to know you are the best yet.

June 3

I asked Ashento for a message. My sweetness, you sense familiar feelings. It is the entering of the shining one, into the essence of truth, allowing your concentration to relax, to feel your breath, to listen to silence, to the wisdom that reigns within the senses.

Keep going down within the tube of light that is always shining bright, on the journey into the realm of crystalline transformations.

May the rhythm heal and unravel all the places within.

Let your body touch the sweet essence of your song, as you sail into the chasm of spiritual beauty, softness, and serenity.

Call in the source hidden in the recesses of the silvery magnificence of the starry realms of above.

Drink of the fountain of magnificent beauty and liquids of love.

Let the light in as it shines brightly over mountains, oceans, rivers and streams, into the wisdom of the depths within.

Let the games begin as you hold the staff of light, swirling it to shine brightly upon the majesty of this holy sacred ground.

Return to nurturing the ways to bring healing and maintain the sanctity. One must not rush. There is always time to choose wisely. Imagine sharing with everyone, the dance of love.

August 11

Last night, I pondered where I was going? I heard his voice and saw his sweet smiling face, with blue skin, long dark hair, and sparkling stars over his tall handsome body. He gave me this song.

Who Am I?

Oh, my sweetness, you know who you are
A shining radiant star, oh yeah

Nothing to fear, nothing you can't do
Nothing can take away your shining light
Radiant light, radiant star
You're always a sparkling, radiant star
Let your voice sing and your eyes shine with joy
Oh yeah, you always know who you are
Nothing will ever take that away,
So, sail away, high into the heavens
You know who you are, a radiant star
No need to shed any tears,
Come fly with me into the heavenly realms, so pure.
Yes, you know who you are, my radiant star.

Dream- *I'm a star priestess with golden wings open wide. Radiant lights sparkle everywhere as I sail from heaven, on a winged white horse, holding reins of golden light. As I returned to my body, I heard; "Share the melodies heard in the realms of heavenly splendor."*

August 26

Sleepless, I'm wired as if by magic, so I listen, to unwind, drifting away slowly into peace. I am one within my heart and soul, as I feel the world swirling, and my body throbbing with the energy of the night.

I am free to unravel, to find the deeper way in, to the path of love, to instigate new ways of healing, to release tensions, to feel our powerful true selves, to reestablish the missing link with the source of love, to reconnect to the long lineage of healing modalities, encompassing the vast greatness, along our journey of magnificent realizations of all.

May we mobilize into oneness, steering in directions, to feel whole, to be sure, we are on the right track home.

Thank you for gifts of truth and wisdom, for showing us how to follow the path, to align with all that began, way before us, along the edge of time, so long ago in the universe.

Thank you for leading us, to sail through the doorways of life. I am you. You are me. We are free to be.

Yes, my sweetness, you, and I, are one in communion, in total alignment with the truth, in all evidence of being - ness.

As you breath in bask in the power of the golden sun, to feel the change, to know the presence, from this oneness, one pointedness.

Into the starry realm we explode with joyful radiance, bursting forth with glorious light-filled love, to head there is darkness, to heal ourselves and the others, all at once.

September 18 - Let's Light the Candle

The deeper I go the more I flow,
to the essence of my soul
to the beauty of the day, to the way of life.
Oh, may we open to the splendor of it all,
to journey on the path free of strife,
with love, grace, hope and peace,
going higher, higher in every way, hey hey hey
. Oh, may we light the candle of our dreams,
to shine as bright as the stars,
flowing like the streams.
Oh, may we run swiftly like our rivers, on and on,
to the seas of peaceful harmony, and serenity.
Oh, may we be like children playing free, flowing, just free.

October 5

As long as you are in this world, you are to be part of it, to actively participate, as a powerful spiritual being in human form, free of chains, believing in truth, honoring the goodness of life, the sole reason, to be here.

We know it can be a challenge, so look within, to see, feel and know that all is flowing, for you know the way to go.

As long as you are in this world, follow the path of least resistance, the path of love. So be here now, to manifest true expressions of harmony, creation, pure intentions, holding sacred, the essence of life, to make magic for all to see, feel and love.

Oh yes, as long as you dwell in this world, cultivate peace, contentment, dedication, acceptance, say often, "I am peace. I am love and light filled. Yes, I am of this realm, to be free, free, free. I am love filled light, one with all there is, without confusion."

October 12 - 31

Come gather round, I'll tell you a story, as you sit on this sacred ground, or stand in a circle with your arms, held high.

Open your hearts and minds, way deep, to the only spiritual home you've ever known. Long before you opened your wings and flew on down through the silver rays of light and love, into the body, right from Source, from far away above.

Everything you ever need is right inside your heart. Yes, right where it's always been, where it's always going to be, in the bright light of your sweet soul.

It doesn't matter what you do, for just ride the waves of love, the best that you can, smiling as you sail along.

Yes, the concerned ones are gathering, at this moment to rectify, the affront against Mother Earth. All is well in the high places of heaven. Yes, we're searching to find love in the hearts of humanity.

What is it that each person seeks in their day, in the vibration of the moment? Isn't it the wisdom of love, which is nurturing, and all encompassing, just like a warm day?

A peaceful solution is the fairest way to restore balance. It is like planting a seed, with nurturing rains following and then bursting into life, from within its' shell, to carry on, through myriad illusions, to express its true destiny. That life force always seeks the energy necessary to anchor it deeper within, the body/ mind.

Practice non-aggressive solutions, when protesting, to overcome everything out of balance. It will make a significant change for humanity. Stand strong in this way despite the obvious deceit and willingness to destroy through violence.

The chaos ensuing, all the dissenting voices, the shady characters that are running things, the truth will overcome. The shadow side will fall and fade away from powerful positions.

December 11 - 18

Concentration leads to liberation, through opening to the highest expressions that one can do or be. You will return to calmness and reflecting inner light. Fulfilling agreements, contracts, listening, keeping connections, and constantly inspiring you to do your best.

The Sandman is coming to sprinkle a little Earth and wisdom in your eyes, to help you see through the smoking mirror, to realize the true colors of the distant stars, as they shine above, under and through, reflecting the glorious sensuality of the midnight skies.

Set your dreams, to fly away, high into the universe.

Where does one go to be free of everyday dramas?

Oh, the sand woman is dancing in the rain, even in the night, she sings a sweet melody even in snowy winters' light.

May you find ways, to unify the broken pieces with vibrant visionary songs of spirit, that gather momentum in the pure light.

Dynamic love is rising, causing those who do not honor this energy within, to see their false illusions fall, crumbling into ashes.

Reclaim yourself, my sweetness, we see each other now, as the veil is ever thinner in all its glory, releasing and relaxing.

Oh, for the vision to carry on, now more than ever, so return to the magic of spiritual practice. You are free to be one with me.

Gratitude for what you have released, for your strong endurance to continue, pure to you word, setting your course, with oneness.

Jan 5, 2018 - Full Moon Glory

What a mystery, full moon, so white and bright. I'm grateful for the silence, for warm stoves, for restful nurturing sleep, soothing body and mind. Oh, bright one, thank you for your unlimited light. I love knowing you're there, blessing us, as a majestic star traveler.

Yes, we are always here, to help fashion lives in positive ways.

Thank you for seeking and appreciating every moment as a treasured pearl to behold.

Feb 4 - Calling Us Home

Let's sing to those places where the flowers shine.
Let's sing to the faces in the clouds.
Let's sing to the glory of the moonlight.
Let's shine every moment, for there's nothing
, nothing they can ever hide from us.
There is nothing that will ever keep us away,
from our deep dark, holy sacred place, inside.
So, let's keep on believing, that we can change the world,
for we know who we really are,
with the swirls of goodness,

Blessed By Light-filled Love

all around us, with the magnificence of creation.
Oh, the dream is real, that we all have inside.
We're holding to the beauty,
We're listening to the midnight rain.
We're calling our hearts home. Calling our missing parts.
Flying on the comets, on the sparkling stars that shine,
flying home to our hearts, home to everything we hold dear.
Come on home, to every part of you.
Sometimes we forget that fragments fly away,
or sometimes are taken away.
So just keep holding onto your dreams.
I'm returning to my holy place within,
to my sweet soul's treasure. How about you?
Come on, lets' all walk together now,
into our sacred places.
I'm returning every part of me, to all of me right now.
It's flying home, every part, all the pieces of my soul.
Did you say, okay now?
May the rain wash away, touching all the rays of love,
wherever you are, whoever you are.
Oh, let the rays wash over you,
all the beauty, healing you.
Oh, my daughters. Oh, my sons, my returning ones.
Oh, let the wrinkles of time unwind,

Mariam Massaro

smoothing out your minds.
Oh, may it rock you like a baby, in the arms of love.
Sometimes it takes a quiet mind to hear.
Sometimes it takes a quiet moment to understand,
how to really look within ourselves.
How to keep on walking. How to keep on forgiving.
Look at the rain, how it keeps on being rain,
even if it turns into snow.
Pay attention, now. Did you hear its time, oh, yay?
Oh, I feel it calling me home.
Oh, I feel I'm going right home,
into the realm I love so well.
Oh, may we find our way,
May we feel the hope within,
for the way, to open wide, to fly away free.
Say goodbye to what you leave behind. Goodbye.
I only want my pieces to come home to me,
to my body, mind and spirit,
to celebrate the beauty within me,
for the music to flow, for the lessons to learn,
for the memories to tuck away,
for the rainbow colors of light.
I say, hello, to the good life I want to flow.
Hello, to all my parts, I'm bringing home,

just like the waves flowing to the shore.
May it take us down deep inside, to the treasure within,
of being alive, right here, free,
Just like the waves washing to the shore,
there's so much more.
We're all part of this holy life,
flowing like the waves sweetly home.
So, snuggle in with your body, mind and spirit.
Fly home deeper than ever before.
Let it unfold in powerful ways,
celebrating in a good way,
every moment, sound and breath
Calling us all home, home.
Release - CD, 2021, Spirits of the Sun Music

February 11

Just finish what you started. Nothing new, no matter what you must do. Unravel all the opportunities that have come along. No more searching or seeking. Make a rhythm to fill your life with greatness, every sweet way you can. Believe in completion.

Feb 25 - We Can All Come Home Now

We can all come home now,
back to the womb, back to the nest.
We can all come home now
Back to the treasure chest within, your peaceful heart
We can all come home now, oh yeah, let's start.

Mariam Massaro

Let's go to the place of nurturing
Of standing tall, in the cold wind.
Let's all go home to our sacred spaces within
to transform, shedding what no longer serves.
What do you see when you look with open eyes?
Is it a shadow, or the reflection of spirit in human form?
Keep your light shining bright inside, with every breath
Let's go home to that sweet space within,
to snuggle deep inside our core where we know
there is so much more yeah.

April 24   **We're the Ones**

We see the cycle of change coming,
The shadows are turning counterclockwis,
Going the wrong way, imploding, falling, disappearing.
We're the ones, who care,
As we sail along the love channel of life,
Like rainbows spiraling in a miracle of love.
Let's say goodbye to the ways, that do not serve.
Leave them far behind,
Just walk on with no more in your mind.
Let's sail higher, beneath the lovely sky,
There's no one to stop us either way.
So, lets' all journey into the mystery
Don't let it slow you down, or take you anywhere,

Blessed By Light-filled Love

except on the path of love, love, love
Breathe it in, deep to spiral into the golden light,
into the miracle of life.
I'm open to hearing from you, Ashento.
Yes, I'm always within and listening. I love the way you look at life differently, transforming issues from one moment to the next.

Moving things like the wood pile, that needed to be rearranged. You just do it rather than put it off. That is your gift, unsticking, unused, dysfunctional piles, everywhere in life.

You turn it around, to find the way through the mire, to release and change into art something useful.

June 8 - Are We Ready?

Are we ready to motivate beyond, beyond?
Where we are right now?
We're gaining strength, moving, flowing, growing,
just like the mighty mother Earth in the summertime,
changing right before our eyes.
Oh yes, we are gaining and learning, as we rise.
We are the ones to make a difference.
How we greet the day, how we sail above,
showering love in every way.
Filling the gaping holes, from the depths of our souls.
So, let's be ready in a moment's notice,
to gather around, to flow beyond, to that place of love.

Mariam Massaro

July 10 - The Dragon has Landed

You are the one, to heal your life, to start again.
It is always good to renew yourself, in whatever way you can.
So hey, come on now, lets' clear it all away,
tear down the walls of shame, there is no one to blame.
Cast the net, the web of magical light,
as you set your goals in sight.
The rainbows colors of delight, let them flow
It's easy to let them go, to release illusions of grandeur.
Oh, how they fade when the pillars of truth take us deep,
setting us free of strife, to cherish life, to make it right,
to be winged warriors of peaceful light,
to keep on growing and flowing hey, hey, he,
Hold on strong, here we go, flying along

July 28 - Over and Over Again

I'm writing my story, that I carry inside
Just like the morning, how it always comes again.
Won't you walk with me, down the road of serenity,
into the light of the mystery?
You don't have to turn around,
just to walk on this holy ground.
We can leave it all behind, for peace of mind,
just like the morning, just like the night,
always coming, happily, free as light.

Blessed By Light-filled Love

Did you ever see the morning late or the night far behind?
Speaking words of regret?
No, they just flow again, one day into the night.
Coming, never changing anything in sight.
They just keep flowing on, over and over again,
while people play characters in the game of life.
Lets' all take a deep breath, as we open wide our eyes,
for the morning, yay, its' no surprise.
So many good days, no more broken records,
no more fallen dreams,
no more hopelessness, only clear truth,
flowing like the streams.
Sweep it all away, the doubts and fears,
with no more tears.
There's nothing we must do,
for life, to unfold the way,
we want it to. Just open our eyes,
to listen more,
to love, to live, to forgive. Yes, so much more.
Releasing doubts or despair.
Just feel the sweetness of fresh clear air,
listen to the rivers always flowing,
just like nights following the days
Look at the years fly by, under the blue, blue sky.

Oh, to walk upon the sacred ground beneath our feet.
Until that day when your last breath says goodbye,
and you fly away never to return in this life.
Take it while you have it, to be free, so free.

August 7

Come, my sweetness to the table of light, as we learn how to rise higher and higher.

May we swim in the river of love, to the sacred treasures within.

May we lean towards the strength that we carry inside, fueled by the power of the almighty.

Oh, what a dynamic concept, the vastness of this universe is beyond, beyond, beyond.

Comprehension, portals careening, planets sailing, light speed, sweet softly singing, serene solitudes, magnificent mountains of mysteries.

Undulations of silence, spiraling into a vast array of colors.

Swirling orbs of radiant light, flowing, swiftly, silently, around,

up, down, and in and out.

May we energize, nurture, come together and flow apart, always

in healing balance and harmony, sweetly, oh so sweetly.

The shadows aspects of life are merely reflections of illusions. May the ones who are called, find one another, for the glory of creation, is inherent within each of you.

Magic happens when like-minded beings are in alignment focusing their peaceful intentions, with far reaching effects.

Unity creates a musically celestial resonance, that reverberates with greatness. Yes, simply greatness.

Blessed By Light-filled Love

The Gaea Star Crystal story is richly engaging and expressive of the truth. May it raise awareness in a pleasing joyful manner.

I love how you appreciate raindrops transforming into gushing waters -magnificent and mighty, as they flow into the oceans of life.

August 11 – 13 - Onto Something New

I'm onto something new,
within, within, so deep within.
I'm letting go, moving with the flow,
focusing my intentions.
Realizing that dreams only manifest when I
take the time to complete, fulfill and finish
everything I started, regardless, when.
I know I am the only one
who plants seeds of manifestation,
what it needs for fertilization,
who longs for the materialization, so deep within.

May We Always Shine Brightly

Sometimes to finish what you started,
you need to open the door, to let it all flow by.
Release, relax, relate, reclaim and nurture.
Be grateful for the day, to stay home and play,
to walk in the misty rain, underneath the grey clouds.
Take care, to replenish in this peaceful way.
Unhook, unplug, say hey, I'm here today,
with nowhere else to take me away.

Mariam Massaro

Oh, to hear the rain, flowing into rivers, onto the seas.
May we fill up easily like the rain's coffers, with love,
abundance, acceptance, and forgiveness
Let's be kind, considerate and respectful.
Let's open the portals of compassion
to weave a peaceful ribbon of light around this world,
to find our way home, through the mist into starlight rays,
to listen to the melody of the rain, falling gently,
in the dark night, lulling sweetly, so peacefully
May we all fly deeper than ever before,
to the center of our core,
blooming like a gorgeous flower
or ripening as delicious fruit on the vine.
May we listen to the melody of the divine,
Like beacons in the night, may we always shine,
tapping into our soul's deepest longings.
May we release the pain of no direction,
with renewed surrender, with willingness,
to sail flying free, for we are the ones,
to lead our lives onward so,
to make our lives worth living. Yes, it is so.

August 16 - 26 - Radiant is Our Love

Radiant is our love, as it shines from within
Just like the blue jays singing in the trees,

Blessed By Light-filled Love

Radiant is our love, that we feel from the wind,
whistling, dancing in the breeze
Radiant is the symphony, our fountain of love,
bursting from our hearts in the morning of new life,
free, free, free of strife.

Sayings for Gaea Star Crystal radio hour :

Accentuate the positive. Uplift your spirit.
Give it another punch. Raise the bar.
Smile at someone today, to show you care.
Always see your cup half full, not half empty.
Don't settle for less than what you want.
Follow in the footsteps of those who already did it.
Savor each moment of one more day.
Open to abundance today. Be grateful for everything.
Believe you can do anything you set your heart on.
Walk on the bright side. Hold fast to your dreams.
Count your blessings. Keep your hopes up.
Know you are always loved and never alone.
Climb every mountain joyfully. Keep life floating.
Return a favor of kindness. Just give a little.
Reach ever higher. The sky is the limit.
Change is for the better. One step at a time.
You must start somewhere. All life matters.
Cherish everything dear to you. Treasure nature.

Set aside time to go deep within. Never give up.
Shine like a beacon in the night. Help those in need.
Express your passion. Seize the opportunity.
Walk with your head high. Finish everything you start.
Greet the day with love. Silence is golden.
Worry no more. Breathe deeply the essence of life.
This is the moment to catch the wind, to sail away free
. Set your intentions to manifest right now.
Don't worry, be happy. Be available.
Say yes, welcome life. Start small, end big.
Sing your soul's songs. Never stop trying, just do.
Learn to say, you may be right or I'm sorry.
Practice living your truth. Return to wholeness every day.
Everything is going to be alright, no matter what they say.
I am full, richly blessed with all that I need and want.
I walk in beauty with happiness flowing, for the days to come.
This too shall pass.

August 30

I ask to heal the pains of humanity. Saying yes for love to flow, in all ways. Oh grace, lead me to the wholesome, healing lands of colorful blissful moments as I breathe, hear, and see.

May I always know you God, Goddess, all that there is.

May I find the way into the deep place within my sweet soul's treasure, into the knowing essence to sing of the sweet love I feel for you. Holy creation, we are one in the essence of it all.

Blessed By Light-filled Love

May I be like you, soft, sweet, silent, still, and at peace.

I release confusion and restore my energy to peaceful bliss as I

grow richly full, like the beauty in every moment.

September 5 -14

May I circle around as you rest beneath the starry sky.

Great destiny awaits those who attune to their divine missions.

Mighty Wisdom Channel

Every day starts the same, as the pages turn,
they never speed up or end the day before it's time.
Are we letting imagination manifest our dreams?
There's little that we need to do, to make our days flow.
So, let's all share what we see, feel, or learned.
Come see the moon perched like a precious
jewel, high in the night sky.
May we unravel a little every moment,
letting everything pass through, flowing along.
Let's keep sailing, writing our stories, all
the way from the bottom, to the top.
Answer no more questions, solve no more problems,
just open to the circles of love,
to the circles of light,
all around on this holy ground.
May we just surrender to life,
to accept, to be free,

to let it rise higher, everyday toward the one,
into the mighty wisdom channel,
into the land of wisdom and goodness today.

September 24 - May We Remember

May we believe in the mysterious grace of life.

May we be grateful, as we remember the ways of peace, love and healing, tapping into pure divine love.

May we be like seeds of grain, full, ready to burst forth, to enjoy the nurturing aspects of life.

May we remember when we planted ourselves in this realm of

Creation. To be born. To learn. To give and receive love. To sprout with new energies manifesting.

May the fountains flow from the depths of love, rising high, touching the temple of true peace. No more searching, only healing and touching the deep places of our souls.

May we discover who we really are, why we came into this promised land from the distant stars. Who accompanied us at the final boarding call, to guide us along this miracle of life?

Let's climb up and down the mountains as we forgive, accept and understand this amazing procession of life. Serenely, spiritually, listening, loving, touching, smiling, and creating.

Let's all dance, celebrate and sing a gentle song, as we learn to live in balance, to surrender to the days ahead, to leave the past behind, to never give up, to sail into the realm of the silver lining.

Let's hop on board the train of love, to be here and now, to set our lives free. For this is the way, to change it around, to live like a radiant light filled star on this sacred ground.

Where everyone is respected and encouraged to walk the path of freedom, cherished for who they really are, no matter what they look like or who they choose to love or be.

October 29 - The Castles of Our Dreams

Let's return to the castles of our dreams,

to the realms of pure love, where we sailed on a moonlight night

that was illuminated by the fires of before.

Oh, yeah, way back when you opened the door, that was covered

by eyes of the all-knowing, the all-flowing.

You'll hear the purring cat that guards the portal, with yellow,

black eyes and long whiskers, watching, transfixed.

You know, you never walk alone. Everything you ever need is provided by Divine source. Pure, rich, full, nourishing and sustaining.

Yes, its' all here, there or everywhere. You only have to walk gently with grace, forgiveness and strength of conviction to live, to return, to the feeling of love.

Just let it flow from your treasure within, from your heart of gold,

the home of your soul.

Oh yes, someday you will return, to the source of love, until then, be well my friends.

Open to the softness, to the snuggling ones who share the journey as companions, brothers, sisters, lovers, to cherish, to flow in union.

Return to this high place, completely, deeply, to the castle of our highest dreams, illuminated by the fires of before, before, way before.

October 31 - We're Coming Down

We're coming down from heavens realm right before your eyes.

Coming to help you realize the good ways,

to live out your days, with sweet tenderness

from deep within your core.

Now is the time to realign with being divine.

We're coming in the flowers, in the breeze, in the leaves.

Yeah, look around, you'll see us touching down,

Just like the cold frost covering the ground.

Just coming on, like waves of love, washing over this holy life with gentle, soft touches, from the divine.

You'll hear us in the whispering wind or see us in the mighty mountains or feel us in the sunshine's warm rays.

Now is the time, to rise, opening wide to a peaceful new dawning, to receive what's coming your way, to shine brightly, like the starry night.

Let your wings take flight. Yeah, every day, every night, let your dreams take flight, high into the realms of pure delight.

November 11

May we manifest the essence of all that there is, deep within the

magnificence of the sacred journey of life.

Bring on a new wave of understanding, of acceptance, of surrendering to the truth, that there is a better way.

Let's walk through the portal of peace, for all nations, to stand strong, to cherish the precious resources, all the rivers, trees, animals and the last tribes living in serenity.

Oh, legions of light, brigades of love, helpers of the dawn of peace, lets' change the old leaders, releasing those that do not walk the healing path of love.

We know that love is the only answer, to lead us, into lives of sweet goodness and peaceful happiness.

Lets' sail along the rapids of life, finding the eddy's, changing for the better, cherishing all life, in all ways.

Let's nestle into that healing place within, feeling love rising, flowing, growing, rolling along on the sea of life.

November 24

May we gracefully release boundaries, accepting truth, honoring our sacred visions, using powerful words such as trust, awakening, freedom, liberation, compassion, cooperation, to show we care.

Let's transform like a beautiful butterfly, bursting from the chrysalis, into a sweet bliss filled life.

Let's dance and sing, to bring in peaceful ways of sharing comfort, to live in the light, clear and bright.

Let's open the floodgates of our hearts, collecting, all the pure love, floating in the air, sharing our best together.

May we give life a chance to rise above, as we strive to remain calm and even throughout it all.

Let's take care of the children. They need our love, for they are the most important anywhere.

May we act as one family, rediscovering the only way to be full of serenity. Celebrating the majesty of all that we hold dear, unfurling everything we came with, until we return home to spirit.

Let's set our lives free, weaving strands from here, there, everywhere into a light-filled creation of life, no matter what.

Let's follow the river, that flows on, through the woods, over the rocks, under the fallen trees, singing all the while, "Trust me, take a chance, create every moment, like I do."

Dance alive hopes and dreams, with the fires of desire.

Let it go. Let it flow. Keep on, keeping on, rising ever higher.

Do you see me turning back, stopping in midstream? No, I just keep flowing, there is no other way to be, so just surrender, to be free, free, free.

Always onward, in the flow. Yes, there is someone up ahead, to merge into, to flow even stronger, as members of the same team, the union of life, never turn around, just keep moving on and on."

Dec 1

I'm grateful to rest but not sleepy. I have tingling in my hand and a painful arthritic hip, forcing me to slow down. I put off surgery.

Yes, my sweetness, I am here. I see and feel your afflictions within your body, in the nerve endings and the skeletal body. Stresses from your active lifestyle, perhaps from years of gardening. So many changes are affecting the people of Gaea Star, now.

I love hearing the rain, I remember the moisture, how it changes everything. I sail on wings of light, into the different realms, always returning to the golden realm of oneness.

May we continue to unite softly in loving essence. I love to merge with your music and songs.

Open into the portal of noble healing, where cobalt blue rays and luminous purple rays bathe you from your toes, to the top of your head, letting colors invigorate, realign, reestablish, and reconnect.

May blessings nurture and sustain the goodness in your heart for the work, you do so well. Remember to rest, to return to the healing love whenever you can.

Dec 10 - Dream - Omajina

I hear, "Omajina." I see an exotic priestess, in a magnificent, silvery blue, shimmering, iridescent gown with long gossamer sleeves, hanging, floating toward me, singing sweetly.

"You and I are one, oh my sweetness." I laughed in disbelief. "Ashento?" "Yes," he says, "Remember, when I was the Diamond eyed woman?"

"Yes," I said. He transformed into another beautiful female incarnation that was different then when he appeared as a goddess, singing the 'Diamond Eyes' song.

(Ashento/Omajina) smiles, waving her sleeves, to float softly and silkily, "Yes, I love shapeshifting into a new form of expression to enjoy."

We laughed. Omajina is a pretty name. What a dream. I performed it in the radio show with the Gaea Star band.

May you be at one with all that you seek to do.

Rest and drink pure water, for thirst. That is best for healing.

I send blue rays of healing, to flow through out your body.

Oh, how life unfolds in grand and glorious ways.

As you and I become one, we give our magnificent love to the world, my sweetness.

May we spend precious moments with loved ones, nurturing

in the fields of love together, until then I wait, loving you with light.

December 13.   Still Searching

I'm searching for my lover, but only in my heart,
only in my soul, for I know I'm already whole.
I'll light the fire in my mind,
It's been such a long, long time.
I know to keep busy, to create, to serve,
to write, to sing, to do.
Yeah, I'm sailing along,
just fine without you,

on this new morning, thinking, were you
ever going to fill that shoe?
Even as the sun shines,
I'm thinking in this glory filled life, when will come the time?
If we'll meet as planned, back when we were in the Divine?
Yes, I remember the pact we made,
to walk as lovers in the forest's glade.
Humming softly in the essence of pure love.
Yes, are you still sailing in the realms above?
Am I missing the clues, we laid for each other,
as we sweep away all that has settled over?
May our love burst through the hard soil, after all this time,
becoming moist, rising high, free, totally sublime.
Oh, dance with me in the glory of the new day,
loving, playing, you and I, sailing, flying so high,
unraveling the knots, in this new way,
releasing all the crossings, all the confusions.
Yes, here at last, right in my loving heart,
Come now, let's make a brand-new start.
Together in this peaceful life, Let's just settle down.
My dear sweet kin on this holy sacred ground.

January 22, 2019

Early morning sunrise over tall trees. I finally finished writing the 'Gaea Star Crystal' into a novel.

We see you focus, setting your mind and heart into creating the story, with interesting, and thoughtful new aspects.

We are pleased for your willingness to complete it, to flow from one to the next. All endeavors unfold with driving intentions.

Reweaving, redoing, inspires the much-needed messages.

Each time you write, is another way of saying, all life flows, restores and renews.

Yes, let the rays of sunshine bathe you with healing light.

Its' one long silvery wide swath of glowing light, from here to there, flowing in love.

Let it slowly evolve, whenever you sit to write, light a candle, say, "I release the light even more, on this glorious day or night." You have much to say, so fly into your day from here to there.

Loving, warmth, touching deeply your sweet soul, as we are always in alignment. Love to you.

Yes, shining brightly, as the star lights that you are, taking paths laid out long before.

Oh, may you all remember, as you gather smiling, sharing, once and for all, pure radiant love. Oh, let it shine so.

I am onto a distant star, to a magnificent, crystalline realm.

February 20

Clouds, cover, the snowy morning, after a luscious full moon cast silvery rays last night. I decide to have my hip joint replaced after trying without success to heal it naturally. I want to walk, hike and do what I can normally. It's time to accept surgery as a form of healing.

Hello, my sweetness, on this day dawning. We are in oneness, as always, returning, realigning, remembering our divine union.

Thank you for diligence in rewriting these teachings. Interesting, to review, seeing maturation.

You are capable of fabricating and editing worthy text now.

Yes, to release all distractions that prevent self-expression, to rest and heal, in preparation for the needed surgery.

Life flows on, even as one ages so. Some parts age differently.

To accept this, to not resist the inevitable, brings relief. Titanium is a useful tool, imparting strength, and longevity. It is new methodology from the stars and is remarkable for a speedy recovery. You will have many more Earth years, pain free.

Being consciously awake during, is a healthy approach, causing easier acceptance of the new hip within.

Thank you for your intentions, prayers of love and peace, and for dismay over the unkindness of your volatile government.

As you know though, love is the only way to achieve balance for all living beings, all else will implode upon themselves soon, dissolving into their own chaos, never to rise again.

We know how challenging this time is for all who are, sensitive, caring, loving and only filled with good intentions.

Softly, gently, willingly, the tide is turning, the mother ship of love is sailing home to safe harbor, through the goodness channel, to the port of love, breaking through the floes of shadowy icebergs, bursting through the last of the shadows of illusion, that the dark forces keep throwing out, in their last feeble attempts to smother, to cover the light.

Oh, you are all rising above, courageously, undaunted, willing to stand strong, resisting.

Oh, let it all sweep away, returning to sweet, soft, love from deep within, fueled by abiding love from above. It is happening all over the world, this rising up, to wholeness, to balance.

Yes, you are all going deeper into the essence within one's soul, to express the truth of warm, caring, love, and nurturing compassion for all life, regardless.

Yes, this is the moment, the reason you came, to shine, to glow, from within, to realign into graceful oneness, with the sole purpose of committed loving acceptance, articulately expressing messages of love, for life, through actions, words, and healing music.

March 9

Yes, my daughter, my sons, we are realigning with communion, with great magnitude, omnipresence, erasing all the years of inaction, replacing with movement and assertive, assimilation, into the pocket of true expression.

So, stand strong, for what you feel deep within, on the hilltops or in front of a camera. Speak in positive profound ways. Going deep. Making requests to save precious resources - to exchange, to communicate, to walk, to swim through the murky waters, and to grow, with all the uplifting, supporting actions for a peaceful place.

These are the achievements of the new green way, for the green

Earth, for the healing of humanity.

May everyone listen, restore, remember and realign rather than anything else. Go into the deep recesses within your hearts, to reestablish healing, harmony, strength and courage.

Yes, let it all settle in high, low or mid-range, we are all in this together, wherever we are, in this grid of life.

April 8

My hip surgery went well. It seemed like all they did was change a part. I did not have any pain except around the incision. I am grateful I did it and feel such new release.

Cast aside any misperceptions, of who or what is right or wrong, for yes, underneath what is visible, is the incredible resilient foundation of love, which supports and nurtures everyone, no matter who or what they are, for everyone is affected by the grace of love. Thank you, my blessings.

September 20

Yes, my sweetness, as we are nestled together in the stillness of the night with sparkling distant stars in sight, with a few clouds mixed in. Yes, there are moments of the day when even if one is being busy, it is good to call attention to yourself to your spirit within, to your central core of beingness.

Align by saying, "I align myself with spirit, with the divine essence of life. I am one essence, one breath, one being."

How may we center ourselves? How do we touch back or touchstone ourselves?

What can help us remember, to pay attention, to attend to caring for ourselves? The easiest way is to slow the breath down.

Oh, yes, just relax. Know that to rest and allow ourselves to come to the place of stillness, brings a freshness every day.

Surely, we can remake ourselves into a powerful present phenomenal being, fully illuminated shining through all the crevices, weaknesses, and cracks in places with strength.

Yes, how we dip. How we dance. How we weave. How we express ourselves. It all comes down to how we know ourselves to how we show our simple peaceful gentle easy ways, even to ourselves.

What brings us to demonstrate who we truly are?

What makes us shift, create, do, be, laugh, cry and love with a real sense of life itself?

It is the breath of life. How it all goes in and soothes all of our alveolus, the little nerve endings in the lungs, all the electrical pathways that can easily be set alight.

Yes, it is the dynamic energy flowing after running, exercising, climbing, swimming or dancing.

Yes, it is in the beats of the heart that accelerates and flows more oxygenated blood to the organs, pleasantly strong. They say let's get our blood pumping to keep it flowing and circulating.

All of this demonstrates a sense of balance, oneness, graceful togetherness and unbridled passions for life.

It is the willingness, a movement to go deeper and deeper, with a fondness for creativity, for nurturing and shedding of the old ways, releasing difficulties through forgiveness and compassion, gentleness, nurturing and surrendering.

Here's to the highest most gentle way, to climb high, to overcome and to set your lives to the highest of which it can be.

May you witness, see, and feel the next phase of your lives.

In a gentle expression of graceful acceptance of all things and all beings, from the depths of our hearts to the depths of yours.

We say search no more as you find the way to dwell within your core fully capable to reshape, to set the theater, to open wide the into the dawning of the new beginning and say yes, it is so indeed.

Here is to life in its fullness. May the grace and blessings of a pure full life finds all of you at peace oneness.

October 31

Sleepless, snacked on blueberries and walnuts. I received a call to sell the cottage site in NY. A kayaker tracked me down by going to the shore to the difficult neighbors who hassled me about the easement through their property even though it was in a deed from a hundred years ago. Is this a sign to say goodbye to my dreamland? Hard to do as I loved its' magical moments there. Life how it unfolds.

Yes, my sweetness, it is the momentous time to release all that binds, distracts and deters you from the pure essence of who you are, like the monarch butterflies who burst free from their chrysalis and mysteriously know where to fly instinctively.

It is all right, there will be other wonderful wild scenic watery places to enjoy. It's not in your energy field anymore. The doors have slammed shut as if to say, no It's not your place.

It's far to travel alone and the unfriendly neighbors, all the dramas for that piece of beauty. Too unsettling. So come home, release what no longer serves your joyful self. Set it free so you may join the higher forces that seek your assistance to guide humanity to walk through the coming tumultuous times of changes.

Oh, sweet one, return to your holy sacred place to help heal the fragments of your fractured fragile souls. Weave it into a web of oneness with the highest intentions of nurturing self. You are calling the pieces of yourself home, remember? They're returning to solidify together for the next phase of your elder years.

May the winds of change blow away my fears, and desire to hold onto the idyllic waterfront land. I hear words, "I set myself free as desiring to own the land fades. No more worrying anymore.

Thank you, Ashento, lady of the lake, archangels, and the source of love. I release it all to express my souls' sweet songs. I want to be free as a bird or butterfly, these angelic beings that flow everywhere. I will follow this way of healing. I sense it is an opportunity to let it go and move on to the next powerful phase of my life, free from strife.

November 7

The cool air blusters in the muffled moonlight. Walnuts and Blueberries again. The quiet stillness of nature thrills me every time. I love being surrounded by it all, resting in soft beds, grateful for warmth and our homes, for a sense of place.

We feel your confusion at the chaos abounding in the places of foment in the world. All is in order as you seek spirituality, taking back your power, for that is the best action to do at this moment.

Seek the smooth way as one searches for the answers to the confusion that lies within. Where to go with all these choices?

Release the irritations brought on by issues. We see how strong you swim through the currents. Take yourself into the eddies to breathe in the beauty, to hold to the passions of deep pleasures.

Find moments to go into the serenity to enjoy the forest, oceans, or lakes. Focus on prayers for healing humanity, to awaken the children of the sun, lost in the veils of their own illusions.

Let yourselves be free, to heal from within, to seek the simple pleasures of love, connections, family, and nurturing. The waters of life keep energies flowing into the light of a new era dawning.

Onto the next horizon where the center of gravity is changing even as the poles are shifting in massive waves of transformation. There are more books to flow. Keep on, reweaving all that you do.

A new song, **I am One**

I am with one with thee, I am, I am, I am.
I call in the ones from the ancient past,
into this moment right now.
I am one with spirit as I release my soul's dreams.
I open my heart to the realms of the sky so blue,
seeking a brand-new start,
where the winds of love ring so true.
I hear rain turning to snow upon the dark windows
as the powerful cold descends again
I relish the comfortable warmth within.
It's time to slow down, to create, to write,
to read, to sing, I am one with the spirit of the night
As I sail into my soul's dreams, I am, I am, I am

December

Oh, my sweetness, you and I are one in this holy creation. We are healing and sailing sweetly throughout the realms of love and light. You and I are shining bright, so full of delight.

May we call everyone home to the glory. Hail to the sweetness of the misty rains of love showering from above, from the East, the West, North and the South.

All of it reaching far and wide as we circle the world so wide. Calling those who long to come home, to return to the light, to the eternal ways of love, to the realms of love.

Thank you, Ashento for your devotion to guiding our waywardness through thick and thin. We are grateful for the blessings, and for awakening to my divine radiant star self.

I have stars in my eyes and stars in my heart. I'm always ready for a brand-new start. Yes, higher and higher, I rise, letting go and learning what makes me flow, here there and everywhere.

We only have one way to go, always deeper within to that holy peaceful place within. Free of the shackles of self-imposed constraints, to set ourselves freer than ever before. Seeking the place of peace, gentleness, and of truly living in a state of grace. We are one.

December 25

An idea for Gaea Star Crystal, book 2 - after the rainbow brigade arrives on Gaea Star, they are invited to Arynylle, the faery dell, which is close to where their crystal ships landed in lush wildflower fields.

January 2020

I enjoy developing unusual characters and their adventures on earth. I have faith the Gaea Star Crystal story will become a movie. May the grace of the goddess inspire us to manifest our dreams. Glorious blue sky sunshine morning. Congrats to me, the _Gaea Star Crystal_, book 1, is published. What a journey to manifest this dream to life.

Blessed By Light-filled Love

February - You and I

You and I, together as one
Weaving a new life in celebration,
of healing, growing love
Embracing ancient ways with feelings,
of love from above
You and I, together as one
Going deeper than ever before,
we know there is much to share,
to show how we care
Let's follow our hearts weaving love
with a brand-new start
You and I, healing each other, releasing love everywhere
All the loneliness disappearing in the winds of change
now that we are united in love.
Memories of ancient times in realms above
Hold me close as we rebuild our love again.
As you and I embrace our love
let's sing new melodies of sweet surrender,
in celebration, in unity as one

February 6

Every day I learn more of myself, as I go deep into my core. I hear wisdom, sometimes loud and clear, or just barely, saying,

Come home. Open wide to the path of divine love. Yes, my sweetness, you are learning to be like a seed bursting through the moist soil, from the warm sun and nurturing rains.

> Oh, bring it home. Come on now, let it shine through.
> Keep on growing on, higher, and higher.
> Yes, you, and I are getting stronger, ever deeper.
> You know who you are, nothing holding you back ever.
> Just keep on bursting on through.
> Every story has a beginning and an ending, so step by step,
> keep on growing, ever flowing.

February 14

Early morning glory. At last, a copy of <u>The Gaea Star Crystal, Awakening the Tribes of Light,</u> book 1, is in my hands with its' vibrant color cover. What a profound sense of accomplishment to see it in print, to give to the world that is awry with chaos. Especially after the first inspiration for the story came in 1998. Such a process to manifest dreams.

Spirit gives us strength to carry on despite what is happening.

Waves of change are sweeping us toward the shores of life, through places of unrest, and dissention in this election year for America.

I am going for the gold by writing daily, hopefully for at least two hours, to complete a passage, chapter, or theme with amazing inspiration from immersing in the pristine tall forests nearby.

I am drawn to explore beyond where I have been, following the whispers from the spirits of the forests.

They led me to a fantastic promontory point, an ancient grandmother golden birch tree and another golden birch tree that formed a cave as it grew over a stream, rather than get its roots too wet. Each discovery has served to empower me even more to integrate these ideas into the text.

Now to carry on to the next story. The rainbow brigade arrives to Gaea Star to help humanity. Are they reborn as babies or do they remain in their celestial forms, even if they have no prior earth history? Will it make the story far-fetched? If it is a fantasy, I can make it flow smoothly.

Yes, of course, my sweetness. Everything is possible for the story changes, just as every day unfolds in serene beauty. As the writer, organize your and rework the theme by bringing the past ideas into the present. We love your inspiration and where it leads to. Completion is the real success, just keep on.

February 16

Open to the wildness, to the treasure deep inside. Where else can it be as you sift through the ashes of transformation from the fires passing like pages blowing in the wind?

Hold onto nothing, except the warmth that rises when thinking of love. See how it fills the heart, seeping into the crevices that ache for solidness, saturating so completely. Only love fills the emptiness.

Breathe it in, to reaffirm, your sacred connection to the creator, to the essence of life. Love in all forms, rings so true, Does it not? I am you. You and I, sing in harmony together.

No longer do I seek solace outside of myself.

Don't turn aside for the magical moment is going to rise. No more saying, if only or could have, should have, would have. There is no more waiting. Move onward, like the river always flowing to the sea, around, over and through. You are one part of the grand creation.

February 22

The rainbow brigade is invited to Avalina, the land of healing waters in the faery realm with a mermaid family.

It is appropriate to change the story. You are the creatress, weave your inspiration by utilizing points of wisdom, through their adventures. Express the all-seeing, knowing, glowing, radiance of love that dwells within one's inner depths.

Those who resonate will recognize it. The creative journey is to rework ideas. This is how one taps into their inherent power to transcend the spiritual teachings for all to see regardless of faith.

We are one family of loving light, seeking to return to the heart of love, to be appreciated and remembered for the loving service we provide. You will be rewarded.

March 4

Into the day I follow the way of truth, aligning with creation, with the sun's rays, and birds singing, even in the strong winds. I am grateful for a peaceful life. I am alright. I greet the fresh air and feel the wonder of breathing, seeing, and dancing.

I'm grateful for it all, for the mighty presence of spirit. I am free in this sweet serenity, as the days flow one after the other. In time this too shall pass into memories. I am content to love myself above all else.

Thank you for the goodness, permeating through this glory.

May I rise from my peaceful slumber to be guided by divine strength with no fear or regret. I accept all things that come, to teach, heal, assist, and help me to flow on in this powerful moment.

I receive wonderful blessings from the vibrant life force to live with juiciness from the magnificent manifestations in all ways.

March 6

To be aligned with my destiny, is to be one with what comes along. I received an email from Net Flicks about the Gaea Star story for a TV series.

Blessed By Light-filled Love

I am thrilled if it turns out after first writing this story as the 'Rainbow Crystals of the Earth' play in 1999. Performed once, then converted into a screenplay in 2009, and now divided into two books, with book 1 published. May this saga keep surging like a river to the sea, taking its own sweet time.

I saw a gorgeous green gold sparkly fun dress in a window for sale. I went in and to my surprise, it fit. I bought it as a reward for the hard work manifesting this dream into reality.

I sold the waterfront cottage site in Ny, even though I loved that sweet idyllic watery treasure. I was ready to move on. Love to the Lady of the Lake. I will miss her.

March 7

Snow covers, river rushes, blue sky, sun shining, prayers of peace and healing for the world. May we awaken on this glory filled planet.

Yes, may I catch the essence of my dreams, to share the message that there is a purpose to be incarnated as a human on Gaea Star.

We are here to share serenity with all beings. To serve, not only ourselves but each other in all manners of love and healing with the power of acceptance, nurturing and a willingness to climb out on the thin branches, to reach for our dreams into realities.

It is a sincere effort to realign with the highest truth, to love oneself first, then transform that into love for all beings.

Thank you for learning, for feeling the warmth of the sun warm, for strawberries, for walking the earth and for a radiant star filled life.

I gather the impetus to go into the calm where I am free to be. May we all have great days of just being.

March 8

Wind whistles through the windows. Life is challenging the world. A raging pandemic, school closings, Olympics cancelled, on and on. Can we rise above to unite as communities, to take care of the elders and the children, to support each other in health and love?

May we hold all families in living love.

Let's not let the magic fade. Let's return to when simpleness reigned supreme, of playing in the summer breezes, in the forests, the rivers and the fields. Let's stay home to wait out the storm. We'll make it as one family of loving light if we hunker down through this challenging moment.

It's the change we needed, to look within, to realize what matters is to return to sail along on waves of love through it all.

Let them wash over those places to help us with peace of mind. We're alright to stay home, to revel in our lives, to go deep in to see who we really are and what we're going to do.

Yes, some of us are alone but it will be alright as we learn to nurture these warm places of love and peace. Holding on. Staying strong. Letting our hearts heal. Caring for the children rather than rushing off to work and school. It's a change but we can do this as we tap into the pure places within our hearts.

It's a rhythm of peace, of goodness, of returning to that sacred space, even if it's changing in ways difficult for us to accept.

Yes, this great shift feels like what we've been calling for, to let go of the shadowy grip, that's had a powerful reign for centuries.

Let's climb out of the crevices of darkness. We can rearrange, reconnect and reclaim all that is flowing away. Yes, it will be vastly different, for we have to rebuild our lives in a brand-new way. Oh yeah.

March 11 - 12

Lots of changes in the world, Mother Earth is stepping in to show what is wrong with humanity on a grand scale. May we all get the message, to cause less pollution.

Cloud's cover, waters rushing, birds are calling as all the llamas are resting in the field where I see them from my bedroom. Sweet Nia is nestled on the bed waiting for me to get up.

I love immersing myself in writing the Gaea Star Crystal, story. It is such a joyous experience developing this fantasy again.

I never know where I am going to end up each time I write. It has a life all on its own, evolving as mine does. I am grateful for the guidance and the many connections.

Chickadees call in the oak. Woodpeckers and Tufted Titmouse too. I am one with you, Ashento. Thank you for the inspirations.

Yes, my sweetness, we are flowing in union despite all that is happening. We are one as we fly in harmony. Thank you for your focus to write the Gaea Star Crystal stories, to share everything you are transmitting, transcending, and transforming.

Honor your deep strength for seeking, searching, trusting, and trying. Into the day you flow, aware of all that you are.

I'm always united with you. We are on our own trajectory, manifesting powerful dreams, being of service in both realms. I am grateful to experience your home land, with geese flying by singing, and bluebirds, nesting near the lush abundant gardens.

I am honored to dwell in the delightful celestial essence of spirit so far from you. It is only brief. Are we fixed anywhere? No, for life is always growing and evolving, sweeping us slowly but surely back to the source of eternal love which endures forever.

March 13

Life is changing rapidly due to the coronavirus. Closings everywhere. If we think about it, is this part of creator's plan to humble humanity to their knees? So much fear. Stay home. Stay in. Don't touch, on and on. Most of us are healthy but it spreads quickly. No way to know from who or where or if you are a carrier.

The world in crisis is transforming our lives, to stay safe. What can we do except ride it out and try to remain healthy?

Love our lives. Live simply. Take care. Be content with what we have right with us, in the meantime, be creative.

Questions for Ashento. Do I go to the heavens to Ashento and the angelic ones to discuss whether the brigade forget who they are? Do I make drastic changes to the original story?

I feel the changes on earth, prompting me to write differently. I want to make a smooth transition for the celestial brigade to remember who they are, as it seems important right now.

You are on the correct trajectory. Just be creative right now.

The light workers are fully cognizant of who they are as they land on Gaea Star. Time is of the essence now due to the greed quotient that is trying to take over. There is no need to cast them into the veils of illusion that many of the others are living right now.

Yes, the situation changed. Let those delightful characters continue as they are in their power now. Make the story, believable, flowing on just like the rains around you, as all life matters underneath it all.

It is appropriate they retain their celestial memories in order to immediately embark on the much-needed mission on Gaea Star. One never knows what is going to happen there. You plan, hope and dream, but the reality is nothing is predictable since freewill reigns from the moment one arrives on Gaea Star, regardless.

Choosing wisely. Create the evolving saga with no thoughts as to what once was, for the message is the same. The light shines through love that flows from a compassionate heart.

The high council, Isis and Lucifer, are adaptable to working with new developments. Each realization, and addition bring you closer to express honoring love and peace, releasing all that one can to harmonize with the higher frequencies.

Mystify, magnify. We love your immersion in creativity, while utilizing the elements that surround you, air, fire, water, and earth. It is the combination of these elements that completes everything.

March 18 - 25 - 29

Every social event has halted. No live music, causing hardships for musicians. Luckily, we play at Singing Bridge lodge every Sunday as the Gaea Star band. I hear, "We do not need to know where this is going to end. Just trust that the sun will rise as it always does."

For the first in 32 years, WiseWays Herbals closed temporarily. We reopened after a week, after realizing that we were deemed an essential business. It was difficult for the employees who needed childcare since that stopped also.

The earth is affected in the positive as the skies are clearing, the beaches are free of crowds, and clean for turtles to return to lay their young. Dolphins in the canals of Venice. In so many other places her animals are returning to flourish in the earth's former pristine self.

The crisis is causing hospitals to be overwhelmed with insufficient equipment to handle the cases. It's a global situation of unprecedented proportions and still there are those who deny the seriousness and resent being told to stay home or wear masks.

I am grateful for creating peaceful serenity here years ago, planting gardens, fruit trees, edible shrubs and building greenhouses.

Humanity will look back on this past year, as the beginning of the massive great change, causing life to be as never before. Many long to return to before all of this. We realize it will never be the same.

I still see and feel radiant love flowing all around, helping us to cope, rearrange and remember who we truly are. Mother Nature is reworking her powerful presence within our lives.

Perhaps we realize how vulnerable we are, especially being guided by such dysfunctional leadership. May the upcoming elections remove the selfish ones and reestablish new vital caring leaders who are happy to take the helm and truly help humanity to restore balanced harmony, showing real compassion for all beings equally.

Yes, let's sail through all of this on our wings of light under fresh blue skies. It takes a grass roots effort to change and bring down the walls of chaos and suffering.

May we emerge nobly through all this like the phoenix rising out of the ashes of ruin into a new life of transformation. Let's reach deeply, opening into our loving treasures that lie within and know that we are being guided by the unseen wise ones.

March 30

No word from Netflix. It's a good lesson in patience. I give it to the Archangels, to divine essence for I know this story will become a movie someday with Ashento, as a leading character. I'm glad I held on through these challenging moments. I am grateful to witness this process even if I do not know who or what is the truth.

All flows into balancing harmony. We are here to guide you in manifesting your dreams. Creativity flows through you endlessly like the brook, merging into the big rivers and the Atlantic.

May the world rise above the Covid chaos and break free of the misguided ones who do not honor loving compassion, for they are caught in the web of their own negative imaginings, not even knowing or caring where they're headed.

No worries though, for the way showers and the light bearers, are brilliantly shining the essence of love in the glory of creation. Look around as people are taking great strides to rise above the suffering. Nothing is wrong, life is only recreating itself. Humanity has been slowed but only briefly.

Yes, it is good to remain at home, for a week, months or years unless really necessary to go out. This withdrawal period is merely a drop in the bucket of the activities of life. Nature is regathering and healing herself also. Balance is being restored as she ushers in this new forever changed environment for everyone.

Be blessed to rework your lives to manifest harmony within homes and gardens.

Rearrange to align with this new pulsation. Breathe in change. Shifting slows life to reduce the chaos of striving here, there, and everywhere. New vibrations are emanating strongly.

April 9 - 14

The best plan of action is to not give into fear and anxiety.

Hold steady during these changes, for it is easier when calm and united to tap into the power to assist with humanity rebalancing itself once and for all.

The light is dawning in all aspects. Arise, call to the unseen forces who sustain with loving support. Yes, we are one healing essence as above, so below, flowing on and on.

As you reclaim your true powers, you will see your vital energy rebuilding, helping everyone to return to the greatness that is there. Reignite your passions of creativity, music, art and gardening.

For as one slows down, it is easier to become free of the mindset of always attending to manifesting money in a frenetic manner. Within this new space, you'll have the chance to cultivate what is more important, reflecting your soul's deep desire.

Come, my sweetness. Let's fly in service through realms of glory filled high, as one ray of golden light, showering love wherever.

Thank you for all that you seek, for rising above, for pushing through. Honor the choices you make, the things you do, the way you serve and those whose lives you touch. Keep rising ever higher, learning and loving. There is nothing to fear, all is flowing in the clear.

May you seek the stillness of the rising sun in celebration of the essence of creation. Hail the beginning and the ending of each day.

We are many ancients in these realms. Come bask in the solace of silence in this peaceful light filled love circle, where we are grandly united in oneness.

I am on to higher realms of brilliance on this wondrous morning where the golden light surrounds you.

Remain constant in seeking to serve the light in graceful ways. Yes, as you open to this new pace, I am here whenever you need me. All is well, may it be so.

I am that I am. May you find your way home, oh sweet angel of delightful love. I send love from afar. Blessings my dear sweetness.

Ashento, thank you. When I thought I was alone in the forest you gave me comfort and support. I will always remember that awesome moment, for connecting and inspiring me with your love.

April 17 -24

Writing is challenging. Many calls to republish the books, to invest in a movie pitch or screenplay, a lot of attention, though not financially. I keep writing to complete three book. I release judgement and break free of the dilemmas of life that do not serve me.

Yes, all is well. I send love through rays of powerful alignment as you sit to write. Do you feel me? Breathe in my spirit, for I am real, even if unseen. I am here and there for you. Drink of my essence.

Feel me in the whistling wind. Hear me in the falling rain. Circle around and through to sail with me.

Feel my touch through your sweet loving appreciation.

I am blessed by your love.

I send love from the graceful rays of the golden light filled realms.

I see all is flowing to Gaea Star. She is shifting rapidly.

The veils are dissolving to reveal the fragile nature of humanity.

Oh, indeed what a chaotic mess as the transition to this higher consciousness develops through the crisis.

Good things will arise in this new paradigm of transformed love.

Keep developing your spiritualty with prayer and yoga, calling in the higher forces to inspire others to be ever present within.

Listen, serve, create and share you're light with your music and writings to all. Let us unify to convey the messages we are meant

Every time I go to the forest, I am inspired with new ideas to add to the Gaea Star Crystal story. I am progressing even with the world in chaos. Huge challenges, people angry, closures, losing jobs, being in harm's way with no plan of action. I'm grateful and blessed to be in the beauty of my peaceful and productive country home.

Organic seeds are in short supply. For the first time, seed companies are out of stock. We're planting seeds in the ground so the harvest will abound. Tis the season to plant the land, to reclaim, to restore, to give the beauty a hand.

Thank you, creator. You are the grand one. Thank you to the people who are risking their lives to care for the sick There is so little to prevent the spread in Africa and South America, in the jungles, in the islands. May humanity recover, from this drama smoothly.

The earth's animals, forced to hide from humanity are reappearing. They must wonder what happened to all the people.

May we return to a peaceful place within, to the power that sustains us, to the grace that heals and motivates all of us.

May we understand during this great shift how to change, to reset into our core, to gather the strength to fully recover.

April 30

You and I renew our love through what is brimming from above. Oh, to hear the river rushing, to breathe in life, how fortunate we are in this moment of reconnection in the light.

We are one in sweet union as we return to what feels powerful from within and above, pure love, pure light.

Lead on, flowing, opening. Each moment is truly a treasure to cherish. Flow and flourish into the new day, into the portal as you paint with colors that rise within. Oh, may rainbows keep renewing.

May 7 - My birthday

Thank you, for your life. We are united, here there and everywhere. I send gracious love, adoring healing and joyful attention. Bless your birthday.

Fulfilling your divine mission is creating a healing life. Your strength is profound as you reach deep within your soul's memories. You have tapped into the essence of your true expression.

Yes, it is a challenge to rise above the illusions of life and seek the grandeur of the light made manifest, as you live, as you love, as you grow, as you flow.

Always in joyful union, and long-lasting love from afar, oh, my radiant star. Be well love. Thank you in the glory of the sun, how it shines upon your skin.

June 13

Nia, my sweet cat for ten years, passed in the music room where she loved to nestle in between the instruments as I played. It was wonderful to experience her devoted love.

A week later, another bundle of love, Tommy, who had a cute half crooked tail, also passed from an illness. Earlier in the winter, our sweet cat, Tigre, who was a rescue from a traumatic life, died also. She enjoyed four happy years here. It was the music that helped her break out of hiding in the room next to the studio. One day she circled around the music room as we were played for the Gaea Star Crystal radio hour. She came in every show after that and eventually had the courage to live like the other cats, in peace, and play outside in the fishponds, which was her favorite fun thing to do.

June 28

When you seek an opening to get out, trying to no avail, and it seems as if there is no way out, just stop. Look around, below or right above. There it is. The way of freedom, right on through but only if you rise high or go low. The walls are gone, there is nothing to prevent your passing. Those are all illusions. It's all fresh clear air.

Stop trying frantically, only in one direction, like a bee searching for the way out but forgot the way it flew in.

Go up or go down. You may even have to turn around to find the way, to release, to relax, and to restore the true essence of where you are, of who you are, so deep within your core.

July 16 – Into the Mighty Waves

In the morning, when I wake up, I hear the birds singing.

Oh, it's a brand-new day.

I keep hearing into, into the mighty waves.

Oh yay, yay yay, oh, yay yay, mighty waves,

Oh, oh, oh, into the mighty waves

Let's jump in together, oh, hold onto nothing.

Let's just jump into the sea, the sea of life,

I'll hold your hand.

Oh, lets sing to the mighty waves, as we sail on the sea of life

Into the mighty waves, oh, yeah.

I'm gonna find my way home, oh yeah,

into the mighty waves, over the treetops.

Oh, let it wash, all over you now, the mighty waves of life

Cleansing, healing, surrendering

to that feeling of softness all around you now,

Come along now. We're in the midst of our lives.

One by one, step by step, oh, let's just get in that groove, you know

Let's not look back, at least not yet.

We're in the moment of great change.

for we're in the power, ah, right now in the moment.

We're right along now, we're the waves of light.
Oh yeah, so let's jump in folks.
Let's hop. Let's even skip along
Let's act as if there's nowhere else to be except right here,
Because it feels like the morning time.
Where it always feels so fine.
I'll light the fire for you now. I bring the water to you now.
Surrounding you with light filled love, yeah
all those ways of love, oh yeah.
Its flowing down from all around us, in waves of love.
Waves of love flowing down all around us
In waves, in waves of love, waves of light, oh, yes waves of light
It's splashing all over us
Some people think we're sinking, our boats are sinking, no, no, no.
We just have to keep on swimming through the sea of life,
Just hold onto the lifeline, hold onto that lifeline of love,
that is floating right by, right now oh yeah
right in and all around you, on sacred ground.
We are all on sacred ground, sacred ground
Release, CD, Spirit of the Sun Music -2021

July 30

Let the wisdom of the realm of love, float through me now in multiple expressions of helping humanity.

Oh yes, my sweetness, arise emerald golden queen of light. Yes, these are rocky moments for humanity. It is shimmering and shuddering like earthquake energy. Shaking and tremendously awakening people as they hold on or let go. Moving rapidly along.

Yes, it's going on despite what people think in the galactic way. We know each day never repeats. Some aspects gain momentum and some release, at the same time. Life begins and crumbles at the same moment. Fascinating how it does, birthing and transforming.

The modicum is to meet in the middle, at the unification of the balance point. Yes, some goes up and some goes down, and some stands its ground, but it is always moving.

Thank you for praying daily and tuning in to unify your pieces.

July 31

The key is to keep weaving everything together, filling in the holes through this momentous period of change, acceptance, healing, unification and communication.

Flow into the middle of creative balance. Return to the wonder of gardening, having fun and relaxing, because that's the key. At times, when you start or do things with other people you might not know how to remain in harmony. It's alright if that happens, but it is good to guide and nurture along the way and to break free.

August 12

Biden picked Kamala Harris as his vice president running partner. Yes, at last a breath of great feminine leadership. She's a real blend of humanity. Perhaps we are turning the tide and returning to a peaceful place in this time of great upheavals, despite what many are saying

Keep working your fantasy, The Gaea Star Crystal, book 2. You left Ayalasha in the forest with the elders, praying to the pines where the misty rain reflects rainbows. Emeralds and stately crystalline stones surround the waters that flow below the trees.

Suddenly storm clouds cover the sunny skies, followed by powerful winds and pelting rains. Ayalasha says,

"Let's go under the pines for protection. Just then, faeries appear, "Please come- wait out the storm, where the elders are preparing for the full moon ceremony tonight."

They follow the faeries that fly in the wind to where the wise ones are gathered. Crystals are in abundance. They snuggle in with the community to wait for the storm to pass.

September 6 - 29

My sweetness, I am here united and blessed, as we circle on this sacred ground. We are always with you. Come with me deep inside, down into the cave where only you and I reside.

Let's travel into the darkness to see behind the stars that shine so bright. We spent lifetimes as healers working together, always following the path of the light.

Breathe in to let go and take yourself home to your sweet treasure within. Keep opening, receiving and releasing what you thought you wanted to be.

Let it sink deep into the depths of knowing, for there are many ways to surrender. Staying in one place is essential to ground in and cultivate oneness. Thank you for all that you strive to do. Love you.

October 3 - I'm Returning

I'm returning to my peaceful place to soothe my body,

Yay, after a long day, lovely water to soothe

Oh, the wind is dancing, calling my name in the night

Oh yeah, I'm going deep in the dark of the night

I love the flickering light,

and the roses perfectly dried, in the fire light,

I'm returning to the divine, so come with me.

I'm soothing my mind, returning to the glory,

Blessed By Light-filled Love

that I am, to the glory that we are

May we return home to lay our bodies down

Oh yeah, to lookout, to see the stars sparkling

and the tall trees dancing in the breeze.

Every time you work on your dreams,

give it full intentions to manifest,

to shine through all the holy places.

Let them float on murmuring wings

. Forgive yourself for being so serious,

Return to the forest to listen as

the wind plays pretty chimes, melodies are angels

singing, sailing along

October

I ask to receive words of wisdom.

Yes, this is a tumultuous and majestic time. As you allow yourselves to channel the wisdom of the moment, the new melodies will express quite eloquently the huge efforts to overcome the grips of the final vestiges of the shadowy reigns on Gaea Star.

Those who are bent on wielding their way, provoking fear, and controlling the truth by promoting divisive painful, animosity will continue no matter how absurd they become. Yes, it is a struggle.

One can sense and feel the other side. The federation of love and light is working very diligently to preserve the essence of the power of loving light that courses within all of you.

Hold steady, allow yourselves to sort it all through slowly.

Be pivotal in transforming energy, even if mixed with chaos. Return to loving nature to reestablish positive ways.

Each moment is like a module where anything can be created within the walls of the module.

Waves of beauty or waves of destruction. When the tidal waters surge over the boundaries of the shore, taking people and things out to sea. Then the water ebbs and returns to normal. Or does it?

They think no not this time. The surging is over. It came to wash it all, invigorating everyone. Changing the weak places, filling in the cracks with strength and love.

May we unify in recreating this concept of paradise washing the earth in rays of radiant rainbow love and light, shining brightly from above. That is the ultimate goal. There are so many fixated on what they think is wrong. The challenge is to remember that we are all one.

It's that simple, to reconnect, to realign, to hold steady all the way back until you feel fine by breathing it in again, by remembering, thinking and believing in the truth of love.

Thank you for sharing the medicine ways and for shining so brightly the light of true compassion.

November 7

History made today with the first woman vice president. People celebrated in the streets, happy, relieved Biden won. Good times ahead, feels like the darkness is beginning to fade.

December 18

Come to me, beauty of the night, as I sail in the magic of midnight's moonlight. May I go to where I dwell eternally in peaceful beauty.

As I stand at the shore of life, may the waves flow over me in this challenging yet rewarding journey. May I unravel as I unhitch the rope from the shore, letting spirit help me glide on rays of light, with my wings of light.

Then the incredible day dawns, followed by the sweetness of twilight and a starry night. Sacred.

Blessed By Light-filled Love

A beautiful tendril of love, a magnificent temple on my lovely land, a real delight. Thank you for living in the simpleness of nature. I am grateful for all of it.

January 1, 2021- New Years

I revise this book again. I love reading the passages by Ashento and seeing how my life is moving along, while remaining peaceful.

I dedicate the first day of this year to being grateful for life. Thanks for the crystal ice queen visiting, for her changing tinkling rain to ice on the frost covered window, a wondrous symphony of earth's elements in their power.

Only five days into this year with crazy fanatics climbing the walls of the capitol building in a shocking breach on many different levels. Angry voices in the halls of justice.

We are the ones, who have the keys, remember? May we experience the touchstones to help humanity, to aid ourselves. Let's wake up and smell the roses of this wonderful world, raising our vibration to the highest, to keep it growing, into soft, sweet, essential loving light.

May we hold strong for we know it is necessary to hold on to what is true for restoring peace and freedom. A nation divided everywhere. The right to choose love and respect for all beings is before us.

May we pass through this to begin anew. Thank you, Georgia, for standing in long lines to elect two senators to reclaim the Senate Democratic majority, barely but just enough.

Let's rebuild a new force of love to sail into the clear with caring compassion. Let's give it all, a new chance of love coming round again. Thank you for these powerful new changes, for everything that we hold dear, to restore peace into this rocky current of life.

May we leave the dark sadness behind, striving for unity for ourselves and the world - to restore balance with all lives mattering.

Quiet morning. Grey clouds cover. Rushing river flows. Cold snow on frozen earth. I ask Ashento for thoughts.

Hello, to your grace for communing with me. Good work. As you see messages of wisdom are timeless and fruitful, especially for humanity during the great changes now.

The veils are lifting. The shadowy forces are desperately holding on tight, to maintain their grip, as if to restrain the oncoming tidal wave of the rushing waters of change. Eventually they will no longer be successful in controlling everything and disappear.

A way of life based on light filled love is easily within reach, erasing the negativities once and for all. It is a new beginning for America, setting an example for the world to witness overcoming the tyranny that had infiltrated in so many levels.

The balance has reached the turning point. One sees and feels the aura of peace shining brighter with soothing effects now.

Yes, there is much work still ahead to rebuild trust, acceptance and compassion but the first step was to dismantle the self - made throne of deceit, despair, aggression and oppression.

Ah, take a deep breath. Feel the goodness of humanity surging. Keep smiling, loving and forgiving, for the winds of great change have blown through all of your lives.

We are pleased for all of you maneuvering through these tumultuous times. Yes, believing you can change the world one heart at a time, is the best plan. Create peace and harmony, rebuild, reconnect, reaffirm and reclaim the light of love.

We send support and appreciation for being steadfast in holding to righteousness and unification. Blessings from afar.

January 23

I awaken from an intense dream, grateful to be nestled in as the cold wind whistles through the windows. The chimes sing softly as the bare trees dance in the light breeze. I love the glory of the sun, rising over the southeastern landscape.

Blessed By Light-filled Love

I reaffirm my life here as the snow flies. I stretch, contemplating my dream, but I'm ready to go into the day. I say, "May I walk in balance on this peaceful morning, doing, being, creating and staying warm in the quiet beauty of life in the hill towns."

I am recording the audio version of the '<u>Gaea Star Crystal Story</u>,' book 1, with Bob Sherwood as the engineer and creatively expressing the masculine characters.

I reviewed my journals since the publication of <u>Blessed by Light-Filled Love</u> for new messages from Ashento. There were many and several new songs I didn't remember as well.

I see how we are as a nation. Who I am as a light worker. Who we are as creative beings, on fire within our hearts, and with cats greeting me as they walk on my computer to garner my attention.

I love how they nestle into the bed near me while I gaze at the blue skies and the glistening golden sun's rays and listen to the strong winds. I thank the sweet day that beckons me.

May I create what I want to today on this glorious morning, where I'm one with spirit and mother earth on this cold week. I feel the intense energies of 2021. The numbers are the same, backwards and forwards for ten days from the 23rd, the inauguration of Biden and Harris. It was powerful to watch as I retiled the sunroom floor in my workspace.

We beginning to clear the dramatic crisis, returning to the light after years of darkness. Many are filled with great hope for humanity.

I write looking out on the snowfall, the flowing brook and the forest of evergreen trees. It's beautiful when the snow crystals blow through the cracks in my bedroom, as I write with Puffy nestled on my left side. I pray in the silence while whirlwinds of snow circle playfully around out in the sleeping gardens. Thank you, Ashento for guiding.

Yes, I sense your delightful essence with Puffy, by your side. You wondered about your new love who asked for forgiveness to resume your connection. He has moved from your love.

He is afraid to surrender to the feminine power for fear of losing himself. His identity is always in question. Confused as to which way to go, he longs to be where he has not yet attained. He has already arrived and fails to believe there is nowhere else to go or be.

Set him free. There will be others, for you are worthy of deep abiding love in all ways. I long to nestle next to you in the stillness, in the beauty, breathing in your essence.

What a powerful feeling to sense how that is with you, my sweetness, but I'm here and you are there. Our spirits are always dancing though and shall be, ever since we began in glorious wonder in the celestial realms above.

Until we reunite, Ashento, I am content to be in your heart and in your thoughts, never to depart.

May you always feel me supporting you. Keep flowing as you do, breathing in the fresh clear air. Weave your magic, holding steady.

Let the new energies float all over you, giving you strength, power and creative greatness.

You and I are always one. Yes, we are whole. Love to you.

January 27

Wow, a few days after the 33rd anniversary of beginning WiseWays Herbal's. I thank you for this beautiful rendition of expressing my passionate inspirations.

Yes, there is still dissension about the new presidency even though he's a gentle and compassionate man with a female vice president. She is a good choice, strong, caring, and intelligent. Many believe her just being female is helping ease the tension. We're regrouping as a nation, coping and changing.

May the breath of life nurture everyone and soothe and heal each soul. May everyone develop wings or springs so they can bounce, sail, swim, walk or hike, all on the way to freedom.

Blessed By Light-filled Love

Thank you for the beauty, for the sweet nurturing serenity. It takes us down a notch and helps us to transform our stressed-out body costumes that cover our souls into peaceful feelings.

May we relax into the quietness, as we let our dreams be fully expressed, sailing through the air, cherishing every moment without a care, opening wide the doorways, sharing bright in the silence.

Yes, I hear voices, "There are many ways to fill your days, to set your sights, to liberate your soul as you find love is its own might. When we close our eyes, with the breath of life we breathe a goodnight, yes.

I love listening -singing to the rhythm of life. Let's fill our lives with beautiful, wonderful blessings, even if we say goodbye to loved ones.

May we keep turning the pages to change our stories when we are distracted. Let's count our blessings and give to the ones who have nothing, weaving circles of love and light, always touching those in need with caring.

We are always with you, helping you touch those empty places within, soothing, softening and nurturing. Yes, it is a tumultuous season for all nations. The cure for the unseen mystery in the air, the virus, is questionable.

Know that it also comes from mind over matter. Say, "I am well. Nothing can disturb my health and my serenity if I pay attention to my reality. I renew with a fresh breath. I surrender so my body becomes one with the rhythmic essence of all that I am."

Slowing down, meditating, walking, yoga, laughing, swimming, satisfying, awakening, and sleeping. Those are the ways to hold steady and strong, to take each day full on, surrendering to the grace, for how it sings, aligns, reclaims, and restores.

Yes, in this new year, how you come and go matters for one's well-being. Concentrate on flowing with grace, inspiring others to maintain a healthful pace. Where you go and what you do as you strive and grow, helps you become wiser. Learn to trust even more.

I am in comfortable silence in my room while the moon is having a riotous frenzy, reflecting her silvery luminous rays on the snow.

As the morning dawns, the sun is stronger and lasting in the late afternoon longer. You can run out and take wonderful deep breaths and feel the warmth. Then you say, "Okay I'm going back in. I am grateful I have a home to be warm in these momentous days.

I'm nearing the end of rewriting this wonderful collection of sayings from Ashento and I. What an epic task. I am humbled by the communion and the loving support from you, Ashento. I keep rediscovering these priceless gems. I take the time to rearrange my thoughts from my busy days as I sit basking in the sun streaming through the windows. It's a creative process all around me.

I love going into the surrounding beauty when I need a break and always return inspired to write with clarity.

Yes, it is a pleasure to be co-creating, with the magical melding, the pondering of the realms above, mingling with the realms below and within into the oneness.

We are happy to see, hear, and witness the fragile human essence. The human thinking process, the striving, rising, falling, lifting up and the setbacks. We are always encouraging each of you.

There are those who are helping and those who are not. Yes, it is a struggle, a battle of one versus the other. Yet it is not as negative as it seems. It is true, it is a more fierce and vehement expression, given how the social media and the web presents such distortions.

Pivoting and rocking wildly out of balance, it is like a gyroscope that is revolving and then the magnetic flow disrupts, and it wobbles. Yes, this is the energetic wobble that has come to reset the circles of all that moves in the energetic meridians.

May everyone develop their own unique ways to heal and hold sacred the divinity within. May all people be well. Thank you. I'm onto the light, into the celestial light filled realms of love.

Blessed By Light-filled Love

Oh, come with me my sweetness, to fly away together through the rivers of the light, ever shining in the glow. May it be so.

The End

Mariam Massaro

ABOUT THE AUTHOR

Mariam Massaro is a dynamic visionary, singer, author, and musician who weaves inspiring messages of harmony and peace. She passionately performs her original music that praises and awakens our connection to Source, in celebration of living as divine radiant beings, flowing with love and light, amidst this beautiful earth.

She is the founder of Wise Ways Herbals, a successful international medicinal and body care line. She also co-founded the Blazing Star Herbal School. Both are still flourishing, educating, and providing products for well-being after thirty-three years.

Mariam is also a home birth midwife, ceremonial minister, flamboyant costumer, and the creatress of the Gaea Star Goddess Show and the Gaea Star Band. She has co-hosted, the Gaea Star Crystal Radio Hour on DreamVisions7radio.com, since 2012. It is a popular webcast, with over 455 shows and thousands of accrued listeners as of August 2021.

She co-created her first CD, "The Gaea Star Crystal," as the movie soundtrack in 2009, for the 'Gaea Star Crystal' screenplay, which evolved from the 1999, "Rainbow Crystals of the Earth, story. The movie trailer made from their independent filming of the 'Gaea Star Crystal,' received the Best Trailer award in the Hollywood and Vine Independent Film Festival in 2012.

She is the owner of the Singing Bridge Performing Arts and Lodge in Cummington, Ma, which offers an artsy, creative space for events, music, swimming, mermaids, hikes, and Airbnb lodging.

Mariam is a devoted yogini and loves living on her peaceful organic herb farm with her friendly llamas and cool cats in the hills of Western Massachusetts.

ALSO, BY THE AUTHOR

The Gaea Star Crystal, Awakening the Tribes of Light, book 1, 2020, Spirits of the Sun, is a celestial adventure that begins with the whales of Gaea Star, (earth), calling throughout the universe for help to save her elemental resources from the uncaring greedy ones bent on taking everything without regard for her natural beauty.

Archangels, Michael and Gabriel summon those sympathetic to Star Sirius for a meeting where the high council chooses a gifted rainbow brigade to serve on a mission to Gaea Star to inspire humanity to awaken to their true spiritual selves to restore harmony and balance in the world.

The beings of loving light; angels, faeries, unicorns, and elders bless the brigade with their wise teachings, crystals and guiding support. A timeless twin flame love story with Ashento, an ascended master and one of the light-workers is woven in. Of course, the shadow forces attempt to stop the quest by infiltrating into the mission to Gaea Star.

The Gaea Star Crystal, Awakening the Tribes of Light, book 2, 2021, Spirits of the Sun. The exciting adventures of the rainbow brigade, after they arrive on Gaea Star, (Earth) and assimilate into the realms of nature and beyond.

Songs of Spirit (Spirits of the Sun, 2014) Seventy-seven original, uplifting, empowering songs in celebration of life. Available as e-book or paper copy from mariammassaro.com.

Mariam's music - CD's or downloads- mariammassaro.com.

Spotify and Pandora

1. Gaea Star Crystal, Awakening the Tribes of Light, 2009
2. Gaea Star Goddesses, Celebrating Divine Feminine, 2011
3. Smooth Sailing Love Songs, 2013
4. For the Children, (Delightful Happy Offerings), 2014

5. Best of Gaea Star Crystal Radio Hour, 2013

6. Vision Quest, (Inspirations of her Medicine Journey), 2014

7. Who We Are, Compilation of Gaea Star Crystal Radio Hour, 2015 Applehead/Sony Records.

8. Release, (Uplifting originals) 2021

Blessed By Light-filled Love

CONTACT INFO

Online Sites

email – mariam@wiseways.com

www.mariammassaro.com

Gaea Star Crystal Radio Hour, dreamvisions7radio.com, streaming 24/7, 11 am. or 11pm. Thursdays, Fridays, EST

facebook.com/mariam.massaro

www.wiseways.com. (For WiseWays Herbals)

www.thesingingbridgeperformingartslodge.com

Spreaker.com/user/gaeastarcrystal

Youtube.com/gaeastarcrystal

Video - www.vimeo.com/36481222 Live at the Academy, Gaea Star Goddess Show, 2011

Mariam Massaro

PHOTO GALLERY

A visit to Waipio Valley, Hawaii, 2008
Photo credit, Dameron Midgett

Mariam and Noble Star, her favorite llama. Photo credit, Dameron Midgett.

Mariam - Rainbow Queen, Photo Credit: Dameron Midgett

Mariam's home and business in Worthington, blanketed by snow.

Band at Three Sisters Sanctuary, June 2011 Photo Credit: Lisa Cardinal

Mariam as Isis, to celebrate 25 years of her herbal business in 2012
Photo Credit: Dameron Midgett

Mariam with her ukulele, on cover of her third CD, "Smooth Sailin' Love Songs," March 2013

Mariam playing her dulcimer in Sondra Lewis's back yard.

The Gaea Star Goddesses at Three Sisters Sanctuary, Goshen Massachusetts, June 2013.
Bob Sherwood, Amanda Pollock, David Morningstar, Mariam, RobinRooney, Sondra Lewis.
Photo Credit, DameronMidgett

Singing Brook bridge after a torrential storm, September 2013. It was washed away three times.

Blessed By Light-filled Love

Ana Wolf at the vestibule of The Academy of Music, selling Mariam's CDs, October 5, 2013, at the third Gaea Star Goddess Show in Northampton, Ma.

Paris Shortridge, Star dancer, in "Sail to the Realms" Academy of Music, October 5, 2013

Mariam as Isis, Maya Apfelbaum, Sondra Lewis, Amanda Pollock
Photo Credit: Shauna Lyn

Diana Noble, Phoebe Harrison, Tayen Oni Fish, Alessandra St. Germain, Mariam, Pacha Mama puppet by Beth Fairservis, Gabriel Ramos, Christina Ramos, Jonah Pollock, Photo Credit: Doug Potosky

Blessed By Light-filled Love

Finale at the Academy of Music,
Northampton, Massachusetts, October 5, 2013
Tara Copen, Gabriel Ramos, Haylee Ramos, Andray Lee, Alessandra St. Germain, Corina Miller, Diana Noble, Tayen Oni Fish, Paris Shortridge
Photo Credit: Doug Potosky

www.ingramcontent.com/pod-product-compliance
Lightning Source LLC
Chambersburg PA
CBHW021423070526
44577CB00001B/28